A DOG'S DEVOTION

A DOG'S DEVOTION

True Adventures of a
K9 Search and Rescue Team

SUZANNE ELSHULT, MA,
AND
JAMES GUY MANSFIELD, PhD

Essex, Connecticut

An imprint of Globe Pequot, the trade division of
The Rowman & Littlefield Publishing Group, Inc.
4501 Forbes Blvd., Ste. 200
Lanham, MD 20706
www.rowman.com

Distributed by NATIONAL BOOK NETWORK

British Library Cataloguing in Publication Information available

Library of Congress Cataloging-in-Publication Data

Names: Elshult, Suzanne, 1952- author. | Mansfield, James Guy, 1949-
    author.
Title: A dog's devotion : true adventures of a K9 search and rescue team / Suzanne Elshult and James
    Guy Mansfield.
Description: Lanham, MD : Lyons Press, an imprint of Globe Pequot, [2022] | Includes index. |
    Summary: "This is an award-winning inside view of a remarkable K9 search and rescue team
    operating in the wilds of Washington State whose "principal investigator" is a yellow lab named Keb.
    Keb's story is of a dedicated K9 who can distinguish the scent of the dead from the scent of the living
    and who can detect long-buried bones. Readers will follow this intrepid K9 and her teammates as
    they face the challenges of changeable weather, deep northwest forests, high mountain slopes, and
    menacing coyotes to find dead bodies, missing hikers, and even the bones of murder victims from
    long ago"— Provided by publisher.
Identifiers: LCCN 2022006397 (print) | LCCN 2022006398 (ebook) | ISBN 9781493068715
    (hardcover ; alk. paper) | ISBN 9781493068722 (e-book)
Subjects: LCSH: Police dogs—United States—Anecdotes—Juvenile literature. | Search dogs—United
    States—Juvenile literature.
Classification: LCC HV8025 .E46 2022 (print) | LCC HV8025 (ebook) | DDC
    363.280973—dc23/eng/20220503
LC record available at https://lccn.loc.gov/2022006397
LC ebook record available at https://lccn.loc.gov/2022006398

Printed in the United States of America

This book is dedicated to our search and rescue comrades, Robert Fuller and K9 Peer. Bob and Peer were taken away from us too soon but left us with enduring memories of commitment, leadership, and friendship. Bob gently led our team from the brink to the light.

Peer taught us what a search dog should be. Bob taught us how fragile life is and the need to appreciate every moment we have with our human and four-legged partners.

They will not soon be forgotten.

Contents

Acknowledgments

Above all we thank Keb. Without her keen nose and willing spirit, this book would have never happened. She changed our lives, humbled us, and made us better, both as search and rescue (SAR) volunteers and as human beings.

We are deeply indebted to our respective spouses, who supported us every step of the way. We arm-twisted Scott and June to review and critique our early drafts, and they stuck with us as writing took over much of our lives for several years. We also are grateful to our very dear friends and colleagues in Cascadia Search Dogs. Together, we've faced big challenges while remaining unfailing in our support of one another and of the vision we share to make a meaningful contribution to the K9 search and rescue community, both locally and beyond. We appreciate the dedicated members of other K9 teams in the Pacific Northwest who train with us and our dogs through sun, rain, and snow. We would be sorely remiss in not recognizing the dedicated members of law enforcement with whom we've worked, deputies and detectives alike. Know that when your family member needs rescue, they're the ones who will lead the effort to bring them home.

The Pacific Northwest Writers Association provided us with our first opportunities to learn about writing a book and finding an agent, and we were thrilled to receive their 2021 Writing Contest for Unpublished Work Award for best entry in the Nonfiction Memoir Category. We are indebted to Evy Dudey for her attention to detail, excellent proofreading—reading every single word, many times—for helping us with our early style guide, and for her many thoughtful suggestions. We thank the EPIC Writers Group, particularly Laura Moe, who led our writer's critique group. Susan Purvis, Cat Warren, and Vi Shaffer are all writers of successful SAR dog books who supported us throughout this journey. Susan Purvis is a bad-ass adventurer and writer who helped us be brave in our own writing with her candid feedback and focus on being "real."

Our awesome literary agent, Regina Ryan, with Regina Ryan Books, had faith in our book concept and went above and beyond to shape our adventure memoir into a more cohesive reader experience. We are indebted to Regina for taking our rough idea for a book, helping us turn it into a reality, and connecting us with a respected publisher. Rick Rinehart, executive editor at Globe Pequot / Rowman and Littlefield, saw the promise in our work, and guided us as first-time authors into the world of publishing.

Suzanne Elshult: While my gratitude first and foremost goes to Keb, I cannot forget about all the other dogs I've learned from, not the least my first search and rescue K9, Bosse, who let me make all the mistakes of a novice handler, while remaining a true and loving companion. I treasure my newest crazy Labrador addition, K9 Kili, for keeping me on my toes and making me play, train, and go on purposeful hikes when I get too intensely involved with book writing. My dogs, ever forgiving and nonjudgmental, have allowed me to become the best version of myself.

I am deeply grateful to a whole host of people. There are just too many to mention, including my very dear SAR K9 colleagues in Sweden, Denmark, and Canada, but I am particularly indebted to the many capable K9 trainers/instructors in the SAR community from whom I've acquired knowledge over the past two decades. I have deep admiration for Paul Martin, Mary Cablk, Ben Alexander, and Deb and Joe Hurlburt, who all have helped me grow as a handler in recent years. Cris Goodhue, Catherine Louis, Jane Harlan, and Janet Wilts all supported me immensely as a novice handler in the early years, as did the late Shirley Hammond, a giant in the K9 disaster world, who convinced me to go to my very first out-of-state K9 SAR workshop in Arkansas—an eye-opening experience.

Many others have made important contributions along the way: legends Andy Rebmann and Marcia Koenig, Matthew Devaney, Greg Strickland, Brad Dennis, Lisa Higgins, Ann Christensen, Ann Wichman, Denise Alvord, Jennifer Hall, Kevin George, Norma Snelling, Kevin Huggett, MaryAnn Warren, Roy Pescador, Terry Crooks, JoMay Wyatt, Laurie Strite, and more. Travels with my friend and colleague Sally Olsen to workshops or National Search Dog Alliance testing events as Principal Evaluators in Washington, Oregon, Idaho, Wyoming, and British Columbia have left me with treasured memories. Also, I appreciate what I have learned about partnering with my dogs from my long-time agility instructor Eric Sanford. And I am so very grateful to have been a student of Terry Ryan as I studied to become a Karen Pryor Certified training partner. She not only helped me train a chicken and a fish to perform tricks but opened up my eyes to the immense power of positive training as we work in partnership with our dogs. Although I have never personally met some of the highly acclaimed authors in the dog behavior world such as Karen Pryor, Patricia McConnell, Susan Clothier, Michael Ellis, and Alexandra Horowitz, their books, blogs, podcasts, DVDs, and articles have been invaluable resources as I have evolved in my understanding of dogs and dog behavior.

I have nothing but respect for Ken Lakey, long-term past president of Snohomish County Volunteer Search and Rescue; Danny Wikstrom, the legendary SAR sergeant with Snohomish County for many years; and Mark Glidden, former chair of Everett Mountain Rescue who believed in me and played an important part in me becoming a member of Everett Mountain Rescue. And I would be remiss without acknowledging and thanking my executive coaching clients, whose patience and understanding when I canceled yet another meeting for a SAR mission allowed me to pursue this avocation as a lifestyle.

Guy and I have been a team for many years and our relationship has deepened as we have written this book together. He deserves credit for coming up with the idea of writing this book, even after I hesitated to begin with. In relating our story, we hope to honor other K9 handlers, dogs, and search and rescue personnel committed to bringing home the missing and the dead. We hope to inspire others to pursue their dreams of being purposeful in the world.

Last but not least, hats off to my family: husband, Scott; daughter, Linnea; and son-in-law, Chris. They have all been rocks as I have lived through the high *highs* and low *lows* of being a SAR volunteer. Scott is the reason I became involved in search and rescue in 2001, as he was already in mountain rescue and we were looking for a joint pursuit in the aftermath of 9/11. From Scott—and the Mountaineers—I learned pretty much everything I know about climbing, scrambling, and skiing. He helped me overcome my fear of heights, triggered by a gruesome accident in the Sierra Nevadas, and has been my adventure partner as we climbed Kilimanjaro, Nevado DeToluca, Kebnekaise, and other mountain tops together. Over the years he has been my dogs' volunteer "subject" (some call it "victim") literally thousands of times and has cheered me on without—much—hesitation in the pursuit of becoming the very best human remains detection handler I can be. There really are no words.

James Guy Mansfield: We are nothing without our family and friends. The love and support of my parents and grandparents has shaped my character and will always be remembered. My brother, Gary, was an enthusiastic partner in my early outdoor adventures, from rock climbing the walls of Yosemite to climbing the Grand Teton, to circumnavigating the Wonderland Trail on Mount Rainier. Sisters Kathy and Cris also joined us for multiple adventures. My wife, June—enticed into K9 SAR with the "why don't you just come out one day and hide for the dogs" ploy—has supported me through all of my careers and adventures and has become a strong organizing force for multiple SAR teams.

My academic roots were shaped by Oregon Health Sciences University professors Judson Brown and Christopher Cunningham, who taught me analytical thinking and winced as they critiqued my early attempts at writing. Their influence served me well throughout multiple careers and continues to do so in my endeavors in the sometimes life and death business of search planning and management. Lifelong friends from graduate school, including Kevin Quinn (The Gray Mountaineer), shared some of my earlier wilderness experiences, which formed a foundation for my search and rescue avocation.

Early in my search and rescue career, the encouragement and guidance I received from Bob Fuller and Suzanne Elshult allowed me to expand my skills rapidly, while enjoying the unique comradeship of the K9 team they were forming. SAR teammates Mike Loney, John Morton, and Yana Radenska served as stellar examples of skill and dedication. Local and national SAR experts Donald Cooper, Hugh Dougher, Bob Koester, Robert "Skip" Stoffel, Brett Stoffel, and Jon Wartes all contributed to my search management training through writings, lectures, and personal guidance.

Over the years, I had the honor to work closely with widely respected SAR deputies Danny Wikstrom, Ed Christian, Kathy Decker, and Peter Teske on many searches and rescues, and they helped me understand one of the secrets of search and rescue: I learn something important on every mission.

Preface

Our stories tell of real search and rescue missions in the Pacific Northwest. Some locations, names, and sequences have been altered to protect ongoing investigations, to simplify the narration, or to shield families of the lost. Where names and details do appear, they are those easily found in published news reports. In every chapter, we attempt to honor the sacrifice and service of search and rescue volunteers as well as the selfless contributions of our brave friends in law enforcement. In every chapter, amidst the drama and humor, we write with enduring respect for the departed and their families.

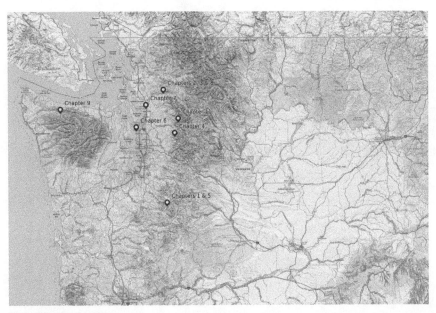

Map of Chapter Locations

Glossary of Search and Rescue Terms

4 x 4: A four-wheel drive vehicle, usually with high clearance and specialized tires, used for travel on rough roads.

AFRCC: Air Force Rescue Coordination Center—a unit of the United States Air Force that coordinates and supports inland search and rescue.

Air Scent: A search and rescue K9 discipline in which dogs are trained to find live people or (for HRD air scent dogs) the odor of human decomposition via scent particles wafting in the air.

Alert: A distinctive change in a K9's behavior prior to a trained final indication, suggesting that the dog is working a target odor.

Assignment: A specific task given to a search team (e.g., search this twenty-acre area on the map).

Base: A location where searchers stage and from where the search may be managed.

Bearing: A direction of travel (e.g., northeast or 45 degrees), typically read from a compass.

Belay: Use of a rope (or sometimes other objects) to prevent (or limit) a climber's fall. A "veggie belay" refers to grasping at roots or plants to haul oneself up a steep slope.

Bivouac: An unplanned, overnight stay in the wilderness. In search and rescue, this is an exciting opportunity to discover if your mission pack contains the gear, food, shelter materials, and extra warm clothes needed to survive the night.

Cache: A collection of gear or supplies. Example: "Before leaving for the summit climb, we cached our food in a small pack, where it was chewed through by hungry marmots."

Call-Out: A request for search and rescue volunteers to respond to an incident. Call-outs most often occur between 11 p.m. and 4 a.m. on nights prior to important business meetings.

Cascades: The mountain range that runs south to north along the crest of central Oregon and Washington.

Certification: A formal test or evaluation of a K9 team's abilities. It does not refer to assessment of mental stability.

Clear-cut: A time-honored and environmentally disastrous logging practice in which every single tree in an area is cut down and removed.

Command Staff: A member of the team (often organized using principles of the Incident Command System, ICS) that manages a search or rescue incident.

Coordinates: In search and rescue, this is typically two numbers: one which specifies a location on a west-to-east axis, and one that specifies a location on a south-to-north axis. Where these two axes cross identifies your location.

Cranium: The upper part of a human skull.

Crew Resource Management: A safety-oriented system (pioneered by the aviation industry) in which there is an expectation that input from *all team members* will be considered when important decisions are made. For example, during a helo mission, anybody in the helo can call "Abort" (typically for a safety concern), and this will be respected by the pilot.

Crittering: When a K9 abandons its search task to chase after, or follow the scent of, an animal.

Cueing: When a handler provides a K9 with subtle (sometimes unconscious) signals to which the dog is expected to give a trained response.

Debriefing: Obtaining a detailed, structured report from each returning search team. This process is onerous to both command staff and searchers (who just want to go home after hours of searching) but provides vital information should the search need to be continued the next day.

Decision Point: A geographical feature (such as a turn in a trail) that provides an opportunity for a hiker to make a mistake and leave the correct route. Careful search planners will try to identify potential decision points and define search scenarios based on them.

Decomp: Law enforcement jargon for the residue of decomposed human remains. For example, liquids oozing from a decomposing body will form a "primary soak" in the ground below.

Decon: Decontamination—a process to wash hazardous materials off of searchers or dogs.

Devil's Club: A large, nasty, spiny plant, found in the Pacific Northwest. Don't touch!

Drainage: A descending terrain feature (usually V-shaped or U-shaped) in which water flows.

Drone: An unmanned flying machine, also referred to as Unmanned Aerial Vehicles or UAVs. In search and rescue, these are typically "mini-helicopter, multi-rotor" devices ranging in size from twelve to thirty-six inches across.

DRT: Law enforcement acronym for "Dead Right There"—the location of a body.

EMD: Emergency Management Department.

Evidence Search: A search in which objects (e.g., weapons, clothing) or human remains (e.g., whole bodies, body parts, bones) related to a crime are the target.

FEMA: Federal Emergency Management Agency.

Field Support: A person on a K9 search team, who accompanies the handler and provides navigation and communication support and also serves as an extra set of eyes on the dog.

FRS: Family Radio Service—radio frequencies reserved for short-range communications among families or nongovernmental groups. K9 teams often use FRS radios to talk between teams on channels that won't interfere with radio transmissions to the command post.

Gaiters: A fabric sleeve (typically tough and waterproof) that runs from low on your boot up to mid-shin. If fitted properly, this will prevent mud, snow, and even water, from entering your boots.

GPS: Acronym for "Global Positioning System"—the United States version of a satellite-based navigation system. Handheld GPS units (or K9 collars) receive signals from GPS satellites and use them to determine their position in three dimensions. GPS accuracy can be substantially degraded by thick forests, heavy clouds, or mountainous terrain—conditions which we often encounter on SAR missions in the Pacific Northwest.

Grid Search: An operation in which searchers typically move forward in a line, with equal spacing between them.

Handler: The person responsible for managing the dog on a K9 team. On volunteer SAR K9 teams, the dog is usually owned by the handler, is allowed to live in the same house, and is often considered a family member.

Hasty Search: Deployment of small search teams to quickly search trails near the Last Known Point and areas of highest probability for finding the lost subject.

Helispot: A location (typically temporary) established for landing a helicopter.

Helo: SAR jargon for helicopter.

HRD: Acronym for human remains detection. HRD can also refer to a K9 training discipline.

Hypothermia: A potentially life-threatening drop in core body temperature. The more severe stages of hypothermia can lead to fatigue, mental impairment, irrational behavior (such as removal of clothing due to a false sensation of warmth known as "paradoxical warming"), unconsciousness, and death.

Ice Axe: A shaft (typically two to three feet long) with a spike on the bottom end and a pick and adze on the top end. Used by climbers to prevent and arrest falls on steep snow or ice.

IC: Acronym that can refer to Incident Command (short for Incident Command Post) or to the Incident Commander (the person in charge of a SAR incident).

ICP: Incident Command Post—the location where the search is managed.

IPP: Initial Planning Point—a search planning term that refers to a location (e.g., the Point Last Seen or the Last Known Point) around which search efforts are focused.

K9 Team Coordinator: The person who leads the K9 Team. This position requires strong experience training K9s, as well as an advanced degree in herding cats.

LAT/LON: The latitude/longitude coordinate system, based on lines of latitude (from the north pole to the south pole) and lines of longitude (west-to-east around the globe). The Lat/Lon coordinate system is widely used in aviation and for maritime navigation but has inherent complexities that contribute to human navigation errors.

LE: Abbreviation for law enforcement or law enforcement personnel. For example, "The area around the clandestine grave is now restricted to all but LE."

LKP: Acronym for Last Known Point—the documented (or sometimes inferred) most recent location for a missing subject. For example, if the child was last seen riding her bicycle toward the lake, and the bicycle is found on a lakeshore path, the bicycle may be used as the LKP.

Mandible: A lower jawbone. When human remains are skeletonized, mandibles frequently will separate from the upper skull.

Mantracker: A person specially trained to follow faint signs (e.g., footprints, bent blades of grass, slight impressions) left by humans as they move.

Marmot: A woodchuck-sized rodent that typically dwells on high mountain slopes. Marmots give a high, clear whistle when alarmed, and these whistles are sometimes reported during searches as false clues: "I think I hear someone whistling for help!"

ME: Abbreviation for medical examiner.

NPS: Acronym for National Park Service.

Operational Period: One shift (typically eight to twelve hours) during search operations.

OPS Chief: Operations Section Chief—the member of the incident command staff responsible for effecting the search plan.

PLANS Chief: Planning Section Chief—the member of the incident command staff responsible for planning *where* to search.

PLS: Point Last Seen—the location of the last, verifiable position of a lost or missing person.

POV: Acronym for Personally Operated Vehicle. SAR volunteers often drive their own vehicles (POVs) to search staging areas. K9 handlers almost always "POV" to the search, because they are transporting one or more dogs in a 4 x 4 packed full of dog-related gear.

Probability of Area (POA): A number (estimated or calculated) that represents the relative likelihood that a missing person is inside a specific Search Region or Search Segment. Example (simplified): "The POA of Region A is 60 percent, while the POA of Region B is only 10 percent. We're going to deploy our search resources in Region A first."

Probability of Detection (POD): A number (estimated or calculated) that represents the amount of POA removed from a search area after a search team has completed an assignment in that area. Note: This definition has been considerably simplified to provide a general understanding.

Proofing: Training a K9 that they *do not* get rewarded for finding (or alerting on) specific types of objects or scents. For example, it is important to proof HRD dogs off of animal bones.

"Read Your Dog": A phrase that refers to the ability of a handler to observe and interpret subtle changes of behavior that might indicate their K9 has detected human scent.

Recall/Refind: The complicated (and hard to learn) behavior chain of a dog when it locates a missing person, then returns to its handler (who may be some distance away), then "ping pongs" back and forth between the handler and subject multiple times as the gap between them closes.

Reflex Tasking: The standard types of search assignments that are implemented right away when SAR arrives on scene. Example: For a lost young child there will be an immediate search of the 100-yard radius from the Point Last Seen, along with searches of any nearby attractants.

Repeater: An automated radio relay station (typically set up on a high point), that receives local transmissions (e.g., weak signals from handheld walkie-talkies) and rebroadcasts them at a higher power so that they can be received over a larger area.

Rig: Slang for vehicle. Example: "I left my dog inside my rig, and he ate half the back seat."

RTB: Acronym for Return to Base. Example: "Team 4 to Command, we are RTB."

SARTopo: An excellent computer mapping program developed by Matt Jacobs that is specialized for supporting search and rescue incidents.

Scent Article: An item (often clothing) that has been in close physical contact with the missing person and likely has absorbed some of the person's scent.

Scent Cone: An idealized representation of scent wafting horizontally from a person—narrow at its source and broadening steadily with distance from that person.

Scent Plume: A three-dimensional "cloud" of scent that originates with the missing person and is then spread both horizontally and vertically by air currents.

SCVSAR: The incredibly awkward acronym for Snohomish County Volunteer Search and Rescue.

Search Region: A relatively large geographic area defined for purposes of search planning. Search Regions (also called Planning Regions) are often defined based on a specific scenario, and theoretically have a uniform Probability of Area throughout. Example: "Based on the scenario that the lost hiker descended into Doom Canyon; we have defined the entire canyon floor as Region D."

Search Segment: A geographic area (typically a subset of a Search Region) that is small enough to be searched by a team during one operational period (search shift).

Self-Arrest: A mountaineering technique used to stop an uncontrolled descent on a steep snow or ice slope. Self-arrests are attempted by plunging the pick end of your ice axe into the slope. When falling down a steep slope in real life, you get about one second to arrest successfully before your speed is too great to stop yourself.

Snow Bridge: A layer of snow that crosses a hazard, such as a crevasse or stream. Snow bridges can be extremely dangerous due to the risk of collapsing under the weight of climbers, hikers, or search dogs. In Mount Rainier National Park, snow bridges have caused the deaths of a number of unsuspecting hikers.

"Source": Short-hand reference to human remains. Examples: "My dog has been trained on large source (large body parts)" or "My husband found jars of source in our refrigerator."

Swiftwater Rescue Team: Personnel with highly specialized training that allows them to accomplish heroic search and rescue assignments in water environments, including ponds, lakes, streams, rivers, and waterfalls.

Trailing: A search and rescue K9 discipline in which dogs are trained to find people by following a scent trail, a method that requires first exposing the dog to a "scent article" from the missing person.

Trained Final Indication: A distinct trained behavior (e.g., a bark or jump) given by a K9 to communicate to the handler that they have found their target.

UAV: Acronym for Unmanned Aerial Vehicle (see Drone).

UTM: Acronym for Universal Transverse Mercator Coordinate System. A global coordinate system that derives south-to-north and west-to-east locations from a theoretical, meters-based grid that covers the planet surface. (This explanation is greatly simplified).

VHF: Very High Frequency—radio frequencies in the range between 30 and 300 megahertz (MHz). Official SAR radios operate in the VHF range.

Waypoint: A specified location on the ground (or on a map). Example: "For any search teams that find bones, please capture a waypoint on your GPS, and then radio those coordinates into search command."

Wilderness Air Scent: A K9 discipline in which dogs are typically trained to find the scent of any human in a wilderness environment. Some air scent dogs are trained with scent articles to find a specific person.

1
What We Live For
In Which We Explain Ourselves

"You think dogs will not be in heaven?
I tell you, they will be there long before any of us."

—Robert Louis Stevenson

The avalanche debris field before us is a swath of icy destruction hundreds of yards wide and a quarter of a mile long. Above us, shadows sweep slowly over ragged mounds of white snow as clouds drift across the southern slopes of Mount Rainier. Tall hemlocks and alpine firs spear up from the slopes, white below, verdant green above, and gray sky overhead. In the distance, I hear the calls of my teammates directing their search dogs. The search incident commander shouts there are three snow burials, and one avalanche K9 team will be directed to each location.

Keb, my four-year-old Labrador retriever is tugging on her leash, more than ready to go. After years of our working together as a search and rescue team, she can feel my adrenaline traveling down the leash and knows what it means. Her nose is sniffing a mile a minute as she takes in the scent of sweet evergreen trees and high mountain snow. Keb loves the snow even more than I do, and while I'm pulling on my helmet and goggles, she sneaks in a luxurious roll and takes more than a few chomps of the fluffy white stuff. Time is urgent and our briefing is fast: safety, situation, safety. My heart is racing. Dan and I do our final checks of our "avi-beacons"—transceivers that each of us wears over our base layer of clothing and under our Gore-Tex jackets. We set them to TRANSMIT. Should any of us get buried by a second avalanche, the entire team will switch to RECEIVE, and with luck, be able to home in on the buried person's beacon, still in transmit mode.

Within minutes, Keb and I are moving toward our assigned location, a huge snowbank about twenty yards away. Close behind me, my field support person, Dan, is on the radio reporting back to search command. A retired Boeing manager and committed K9 team member, Dan is a rock. You need gear sorted? He volunteers. You need someone to hide as a "lost subject" in the cold rain for hours during a K9 practice? Dan will step up. He'll be accompanying me today because my usual search partner, Guy, is playing the role of a buried victim.

I've released Keb on a "go find" command, and right away she's got a live scent. She smells a human. She sprints to close the distance to the snow mound in front of us, moving left, then right, then left again as she narrows down the location of the strongest human scent. In K9 detection jargon we call this "working the scent plume." Keb knows exactly what do to now. She starts digging furiously, pearly snow flying wildly out behind her. Dan and I have our snow shovels ready, but we don't help, we just stand back and watch as Keb burrows deeper and deeper into the snowbank.

A hole appears under her paws, and Keb's digging becomes frantic. Her excited barks ring out across the slope. She sticks her nose in as far as it will go but can't fit through. She digs for another thirty seconds, the hole widens, and abruptly Keb dives headfirst through the hole. Her whole body disappears.

Now we hear a muffled "Woo! Woo! Woo!" from inside the hole as Dan and I dash forward to enlarge the entrance. Suddenly a gloved hand holding a tug toy reaches out from the hole, followed shortly by Guy's face, showing a huge grin. "Woo! Woo! Woo! Good job Kebbie!" Dan and I join the celebration with yips and yells that can be heard throughout our avalanche rescue training area.

Keb's tail whirls ecstatically. Even before she started digging, her nose knew that one of her best buddies was in that hole under the snow. She knew that when she broke through, Guy would be waiting with her favorite tug-toy, for a wild play party to reward her. As Dan and I enlarge the entrance to allow Guy to clamber out, Keb dashes in and out of the snow cave we had prepared in advance. She alternately plays tug-of-war with Guy and rolls enthusiastically in the snow. I just watch with a warm smile and a proud heart. This is what Keb lives for. And, as search and rescue volunteers, it's what *we* live for as well. We search for the living, the lost, and the dead.

A Dog's Devotion is our book. It is about me, my dog, and my search partner, Guy, and our journey of dedication, adventure, and hope as we overcome

With special permission from the Mount Rainier Park Superintendent, we were able to do avalanche rescue training with our dogs.

inner demons, face strife and human frailty, grow as persons, and evolve as search and rescue volunteers. It's the story of my steadfast K9 partner Keb, whose determination, keen nose, and willing spirit lead us every step of the way. This is a tale of belief, passion, being devoted to a cause, and trying to make a meaningful difference in the world. But above all, it's a story of the search for the living and the dead—using hard-earned skills to find what remains of lost souls, to seek out justice, and to always bring them home.

Suzanne's Story

I came into the world of K9 search and rescue suddenly and naively, with a vision of wanting to help in any way possible. It's the morning of September

11, 2001, and the phone rings. To my surprise it's my older brother calling all the way from Stockholm. I begin to exchange pleasantries, but he interrupts loudly. "Suzanne, listen to me. You must turn on your TV, NOW!" His voice is getting increasingly tense, and he sounds alarmed. My TV comes on just as footage is showing the second Twin Tower collapsing. In that moment my life changes forever.

Little did I know that the attack on my adopted country on that terrible day would be the catalyst through which I would find a cause that grew closer to my heart than anything I had ever dreamed possible. It was the event of 9/11 that prompted me to take stock of my life and to seriously explore my purpose in the world. A month after my brother's call, with the leash of my first SAR dog "Bosse" in hand, and high hopes in my heart, my twenty-year journey with Snohomish County Volunteer Search and Rescue began—a bumpy road with high *highs* and low *lows*, but on the balance so very much worth the personal and physical costs.

I was born and raised in Sweden, a small country with vast open space and unexplored wilderness. Who I am today was shaped by growing up in a culture with strong connections to nature marked by berry picking, mush-room hunting, cross-country skiing, and picking wildflowers. Then, as today, I had a happy-go-lucky character. I am someone who laughs easily and loves situational humor; I used to write comedy screenplays in school. I also have always had a serious dimension, which as a teenager led me to write dark poetry and, to my family's dismay, listen to Johannes Brahms piano concertos and Beethoven's Symphony No. 5 "Fate" ad infinitum. My obsession with Erik Johan Stagnelius, a troubled and gifted Swedish poet with strong mystic connections and writings on death, foreshadowed my later preoccupation with K9 human remains detection in search and rescue.

While in Sweden, I studied international relations at the university in the medieval town of Lund. My early interest in conflict management and community building led to a scholarship at the University of California, Santa Barbara, where my master's thesis was written under the tutelage of famed psychologist Carl Rogers, the father of the human potentials movement. After graduating, I moved to Seattle with my husband, Scott, whom I'd met on a blind date when he was an exchange student in Sweden. Among our friends at the university, we became known as "Suzanne and her Yankee."

The Pacific Northwest had everything we wanted. Wilderness, mountains, water, and skiing. Life was good, and my career took off as a senior executive responsible for running the human resources and organizational development aspects of businesses. Years later I found myself mired in a "merger from hell" marshaling an effort to integrate two wildly conflicting business cultures while rubbing shoulders with politicians, as they struck deals that I sometimes found morally reprehensible. Organizational transformations like this enticed me earlier in my career, but many years of stress had begun to take its toll. "I feel like I'm losing myself," I confessed to Scott in a weary voice. "Am I just a money-making machine destined to work sixty-hour workweeks forever? What am I missing out on?" Tears flooded my eyes. "Our daughter is growing up so fast and before we know it, she'll be off to college." Daughter Linnea had been an unexpected gift entering our lives a few years earlier, and we had gladly thrown ourselves into the role as dedicated parents.

Without missing a beat, Scott reassured me with a tender hug. "It's your turn, Suzanne. I know this may be a gamble, but you being happy is my priority." Rocking back and forth I listened to him as he reminded me how I'd been there for him as he faced a difficult career decision many years earlier. "Yes, cash flow may be an issue for a time, but we've faced challenges worse than that together. We'll make it work!" I felt a sense of calm and hope come over me.

With Scott's support, I left my old career behind and focused all my attention on designing a professional practice around what I still loved doing:

growing teams and effective leaders. I also wanted to build a business that would allow me to be me—all of me. To the dismay of many traditional consultants eager to advise me, my evolving brand merged my personal and professional life into "building community" wherever I go. To this day, all my clients know that when they buy my coaching services, they buy all of me—warts, flaws, and all—whether they want it or not, and that includes my obsession with search and rescue. I am so grateful to my clients for the support they have shown for my avocation over the years. "Oh, you have another search mission with your dog? No problem, no problem at all. We'll just reschedule. Please let me know how it goes."

With my redesigned career as an executive coach well underway, I started exploring different volunteer venues. I wanted to find a new and meaningful way to give back. As the first woman Rotarian in my club in Snohomish County, I had broken the glass ceiling for women and was flattered when one year I was given the "Working Woman of the Year Award" by the International Federation of Business and Professional Women. Yet as I excitedly immersed myself in a new career, I sensed *something* was missing. What do I want my legacy to be? What is my WHY? And, what do I want to be known for?

September 11 was just the catalyst I needed to bring everything into clear focus. As I drove to meetings in Seattle, I would see our Cascades in the distance: a range of high volcanic peaks and densely forested wilderness that bisects Washington State from north to south. Suddenly ideas swirled in my head: search and rescue (SAR), disasters, dogs, finding lost people in the wilderness. Why had I not seen this before? The puzzle pieces fit perfectly together. I was elated to find out that Snohomish County Volunteer Search and Rescue (SCVSAR) had a small K9 team. And to top it off, Scott was already involved with Everett Mountain Rescue, a partner organization of SCVSAR. If I became a SAR volunteer, we would have a new joint avocation allowing us to experience more of the Washington state wilderness together. Whooping and hollering as we shared bottles of wine over dinners, Scott increasingly became enticed by my vision: "We will be hiking together with a purpose." I had found my cause.

In the fall of 2001, puppy Bosse entered my life as my first search and rescue dog. As a puppy, Bosse was a little bundle of energy with a bigger than life Labrador retriever personality, which included a voracious appetite. Even now, years after he has passed on, he has a legacy within the K9 SAR community: with Bosse nearby, no hot dog or donut was safe. Bosse taught me about loyalty and everything I needed to know about training a search and rescue dog. He patiently stuck with me as I made all the mistakes a new handler can possibly make and then some. Throughout it all, he loved me unconditionally. He was my true-blue dog.

There are right and wrong ways to select a dog for search and rescue work. I chose Bosse because I fell in love with a cute puppy and was totally unaware that his moderate "drive," and lack of working-line breeding, would cause me no end of challenges. As a dog bred to be a great pet and companion, he did not have the strong hunt drive—commitment to searching—we want in a SAR dog. One day a couple of years into our training, I was told we just wouldn't cut it as a SAR team. "He just is not reliable and drivy enough." Our trainer then secretly scattered a package of hot dogs on our next training assignment to prove her point, possibly suspecting that Bosse would choose the hot dogs over the search. Fortunately, he was on his game that day. He trotted right by those yummy morsels—and found the volunteer hiding deep in shoulder-high ferns. We were given another chance to prove we had what it takes to become an effective SAR K9 team.

Somehow, through sheer determination and many hours of weekly training, we succeeded where many other novice K9 teams would fail. After two years of hard work, Bosse and I received our first certification. As a Wilderness

Air Scent K9 team, we were officially qualified to search for lost persons in Washington State. Soon after Bosse and I certified as an Air Scent Team, we were unexpectedly thrown into our first "cadaver search" on a gruesome murder case that remains unsolved to this day. On that search years ago, a seed of possibility was planted in my mind. Could I train a search dog to find human remains?

Most people don't realize there are different types of search dogs. Air scent dogs are trained to find airborne particles carrying the scent of humans. They are usually assigned 50 to 100 acres to search and can often detect the scent of a lost person from hundreds of yards away. Trailing dogs, on the other hand, are given a scent article (such as clothing worn by the lost person) and follow that scent trail. Specialized K9 disciplines, such as human remains detection (HRD), require a substantially increased level of training and commitment.

In Washington State, all counties have their own SAR organizations, operating under the purview of the sheriff's office. Snohomish County Volunteer Search and Rescue was a large organization with several hundred volunteers in multiple specialty teams. At the time I joined, the K9 team was small, and unfortunately internal conflicts were part of our daily diet. A K9 handler, seemingly insecure and with little experience as a leader, took over and immediately announced that her way of training dogs—which did not account for the fact that all dogs are different and that a method that works for one dog may be totally ineffective with another—was the only way tolerated within the team. Factions formed, with each actively trying to oust the other from search and rescue. Unsurprisingly, this ultimately led to a total implosion of the group, with Air Scent, Trailing, and HRD factions warring against each other. In response, the sheriff's office came within moments of disbanding the entire team. At the last minute, reason prevailed and a neutral group leader was appointed to separate and oversee the squabbling K9 factions.

Bosse and I continued to operate and train as members of the Air Scent team, separate from the Trailing and the Human Remains Detection disciplines. Our saving grace as an overall K9 group was that when called out for missions, all disciplines took the high road and worked cooperatively. This was anything but an ideal situation, but given the political realities within SCVSAR and the sheriff's office, it was the best option available at the time.

Despite this fractured environment, my early career as an air scent handler flourished. While training with Bosse and other team members, I started to realize I could draw on my professional experience and began providing guidance and leadership to our growing K9 team while working hand in hand with our K9 coordinator to build a team respected locally, regionally, and beyond. As I gained credibility with my team, I was also excited to be able to champion science-based, positive reinforcement approaches to training our dogs. I loved my new avocation with every fiber in my body. Getting up at an ungodly time every weekend to drive an hour or two to join my K9 team colleagues somewhere in our mountains to train quickly became the high point of my week. Training together ten to fifteen hours per week became a lifestyle that has absorbed me ever since. Add to that many hours spent as I moved into SAR leadership roles over the years. K9 search and rescue truly became the avocation I hoped it would be.

As SAR volunteers we often joke around that our compensation should be doubled, but of course, all this work is voluntary. In addition to the many hours of training and running our teams, there have been years when I spent $10,000 out of my own pocket on external workshops, conferences, gear, and equipment. "You don't get paid?" my brother in Sweden asks me incredulously every summer I visit with family. "Are you crazy?" My attempts to explain that many Americans volunteer their time in this way and that we don't have the social safety network as Swedes do, seems to do little to assure my Swedish friends and family that I have not gone over the deep end.

As Bosse and I became a seasoned K9 team over the first seven years of our SAR career, I decided to take on another challenge. I had long loved the mountains and wanted to be able to deploy on technical mountain rescue missions in remote and challenging terrain with both my dog and my mountaineer husband. Not only would this allow us to spend more time together, but I also secretly harbored a dream of overcoming deep-seated fears of heights, rooted in a gruesome mountain tragedy Scott and I had lived through many years earlier. I decided to join Everett Mountain Rescue, a sister organization closely allied with Snohomish County Volunteer Search and Rescue. Our county's mountain rescue team had historically mostly consisted of a small group of crusty men with a reputation for being solidly set in their ways. Indeed, they looked skeptically at me when I applied for membership: Not only was I woman, but I was not a young woman in her twenties or thirties. I was in my early fifties! And I had a dog! They were quick to throw out challenges. "What is Mountain Rescue going to do with a dog? Are you fit and fast enough for mountain rescue missions? Where are your technical skills? And, with Mountain Rescue being all male, how are you going to pee on the trail?"

In my heart, I knew I could meet these challenges, but my resolve waivered. In a moment of frustration, I turned to my husband, Scott. "Are they testing me, or have they already made up their minds?"

To his credit, and much to my relief, he and his friend Mark, the chair of Everett Mountain Rescue at the time, supported me wholeheartedly. "You go girl. Show them you can do it!"

Heartened and encouraged, I decided to step up and meet all hurdles and conditions thrown my way. I'd already completed the Everett Mountaineers Scrambling course ten years earlier. In that course I had mastered the art of climbing nontechnical routes to summits of many rugged peaks in the Pacific Northwest.

To meet mountain rescue team requirements, I now enrolled in the Everett Mountaineers arduous, year-long Basic Climbing program, learning about rock climbing, snow climbing, and roped glacier travel techniques. In addition to the physical climbing, my brain was filled with learning mountaineering knots and placing safety anchors for belaying and rappelling. My most vivid memory from the program was hanging for half an hour in my climbing harness fifteen feet down in a crevasse on the Mount Baker Coleman Glacier desperately trying, but failing, to use my ice axe to get over a monstrous overhang, all the while wiping angry tears out of my eyes. "I just can't do it!" I screamed at my instructor who, with a slightly vicious grin, retorted, "Well, you will never forget this, will you?" This response led me to clench my jaw, swing my axe pick into the ice wall, and climb out of the crevasse with a feeling of satisfaction I'll never forget. I could do this! After that, I had a blast in the Basic Climbing program: Scott was an instructor and we got to spend time together. Plus, our daughter, Linnea, and her then boyfriend, now husband, Chris, were also taking the course. It was a family affair, and we all enjoyed spending time in the mountains together.

After a year spent climbing and working on my mountaineering skills, I once again approached the all-male Everett Mountain Rescue board. As I sweated during a thorough grilling, I convinced them of my climbing skills and of the value that Bosse would bring for avalanche rescue. When I was accepted as a member at the end of the interview, I turned to Scott and Mark to see wide smiles.

Over the next couple of years, I was able to deploy with Bosse on "normal" wilderness search missions, as well as on select mountain rescue missions requiring specialty skills such as avalanche training or snow travel. I was later invited to join the board, and Scott became the chair. We ended up playing an instrumental role in growing the team from just over a dozen members to well over fifty. This included many capable women, which reflected a personal commitment of mine to pave the way for women in all aspects of my life.

Guy's Story

My life in search and rescue began on a cold March day in 2008 when I volunteered to join rangers on a search for a missing person in Mount Rainier National Park. My years of climbing and hiking in the California Sierra Nevada and the Cascade Range of the Pacific Northwest had prepared me for that day. We strapped on snowshoes, pulled on heavy mission packs, and spent hours grid-searching through steep, snow-covered forests. As we searched back and forth across our assigned area, we could hear other teams reporting on their handheld radios. We could hear the helicopter whirring above our heads.

I remember teasing my team member, a young ranger woman, as she boldly traversed a high log bridge wearing snowshoes. "Clare, if you fall into that ravine, we're not coming after you!"

I remember being "found" by happy search dogs as we took a snack break sitting in the snow. Their grinning K9 handlers rewarded them, saying "Good boy! Good boy! Now find another!"

I remember how Team 1 radioed to report they were now following a set of tracks in the deep snow. Two hours later, they found our missing hiker, dead from hypothermia.

For me, this began a decades-long commitment to search and rescue. Within a month, I joined my local Snohomish County SAR team. Eager to learn the basics, I discovered that the K9 team held mock search practices almost every week, and I leaped at the opportunity to join. I found myself amid a dedicated group of folks who loved dogs, trained constantly, and responded to missions with fanatic enthusiasm.

In my years volunteering for Snohomish County Volunteer Search and Rescue and Everett Mountain Rescue, I've deployed on SAR missions ranging from wilderness searches to technical rope-rescues, to disaster searches, to urban searches for Alzheimer patients. When not on missions, I worked closely with Suzanne developing a field support and navigation training program for our K9 team.

While Suzanne excelled in training search dogs and providing leadership for the K9 team, I naturally gravitated toward the complex task of search management. I discovered that search planning required understanding behavior patterns, systematically processing facts and clues, and applying probability-based search theory concepts. This was a perfect match for my background in health sciences and information management, and over time our SAR deputies began to call on me more and more to run difficult or multiday search missions.

Suzanne and I became a strong team: in the field on search missions, in our efforts to grow a top-notch K9 team, and later, in planning some of the largest K9 team deployments in the history of SAR in Washington State.

Suzanne

When Guy joined our Snohomish County K9 team, we quickly recognized that his wilderness and navigation skills were perfect for the role of "Field Support." In our county, we deployed K9 teams as a triad of a dog, a handler, and a field support person. The dog would range in front using her nose as a superb sensor; the K9 Handler would direct her and keenly watch for changes of behavior; and the field support person would be responsible for navigation, radio communications, situational awareness, and for keeping an extra set of eyes on the dog. Guy became a master of the field support role in very short order.

Over time Guy also became a master at developing interesting scenarios and planning out our trainings, which were becoming increasingly complex to manage as our team grew. Our trainings would start with a briefing from Guy while we all took notes: "Our plan today has eleven dog teams with different training objectives." He would then pass out a written plan he had painstakingly put together. "As you can see," he'd continue, "we have four rounds of training starting with three dog teams that each have between forty to sixty acres to search, some with significant elevation gain and steep gullies. Be aware that some of your subjects (volunteers tasked with hiding) may have medical issues. You need to be prepared to assess the situation and call in your subject care plans to our command post, which today will be me."

"But," he continued, "before we do anything else, we're doing some run-away drills with all our dogs to get them and you warmed up." Runaways are the foundation for what air scent dogs do—it's a chain of behavior we start with puppies from day one. In short, the handler holds the dog while another person runs away and hides a short distance away. The dog is released with a "go find" command, locates the subject, returns to the handler, and does a trained final response (TFR) such as a bark, jump, or tug to communicate that he has found a subject. "Show me!" shouts the handler, who then sprints after the dog, who has already whirled and is now dashing madly back to the lost person. Upon arrival, the dog's favorite toy magically appears, a *big* party ensues, and the handler and training subject yip and yell to excite and reward the K9.

The trained final response for an air scent dog is designed specifically so that the K9 can lead the search team to a found subject. It's essential that air scent dogs are rock solid on this chain of behavior. That's why we repeat these runaways literally thousands of times to develop muscle memory that will stay with our K9s on actual missions, even when they may be exhausted after searching for days for lost subjects. On a real mission, the trained final response may make the difference between life and death for a missing person.

In my emerging leadership role, I focused on team building and nurturing a strong and healthy culture. Guy, on the other hand, applied his analytical skills to organizing our team functions, to training us in wilderness navigation, and to visualizing SAR training concepts that he presented in a never-ending series of PowerPoint presentations. Where I was social and outgoing, he was quiet and reserved. If you needed someone to be the life of the party, I was your girl. At that same party, Guy would find a quiet corner in which to nibble on a plate of hors d'oeuvres. I'm a dog person. Guy prefers cats.

Keb's Story

Keb entered the scene as my SAR dog when Bosse was approaching retirement. In my search for a second SAR K9, I now knew the importance of the dog's breeding, so I engaged a Pacific Northwest working-dog professional to find a puppy with just the right drive and personality. She found Keb!

Keb is named Kebnekaise, Keb for short, after the highest mountain north of the Arctic Circle in Sweden, a peak we had recently summitted as a family. As a puppy she was quite a handful. She had unending energy, and she was fearless and willing to take on everything she was asked to do—full speed ahead. While Bosse was trained in human remains detection only late in his SAR career, Keb started her HRD training right away. She was an eager, quick learner! Within a few years, we had certified in multiple SAR disciplines, including Wilderness Air Scent and Human Remains Detection, as well as Avalanche Rescue and First Responder Disaster.

In many respects my circumstances when training Keb were quite different from ten years prior when I attended my first K9 SAR training with

Bosse. I had learned much about dogs and K9 training and had even earned a professional designation as a Karen Pryor Certified Training Partner. Karen Pryor is known around the world as a leading spokesperson for positive reinforcement—force free—training of animals. I initially trained Keb as a wilderness air scent dog—trained to find lost people that are alive. One of my first challenges was to find an appropriate trained final response, sometimes referred to as an "alert," for Keb—a way to communicate to me in no uncertain terms when she has found a person.

Oof! Keb impacts me with her jump alert.

For her trained response, I naively let Keb pick a behavior that seemed to come naturally for her: a "jump alert." To my enduring dismay, this evolved into a full-on body slam, as Keb started her jump five feet from me and would impact my body as a small furry missile.

This earned her the nickname Kebinator. Early in Keb's training career, after my annual physical exam with my family doctor, I remember him asking me to meet with him in his private office. I was of course alarmed, and my blood pressure soared as he hemmed and hawed. "How are things going at home? Are you and your husband getting along?" In a sudden wave of relief and embarrassment, I finally got it—he had noticed all the bruises covering my body and now suspected I had an abusive husband.

"No, no!" I explained. "I mean yes, yes, we are getting along fine! It's just Keb, my overly exuberant search and rescue dog."

Although Keb and I have been certified in multiple K9 SAR disciplines, we have always specialized in finding human remains. Think about puppy Keb going through basic obedience training. For her, this was grade school. Even before she was six months old, she was learning more difficult commands, such as an emergency stop, a necessity to keep her from moving toward hazards ranging from traffic to mountain cliffs. This was Keb's high school. Starting before she was just twelve months old, her advanced training to be an air scent SAR K9 was dog college. For Keb, certifications in specialty disciplines, such as human remains detection, which she earned at the age of four, were the equivalent of graduate school degrees. And once learned, these skills required constant practice to reinforce and maintain her detection abilities.

Training for human remains detection builds on, but is different from, air scent training. During Keb's foundational air scent training, she learned to seek out the scent of live persons and return to me with a dramatic jump alert. As she advanced into HRD training, she had to learn that a different command meant to search for the odor of the dead. She had to learn a trained final response (TFR) specific to HRD finds. She had to meet new and more challenging certification requirements. National annual certification requirements have tested our ability to find the odor of human remains ranging from larger sources of odor in wilderness settings, in water, and in rubble, to a few drops of blood on a carpet in a building or vehicle. In criminal cases, alerts from HRD K9s are sometimes used to justify search warrants, and the validity of these alerts may be challenged in court. For this reason, certification tests are deliberately hard. Even after years of training, HRD dogs can fail their tests. This happens in one of three ways: (1) not finding the "source" of human remains odor, (2) not alerting their handler by giving the appropriate trained final response (TFR), or (3) alerting on a nonhuman source of odor.

In the early stages of HRD training, we spend a lot of time imprinting the whole spectrum of decomposing human remains on our dogs, putting in many tedious hours doing thousands of repetitions of their trained final response. Keb's TFR when locating the odor of human remains is to sit, with her nose as close to the source as she can get it (i.e., where the odor is the strongest). We have a ritual when we start an HRD search. She sits at my left side, her gaze focused where I am pointing with my hand, in the direction of where I want her to search. I let her know her ball—her favorite toy in the whole world and her reward for making a "find"—is in my pocket. By now she knows the game is on. I can feel her body tremble slightly as I apply light pressure by folding my hands over her chest. I lean down, see her white eye lashes twitch, and whisper "sök" (Swedish for "search") into her ear.

Keb hears this and shoots out like a rocket, then quickly slows down to search systematically until she gets into odor. She then works her way into where the odor is strongest. Imagine the scent source is a glass jar containing one or two human teeth that has been carefully hidden away in a stump. Once she puts her nose on that stump, she'll make a couple of quick sniffs, close her mouth, and sit her rump down on the ground in a perfect TFR. Good girl Kebbie!

Keb, Guy, and I have deployed together frequently over the fourteen years since Guy joined SAR. We have found victims in the mud of a disastrous landslide. We've searched for the lost on high snowfields of Mount Rainier. We've searched for clandestine graves of murder victims and found bones that helped solve decades-old crimes. We've been called upon to volunteer our services in the dark, the wet, the snow, and cold in the rainforests and rugged mountains of the Pacific Northwest. We've searched in urban areas with homeless camps, drug needles, and thick blackberry bushes, and even as far away as Scandinavia. Throughout all, death has become an ever-present companion.

With Keb at our side and faithful SAR partners close by, our passion for finding the missing and the dead continues to provide us with some of the

Suzanne and Keb happily taking a break in a snow cave, after successfully finding and digging out a volunteer hider.

most moving and fulfilling times in our lives. We fall asleep at night knowing we make a difference for those left behind, and we do so with love, integrity, and professionalism. It's what we live for.

2
The Oso Landslide Disaster

In Which Our Lives Are Changed

*"One of the finest things men and women do
is rescue men and women,
even when they know they are rescuing the dead."*

— NORMAN MACLEAN, *YOUNG MEN AND FIRE*

"Why aren't we being called out?" March 23 is a gray Sunday as our K9 search and rescue team gathers at an urban industrial park for our weekly training. We run our dogs through their exercises, but everyone's mind is fifty miles north at the Oso Landslide, where the media reports that over 100 people are missing in the disaster area. My God, over 100 people?

Yesterday, my husband (Scott) and I had watched in shock as the news reports appeared. On March 22, 2014, death in the form of a 600-foot valley wall hung above the small Washington State community of Steelhead Haven, and then descended. The steep hillside—high above the North Fork of the Stillaguamish River—gave way in a massive landslide, spewing ten million cubic yards of dirt, mud, and debris as it came down, crossed the river, and crashed through the community below. The landslide destroyed trees, vehicles, and homes in its path and left piles of debris twenty feet high where it came to rest on the south side of the valley.

Arriving emergency crews and civilian volunteers were stunned by what they saw. People had been here. Families had been here. But now they were gone, the road was gone, their houses were gone. An entire community had disappeared in a sea of mud. Searchers frantically looked for survivors but were barely able to move through the cold, knee-deep muck. Trying to reach what was left of houses, rescuers themselves became stuck and unable to move.

In the desperate hours that followed, helicopter rescue crews from Snohomish County Search and Rescue, Whidbey Island Naval Air Station, emergency crews, and civilian volunteers from all over the area were able to pull only eight survivors out of the wrecked landscape. And then all became quiet, and along with the quiet came the stunned realization that many more people were missing but none were still living.

But there have been no calls for our K9 team to respond, and some of us fear that internal politics are at work. In our region as in many others, K9 SAR teams do not self-deploy. If there is a child missing next door or a collapsed building just down the block, the only way to get us to appear is to call 911. Our law enforcement deputies then determine if and when we respond to missions. Even within our own county, if we are close by and eager to help, we can't respond without their permission: to do so would end our search and rescue careers. There are valid reasons for this, and we accept most of them. We (and each of our dogs) are registered emergency workers for the Washington State Emergency Management Division and operate under the auspices of the Snohomish County Sheriff's Office. However, there are dubious private K9 handlers who just show up at searches and offer to help. Such people are not suffered gladly by the professional SAR community.

In our county it's our sense that there is an unfortunate history of the sheriff's department not calling our K9 team when we know we could help. Public infighting within our team a few years back did nothing to enhance our reputations. We also suspect that some of the deputies don't think search dogs are reliable. Our team struggles against this perceived bias by training hard, and by deploying only those K9 teams who have met strict certification standards.

It's now been three days since the Oso Landslide. Three days and still no K9 call-out! On the cold morning of Monday, March 24, I am walking across the SuperFit parking lot to my Toyota 4Runner. In my core I can still feel the warmth of the cardio-weight training session that I do with my husband religiously three times a week to stay in condition for our arduous volunteer work as part of search and rescue teams. On my sweat-covered skin, I can feel the chill of winter still upon us. As I open the car door, I hear the beep from my SAR pager and quickly grab it. This is it: the page to respond to the Oso Landslide!

I immediately call Carter, the K9 team leader who is coordinating our response. Carter is an immensely knowledgeable guy and a true asset to our team, but sometimes mission adrenaline can channel his thinking. "We have all the spots filled," he tells me.

"What, I can't go?" *Djävlans helvete!* I fume to myself in a cloud of Swedish curses. Keb and I should be responding to this mission! Instead, several of our more junior handlers and field support volunteers are being deployed to the disaster site. I take several deep breaths to calm myself, then try to redirect his thinking by asking some leading questions. "Carter, isn't this mission going to need dogs with both wilderness and disaster experience—and dogs trained to . . . "

"Like I said, Suzanne, sorry, but all spots are already filled."

I lean my forehead down to the steering wheel in a moment of despair. I can't believe Keb and I are going to be left behind on this mission. We're trained, we're ready, we're the only team in our group with experience finding both live and deceased subjects. We are *the* right team to deploy for this disaster. Then to my relief, Carter, who always comes through once he's had a chance to think things over, calls me back. "OK, Suzanne, can you respond with Keb, and can you also coordinate the K9 search assignments on the west side of the slide area?" Yes, yes, yes!

On the drive home, I call my regular search partner, Guy, to see if he's available to be my field support person. As my field support, Guy will take care of radio communications and navigation guidance, while providing an extra margin of safety by watching for drop offs, spilled chemicals, and other dangers to Keb and to me. "I'm on it, Suzanne. I'm loading gear in my car right now and should be on the road in about ten minutes. This could be a big one!"

At home now, I frantically pull on my SAR clothes: tough synthetic pants, multiple synthetic upper layers, and sturdy boots with Gore-Tex gaiters covering my legs from my feet to my shins. I scramble to pack while yelling to Scott, "We've finally been called out on the Oso Landslide! Can you help me check that I have all the gear and equipment that I'll need? Can you make sure Kebbie's extra food is in the car?"

Scott knows this is our first true disaster mission and gladly takes a few minutes to calm me down and help inventory my gear. "Be damn careful up there!" Scott cautions as he loads my SAR mission pack into the already crammed luggage space.

"Load up!" I call. Keb leaps happily into the backseat of my car, and once again we're a girl and her dog, out to save the world. Soon we are driving north toward Oso and to a search that will change us forever.

The call to respond to the Oso Landslide signaled the beginning of a month-long deployment for me and my SAR K9 Keb on one of the largest natural disasters in Washington State history—a tragedy that claimed forty-three lives and completely erased the presence of a small community nestled along the Stillaguamish River. Oso also marked a turning point in the long journey that Keb and I, and my SAR teammate Guy, have been on ever since becoming search and rescue volunteers years ago. During our long days of searching at Oso, our eyes were opened to the value of our regional K9 SAR community. Most importantly for me, though, my self-confidence and my trust in Keb's abilities grew to the point where I no longer had any lingering doubts. And I've never looked back.

During the two-hour drive to Oso, my thoughts swirl with anxiety and anticipation. Keb has no clue what we're about to face, but she's no doubt noticing that I'm talking to her as if she's human, a habit I developed over the years when under stress. "What do you think, Kebbie? Are we ready for this? What should be our priority as we arrive on scene?" Here, in the privacy of my car, it's just the two of us, and I can avoid embarrassment from getting caught debating the pros and cons of search tactics with my dog. Keb is a great backseat listener and expresses her opinions with soft woofs, nudges to my blond ponytail, or sneaking licks of my neck. Soon enough though, she is snoring softly in the backseat, as the pre-mission anxiety I always feel is not an issue for her.

Nearing the scene, my hands clench the steering wheel, as I pass parked fire engines and rescue vehicles near a Washington State Patrol roadblock. An officer sees the large "K9 SAR" decal on my vehicle and directs us through to park on the shoulder of the highway. The slide area is over a mile wide, and today our teams will be deploying on the west side. I get out of my car, and the first thing I notice is a blue house in the distance. Something is not right. Why is it sitting on the highway? My gaze slowly rises and—my God!—I see the slide itself, a massive open wound in the landscape that starts up at the valley rim and ends in the vast brown sea of mud before us. We've never searched in conditions like this. We've never even seen anything like this. My heart thuds. Oh, Kebbie, are we ready for this?

I see a swarm of activity near the forward staging area, and it looks as if local fire department personnel are in charge here. I'm relieved to see several members of my own Snohomish County K9 team are already here, so I hurry to join them. I see more colleagues from neighboring King County Search Dogs. Among them are Andy Rebman and Marcia Koenig, who are both seasoned K9 SAR pros, nationally recognized for their contributions and expertise. Andy is the coauthor of the book *Cadaver Dog Handbook*, which many consider the bible for training K9s to find human remains.

I have a rushed consultation with the fire captain in charge. He's heartened to see a half dozen K9 teams have already arrived, and he's desperate to get dogs out into the field. I suggest that we leave two experienced K9 volunteers at forward command to coordinate with K9 teams that will be deployed. The fire captain quickly agrees to my plan. We appoint Andy Rebman from King County and Nick Adams from my own Snohomish County team to these liaison roles. Leaving Keb in my car, the rest of us hike up and over the hillside to view the search area where we will be deployed. The fire captain had shown us search assignments on a hastily sketched map, but from here we can actually see the reality of our search area. On our left, we see the huge open scar on the hillside. Ahead of us, we see where the highway disappears under the slide. To our right, we see the wall of trees and debris that has been pushed to the south side of the valley.

With a fresh vision of what lies ahead of us, we return to our vehicles and get ready to deploy. We wait, and then we wait some more. Nothing is happening and continues not to happen for quite a while. Finally, we ask the fire captain what the holdup is and find out that state geologists are still assessing the stability of the remaining valley wall where the slide had occurred. All rescuers have been pulled out of the field until the geologists are convinced that more of the hillside will not come down upon us. Until we get the go-ahead, we're stuck waiting. My anxiety mounts. Keb continues to snooze in the backseat.

As we are waiting, George, one of our Snohomish County SAR deputies, suddenly appears. One of four deputies responsible for overseeing SAR volunteers, he lives only a short distance from the slide; his home community is reeling from the impact. George is usually calm and soft spoken, but the stress of this disaster has taken over. Bristling with anger, he walks right up to me and rages, "Are you self-deploying?" Taken aback, I try to explain that no, we were called out and are here based on an official request. It's as if he can't hear me. Muttering "This will have consequences!" he stalks off to the side to call our lead SAR sergeant. What's his problem! I think to myself. He didn't even listen to what I said! It's disappointing that my efforts to build a credible relationship with George have apparently gone nowhere, perhaps overshadowed by a long history of conflict within the K9 team.

An hour later, George returns and his rage about my possible self-deployment has disappeared. He shifts the conversation to specific "safety guardrails" for our deployment. "While you're out in the slide area, you're to keep all team members in sight at all times. Your team must stay within fifty feet of the outside slide boundaries." It takes me a few seconds to understand what he means. Then I realize that if more of the slide came down and caught us out in the middle, there might be little chance for rescue. Days later, George finds me and sincerely apologizes for his angry outburst. This incident becomes only one of many reflecting the underlying human stress caused by a disaster of this magnitude.

Hours go by. Keb is bored, and while I'm away trying to get status updates, she sneaks up to steal my sandwich from the passenger seat. I catch her stealthily returning to the backseat with it dangling from her mouth. As I hurriedly open the car door to retrieve whatever is left, she devours it in one big gulp. "Bad girl, Keb!" I yell. "*Jäklans skit!*" That may well be my only food all day, I think.

Guy, who has seen this happen before, grins while admonishing me. "You never learn, do you? She's a hungry Lab. You're going to need a K9-proof lockbox for your food!"

Tall, calm, and known for his sardonic humor, Guy somehow finds opportunities for levity during otherwise grim searches. He's been my regular search partner for years now, and I'm grateful for his steady influence today. He knows that my colloquial Scandinavian curses sound harsh, but often translate to old-fashioned farm country humor—an outlet for the stress and emotions we face when searching for the missing or the dead.

A couple of hours later we finally get the "go ahead," put on our helmets, and shoulder mission packs heavy with first aid gear, extra clothes, folding shovels, and water and food for an all-day deployment. We carefully begin to move out into the slide area. On this first day, our Snohomish team, five K9s (Keb, Mav, Sable, Gema, and Odin) along with their certified handlers and field support volunteers, will deploy as five separate search teams across widely dispersed areas. During the long cold hours to come, short snippets of conversation via our team's walkie-talkie frequency will be the only way we have of knowing what our friends are encountering in other areas "out on the slide."

As we approach our assigned area, I'm still taken aback by the total devastation we encounter. I know I've got to concentrate on our search assignment, but my mind starts to imagine the horror of men, women, and children crushed by an unexpected monster of nature. I wrench my thoughts back to focus on the task at hand. Two King County K9 teams split off to search near the blue house we saw earlier in the middle of the road. Ahead of us, we see Ethan Denver, a handler from Kittitas County, moving far out into the debris field with his black Lab, Jet, zigzagging in front of him. Due to the hazardous environment and the sheer difficulty of searching the debris fields, Keb and I will have both Guy and Dan as field support today. As we continue hiking to our assigned search area near the foot of the slide, I reflect that these trusted teammates are exactly the two I want with me.

As Guy, Dan, and I work our way cautiously to our assigned search area, Keb is still on leash. She is impatient, pulling hard, and audibly gasping and choking. While I love her exuberance, I hold tightly to her leash. I'm worried about what dangers she may face. The air is filled with the throbbing of helicopters above us and the buzzing of chain saws cutting through smashed houses. Our noses fill with the scent of wet earth and mud. My mind is filled with unnatural visual images of a world destroyed.

In the distance we see a black body bag being hoisted by a helicopter. Before us, our search area is one expansive sea of debris and broken up houses mixed in with large swaths of mud. As we come upon firefighters and other rescuers, we explain that my search and rescue K9 "Keb" may alert on any victim that is still alive, or on the odor of human remains, and that we will let them know if and when that happens. Standing at the edge of the search area, Keb is now trembling with excitement. Her gaze and whole body are focused forward. Her leash is still firmly in my hand. "You ready, girl?" As she balances on a pile of debris, her tail is thumping against a broken piece of plywood at a frantic pace. *Whomp, whomp, whomp.* Keb's message to me is clear: *I'm ready to go, RIGHT NOW!*

Three days have gone by since the landslide. It's possible that we might still find survivors trapped in the debris. I unleash Keb and decide to deploy her with a "find a live person" command so that her focus will be on the scent of living persons that might be buried. I wonder what will she encounter in this world of devastation, and how will she communicate with me? Will I be able to read her change in behavior? I can trust Keb to alert on a live person, but how will she communicate to me if she runs into the odor of the dead?

I try to imagine what Keb is experiencing. She basically *is* her nose. For Keb, all humans exist more as different odors than visual images. Her olfactory system is a finely tuned piece of biology. She has several hundred million scent receptors lining the caverns of her nose, compared to my skimpy six million. Her olfactory bulbs make up a big part of her brain—a vomeronasal organ sitting above the roof of her mouth. She can smell *a lot* of stuff we humans cannot even start to imagine. The stew of odors she is met with today must be absolutely overwhelming. Sometimes when we are searching together, the only part of her body that is not motionless are her nostrils, which can be seen quivering slightly. It always makes me wonder what she is processing. Science on K9 olfaction has historically told us that dogs catalog smells with infinite precision. Though recent studies appear to suggest otherwise, I always imagined that when I smell stew, Keb smells all the individual ingredients: carrots, meat, parsley, bay leaves, and every other spice. What are you smelling right now, little girl? I'm almost afraid to imagine.

The debris field is wildly uneven, and I'm thankful for all the hours Keb and I have spent doing disaster agility training. She moves quickly and effortlessly, while we mere humans struggle to move step by step across the piles

I'm thankful for the disaster agility training Keb has had. Climbing on ladders and rubble piles has prepared her for this challenge.

of splintered boards, shredded roofs, and smashed furniture. In our assigned area, the challenge is less the slippery mud and clay but more the instability of the wreckage we have to climb over, under, and around. Following Carter's advice, we've wrapped duct tape around the tops and bottoms of our gaiters to seal the mud out. We've also been warned about the dangers of walking in debris fields, so I'm wearing my heavy mountain boots for protection. These have hard plastic shanks that may protect my feet from puncture wounds. But Kebbie doesn't have such protection. The thought of a nail piercing Kebbie's paw sends a shudder through me.

When searching for a live person in a wilderness setting, Keb's trained response is to return to me with a jump indication to tell me, *I found someone! Hurry and follow me so I can get my ball!* In her enthusiasm, she has knocked me down more than once, and I've been known to shove my field support person in front of me to take the hit. Today I've started Keb on a "search for live persons" command, and I'm secretly dreading what will happen if she senses someone alive under all the debris. If Keb body slams me on an unstable pile of debris, the results could range from acute embarrassment to injury. By contrast, when you train for a disaster search, you use a more passive alert (such as barking) for either dead or live finds. This is for reasons of safety, as you typically work in a very unstable environment. I worry now that I should have started Keb with a "disaster search" command, but it's too late; she's started searching already, and I don't want to confuse her by switching.

For as long as I've been in search and rescue, the K9 community has had an ongoing debate about when dogs smell "dead" versus "live." How soon after death does the "living person scent" start changing to the "dead person scent?" How fast is that transition under different conditions? After a disaster such as the Oso Landslide, how soon should we start giving our dogs "search for the dead" commands instead of "search for the living" commands? One possibility is that cells start changing at the moment of death, and depending on the circumstances, may begin decaying even before organs start shutting down. Science shows that more than 500 chemical compounds come off a human body at various stages of decomposition, and more are continually discovered. But we don't know exactly which ones our dogs are responding to or when during the process what compounds are available. Our best guess is that there is a continuum of transition from "live" to "dead" scent, and we hope that varied and comprehensive training will allow our dogs to alert us in the presence of either.

On my first day at Oso, we get three strong alerts from Keb, and one find that will stay in my memory forever. Shortly after 2 p.m., we're searching through piles of debris from smashed houses, when Keb starts slowly circling an area. It looks like she's trying to do her sit indication, which is her trained alert for *scent of the dead here*. I can tell she's frustrated, and she starts barking, something she rarely does except when someone comes to the door at home.

Suddenly I remember our recent four-day disaster training in British Columbia looking for volunteer hiders squirreled deep into rubble piles. Keb learned
that when she detected a person but could not reach them, she was to sit and
bark. I decide to take her bark as a clear signal that she's found human scent.

I look around urgently to see if any other dog team can come over to
double-check the area and validate Keb's find, but everybody else is too
caught up in their own searching. Keb keeps barking. I contemplate running
her in the same area again, but I worry I am likely to cue her—*Oh, you want
me to alert here?*—by bringing her back over and over to the same place.
When searching for human remains, typically the first pass gives us the best
information.

"I think my dog has something! Can you dig over here?" The firefighters
start digging and removing loose boards. They keep looking back to us for
direction as they do backbreaking work, carefully prying up and removing
one board at a time. My nervousness increases: I'm hoping desperately that
we're not sending these dedicated rescuers on a wild goose chase. But time is
critical, and we can't linger to see what they uncover. We need to search other
areas.

Thirty minutes later Dan, Guy, and I have moved on, and less than fifty
feet away we suddenly see Keb on top of another debris pile where she sits
and gives *another* loud bark! She turns and looks intensely at me with her eyes
dark as wells. If eyes could only speak. She is clearly communicating with me
again. Nearby rescuers drop what they are doing and move toward this second
pile to start removing debris. Here, as in other areas across the slide zone, our
dogs are the ones telling us where to search, but at the time, I didn't realize it
would be days before I knew if Keb's alerts were indeed accurate.

As we move on, I notice mud-caked firefighters slowly dig their way deep
into the shredded wreckage of a family home. Helicopters whir low overhead, and the drone of chainsaws drifts across a sea of horrific devastation.

Suddenly I see Keb out of the corner of my eye and realize I've temporarily lost track of what she is doing. Chiding myself for a handler error, I turn around and see her in a crouched, almost stalking position, circling slowly and cautiously in a sludge-covered area ten feet away. Keb is now sniffing intensely from different angles, pressing her nose into the ground, and taking swipes at the dirt. Bits of clay and dirt go flying as her claws rake the surface. My heart gives a small thump as I watch her continue to circle the area. This is not what she is trained to do. She is not giving a "trained final response," such as a sit or a bark, that would clearly communicate she has made a find. Nevertheless, her behavior has definitely changed—it's almost as if she's mesmerized by whatever she is pawing at.

I lean over to one of the volunteer firefighters standing close to me, point to Keb, and ask "Is it possible a body was lying there before it was airlifted?" With the strain on his face showing, he wearily shakes his head "No" and goes over to where Keb is standing. He starts carefully removing layers of loose brown dirt, using first a small shovel, then just his gloved hands. Moments later he turns around and just stares at Guy and me. We move closer, not knowing what to expect. With sweaty palms, I put Keb back on her leash and watch as the firefighter takes out his water bottle, and with a gentleness I will always remember, starts washing mud off a face that is staring at us with the eyes of the dead. Keb has found her first victim of the Oso Landslide Disaster.

As the firefighter calls to his team for assistance, Keb and I retreat a respectful distance and my mind surges with a terrible mix of emotions: the pride of success and the sorrow of human loss. I can't believe it was just seven hours ago when my search and rescue pager went off, interrupting my workout at our local gym.

Keb and I will have only one find confirmed on that first day of our deployment on the Oso Landslide—the victim that haunts my memory as the Lady in the Mud. Most vividly, I recall seeing a ring on a pale white hand. For some reason, that's the image I can't get out of my mind. On the drive home I feel a roller coaster of emotions: sadness at the total devastation and lives lost, ache for the broken-hearted family members that mingled with us on the search earlier in the day, pride in Keb's performance and her find, mixed with self-doubt and questioning: were her two other strong alerts something real, or just Keb's confusion in a chaotic and bewildering environment? Will I ever know?

Two days later, after a mandated rest period, Keb, Guy, and I are driving north to the Oso Landslide for our second deployment. We stop first at the Arlington command post on the west side of the slide. Here, we spy our fire captain, who hurries up to me. "Where have you been? After you left, we found victims in both those other places where your dog alerted!"

Relief, satisfaction, pride, and sadness swirl, as I struggle to respond coherently. "Our SAR sergeant required us to take a full day of rest, but we're back today."

From the fire captain, we learn that our assignment for today is actually on the *east* side of the slide, not far from the tiny town of Darrington. Normally, this would be a quick thirty-mile drive, but the road between Arlington and Darrington is still buried in a sea of mud. Guy and I look at each other in resignation, it's going to take us at least another hour to drive a northern detour route, first farther north on Interstate 5, then many miles east on Highway 20.

Once at the Darrington command post, we learn we'll deploy along the south edge of the slide, with a six-person rescue team from the local volunteer fire department. Search planners have theorized that victims may have been swept entirely across the valley floor to lodge in the southern debris edge. Our other Snohomish K9 teammates are widely scattered on assignments throughout the 800-acre disaster area.

Searchers struggle through the treacherous log pile. One slip could have led to entrapment or a broken limb.

Once our gear is ready, we join the fire/rescue team sitting in the back of a large pickup truck that will drive us up a hastily constructed gravel bypass road, which skirts the southern edge of the debris field. Across the pickup bed from me is a young firefighter, dressed in a bright yellow and blue rescue jumper. Her eyes shine with worry, and I have to resist the urge to give her a hug.

Our ride up the hill is rough, but thankfully short. We unload from the bed of the pickup, and I keep Keb close while we scan the scene. On my right, I see a twenty-foot-high wall of demolished forest. Imagine a game of Pick-Up Sticks, only with broken trees, many of them at least two feet in diameter and some fifty feet long: this is our search assignment. Guy's grinning, but I'm starting to get nervous. I cautiously hold Keb back for a moment as Guy moves ahead of us. He climbs up on a twisted cedar trunk and peers into the wreckage. "Suzanne, it looks like the wall of trees is only about thirty-feet wide. I can see the main mud field on the north side!"

Balancing on tilted wet logs and clambering through fragrant, broken evergreen branches, we try to climb our way in. Keb is eager to charge through, but I quickly realize it's not safe for her. If she slips into a deep hole between trees, we might never get her out. It's not safe for us either. "Guy, we're going to have to back out and look for a different route!" After years of working as a team, a quick glance and a nod is all it takes: we're in agreement. We back out.

Twenty yards to the west, we find an opening in the wall of smashed trees, and as we break through on the north side of the log wall, we're stunned once again by the devastated landscape before us. We can see clearly now how the moving sea of mud swept a mile across the valley floor, pushing trees and debris ahead of it. Having failed to enter the log wall from the road on the south, we're now going to attempt it from the north side, through the mud.

But we can barely move. In most places, it is difficult to walk. In some places it's impossible. I see Guy a few yards ahead, struggling to lift his feet, "Suzanne! The mud here is six feet deep; we need to go around!" If we step in the wrong place, our legs plunge knee-deep into thick wet mud, and there are many more wrong places than right places. Small ponds and streams have formed in the mud flow, and we must find ways around or over them. We adopt the tactic of trying to step on downed branches, or on places where the mud looks slightly drier. This allows us to slowly pick our way closer to the log piles that we are supposed to search.

Guy and I continue to slowly work our way along the southern edge of the mud field, probing into the log piles wherever we can. We then traverse through woods and across small streams to meet up with Carter and K9 Mav. While we quickly brief each other on where we have searched, I see poor Mav is covered with wet mud up to his belly. Later that day after hours of more searching, Mav, wrapped in warm towels, is treated for hypothermia while

Carter holds him in his arms. After two days of rest, Mav completely recovers and returns to the Oso Search.

After searching for hours, Guy and I rejoin our fire/rescue squad at the pickup truck which is parked back on the maintenance road. There we learn that we've been reassigned to another nearby area. We take a short break at the pickup truck, to chomp snack bars and gulp water, then walk down a dirt driveway to a collection of wrecked houses. With less mud here, we're actually able to move around and search more effectively. We walk 300 yards to the west, where we come upon a completely collapsed house. Imagine a giant hand taking a house and smearing it across the ground until only the roof remains. That's our house. I direct Keb to search access routes under the roof, while the fire/rescue squad and Guy circle the house. Kebbie shows no changes in behavior, and we see no sign of victims. We move on.

As the afternoon wears on, we work our way back to the east. We pause to avoid entering a helispot, a helicopter landing zone, where a body is being loaded for transport. Soon, we come to a house that is wrecked but only partially collapsed. "Guy, I'm seeing noticeable changes of behavior from Keb here. It's not a full alert, but I think we should try to take a closer look. Go ahead and mark a GPS waypoint for K9 interest at this location, we can also report this back to incident command for follow up." Reaching the side of the house, Guy peers in through twisted two-by-four framing. He turns his helmet headlamp on and moves cautiously into the wreckage, stepping over boards and twisting through tight gaps. He calls out for any survivors. Even though it's been several days since the slide, there's still a chance. We listen. We watch Keb for any alerts, almost fearing what she might tell us. We get no response, no sounds of the living, but apparently there is no smell of the dead either.

It slowly dawns on me that Guy is crawling inside an unstable structure resting on an unstable mud flow: probably not one of his best ideas. "Guy, I don't think you should go any farther!" To my relief, he shares my realization and starts backing out carefully.

As he reappears out of the wreckage, I see he's carrying a family portrait in a small mud-covered frame. Guy looks at me for an opinion: "I don't know the protocol for this, but if we leave it here, it's just going to get demolished by excavating machines." After a short discussion, we decide to retrieve the picture. It may help us identify whose house this was and may also bring some comfort to those left behind. Guy puts the picture carefully into his pack, and we start back to our rendezvous point.

After a long day of searching, six fire/rescue squad volunteers, along with Guy and myself and a very muddy Keb, all pile back into the pickup truck for the return to advanced base, which is merely a section of two-lane Highway 530 where fire trucks and command vehicles are parked. All afternoon we've been tromping through mud mixed with household debris, rotting food, human waste, and God only knows what else; so we want to get that stuff washed off. However, this early in the incident, the only decontamination available to us is from a small fire hose at the back of one of the rescue engines. A smiling fireman gently hoses mud and ick off our legs; then I hold Keb while she gets the same treatment. I sit down and peel the now muddy duct tape from my gaiters, then return to get more mud washed off my boots. Somewhere there are professional decontamination specialists reading this right now and shaking their heads in dismay, but it's all that was available to us.

On the way out, we stop at the Darrington Fire Station command post to formally check out for the day. In any search incident, especially a disaster, searcher safety is a primary priority, and it's critical to know when all search personnel are out of the field. Before leaving, Guy reaches into his pack, pulls out the portrait we found, and hands it to one of the command staff. She looks at it and is silent for a very long moment. Then she looks up at us, and in quiet sorrow says, "Yes, I know who this is, thank you."

Cookies for Dog Heroes. I teared up when I saw this near our search base.

It's nearly 5 p.m. when Guy and I separate and start our long drives home. Heading west on Highway 20, my body is tired, but my brain still whirls from the day's stress. We've learned that the "thou shalt take a mandatory rest day between deployments" policy has now been relaxed, and they want us back on the Darrington side tomorrow. Thinking about the three-hour drive home and the three-hour drive back for more searching tomorrow, I start scheming. Is there a nearby place to stay overnight? Do they allow pets? Driving through Burlington, I spy a large Hampton Inn and decide to see if they have a room available. They do, so I phone Scott to let him know of my plans. I sort out piles of dirty and clean search clothes and relax for a few moments before falling asleep with Keb happily on the bed beside me.

Up early the next morning, I avail myself to the free breakfast down near the lobby. Sitting in my considerably less-than-clean SAR clothes, I enjoy dry scrambled eggs, even drier potatoes, and considerably less-than-strong coffee. I'm sneaking some eggs into a napkin for Keb when a stranger comes up to me. Oops, has he caught me taking food?

"Are you with the search teams?"

"Yes."

"I just want to thank you for what you're doing."

A lump forms in my throat; I am only able to nod and smile.

Mission Debrief

Guy

In the months following the Oso Landslide, geologic research unfolded an important perspective before us, reminding us that human time is not earth time. We learned that the valley walls on both the north and south sides of the Stillaguamish River Valley were, in effect, loose piles of unconsolidated glacial soils. LIDAR imagery (like radar but using laser light) revealed that the valley walls had a regular history of sloughing off in large landslides. The community of Steelhead Haven had been built under the Sword of Damocles.

Even before the Oso Landslide mud dried, fingers began pointing, blame started spreading, and lawyers' phones started ringing. Geotechnical studies concluded that the main contributing factors were the underlying geology of loose soils, increased groundwater loading due to timber harvesting, and the three preceding weeks of extreme rainfall. Seismic recordings revealed that the slide occurred in two phases. Stage 1 was a remobilization of a mass of loose earth left over from a previous smaller slide in 2006 on the same valley wall. This movement essentially pulled the rug out from under the upper slopes, which unloaded 250 seconds later in a second catastrophic debris flow that swept death across the valley.

When Suzanne, Keb, and I searched across the 800 acres of mud and debris on the valley floor, we simply deployed where we were told. Our focus was on searching through each section of mud or debris assigned to us. In those early days, the search planners at the Incident Command Post had hastily divided the slide plain into large areas, and in those areas, searching around pockets of wreckage was the first priority. It would not be until later that the search planners discovered there was a pattern to where the slide had deposited its victims. When the slide swept through Steelhead Haven, it swept debris and victims ahead of it in a fan-shaped pattern that split into two streams. This was a breakthrough that dramatically improved search efforts and opened my eyes to the world of search planning.

Looking Back

Suzanne

As fate would have it, the day immediately following my first day of deployment on the slide, I found myself on the Edmonds-Kingston ferry, sailing west across the waters of Puget Sound to face an important challenge for Keb and me. We had been scheduled months before to take our human remains detection (HRD) certification test on this day. We were to be evaluated by Norma Snelling, president of the National Search Dog Alliance, a certifying agency providing services throughout the United States. For Keb and me, it would be our first HRD certification test with a national organization, and we were nervous. Well, at least I was. Keb, as usual, snoozed peacefully in the backseat of the car.

As we drove off the ferry and headed west toward the small town of Sequim on the Olympic Peninsula, my cell phone rang. I answered using my hands-free feature (safety first!) and was surprised to hear our SAR organization's critical incident stress (CIS) counselor inquiring unnecessarily as to whether I was OK or not. He's the guy that helps SAR volunteers cope with feelings and reactions after particularly gruesome or disturbing missions. With some irritation, I suspected this was Carter's doing. After yesterday's mission, I had *told* him I was not feeling any unusual emotions, but he decided to have the CIS counselor call me anyway. Grumbling silently, I had to take my focus off our looming certification test and convince this CIS guy that I was not freaking out. While the Oso Landslide was my first large-scale disaster, I carried with me prior experience from the hundreds of missions I had been involved with over the fourteen years of my SAR career.

Most of us SAR volunteers, like health care professionals, have learned how to compartmentalize dealing with death on missions. If doctors or nurses let themselves get too emotionally involved with their patients, burnout quickly looms on the horizon. In search and rescue, we too could quickly become an impediment to the mission if we let our emotions take over. That being said, yes, there are times after previous missions when I shed tears privately and quietly as a way to process the pain I felt for victims and the families left behind. That is healthy. Yes, I felt deeply, and yes, the image of the hand with the ring and a stream of water gently washing mud from the face of an unknown woman was still vivid and recurring. But I didn't need support at this time. Unexpectedly, the conversation with the CIS counselor turned out to be a good one. We concluded the phone conversation agreeing that my feelings are quite normal, and there was no reason for any kind of intervention. What Keb felt about all this is unknown. Throughout the conversation, she snored softly from the backseat.

Once in Sequim, we met up with Norma, and anxiously started our certification test. It was a challenge that required all my attention, with multiple elements taking the better part of a day, including wilderness and road assignments, as well as searching both vehicles and buildings. Five hours later we proudly left with a certificate in hand; Keb and I were the first in our K9 team to certify in human remains detection with a national organization. Our certification was the culmination of several years of training, often ten to fifteen hours per week or more. My heart was soaring, and I planned a steak dinner for myself and Scott, with a generous helping for Kebbie. "Kebbie girl, would you like some steak?" *Thump, thump, thump,* from the backseat. She knew exactly what that word meant and immediately started drooling. Driving home, I pondered the coincidence of the Oso Landslide and our HRD certification. The timing seemed incredible.

Reflections

After each training, after each mission, Guy and I force ourselves to pause, reflect, and learn. What did we do well? Where did we screw up? Our focus starts on Keb and how we did as a K9 team.

Did I keep Keb safe? The honest answer, the answer that still wakes me at night, is no. The mud plains of the Oso Landslide were strewn with chemicals, sewage, and in some places, human remains. All of us, the fire crews, the SAR volunteers who responded, the loggers from the local community who joined the search, should probably have been wearing hazmat suits. None of us did. Boots, gaiters, and gloves were all we had. During disaster searches, K9s are typically deployed without vests, collars, or any covering, for fear that they will get caught by debris, out of reach of human rescue. On the Oso Slide, our search dogs, without protection of any kind, were close to the ground and faced even greater exposure to the toxic environment than we did. Keb did not choose to search under those conditions; she merely went where I asked her. I was responsible for her safety. I sent her in harm's way. That Keb, and other search dogs, suffered few ill effects of the Oso Search softens my guilt, but it does not wash it away.

Did we notice changes in Keb's behavior and interpret them correctly? I know now, that Keb, my Kebbie, was responsible for finding at least three of the forty-three victims of the Oso Landslide. During our searching we marked and reported at least a half dozen locations where Keb showed interest; but there was no organized feedback to K9 teams, and we had no way of finding out if remains were subsequently found at these locations.

Did Keb and I miss any victims in our assigned areas? Although none of us likes to think so, this is possible on any search, and was even more likely under the terrible conditions we faced in the mud and wreckage of the Oso Slide. Weeks later we would learn that all victims had been located and recovered, a fact that brought some comfort to the families and provided search teams with a sense of resolution.

Guy and I thought we and our teammates had done well. While the mudslide terrain was totally new to all of us, we were pleased to see that our wilderness training allowed us to move and navigate through a moonscape of dirt piles and debris. I personally was pleased that Kebbie's agility training allowed her to keep her footing over piles of broken boards and smashed trees. But more than anything, I was thrilled knowing that Keb's HRD training allowed us to find the missing and bring them home.

And for our whole team, well, I was just proud of us. We stepped up to a brutal unknown, we responded professionally, we adapted to an environment unlike anything we had experienced, and we completed our assignments. In a dark hour of need, we, alongside other local and regional K9 teams, became an important resource for our community.

3
How All Were Found

In Which We Return to the Oso Landslide

*"Going on the last three days the most effective tool
has been dogs and just our bare hands
and shovels uncovering people.*

*But the dogs are the ones that are pinpointing
a particular area to look, and we're looking
and that's how we're finding people."*

—Travis Hots, Fire Chief, Snohomish County District 21

It's been a week since the Oso Landslide. Rescue resources from all over the state have responded. The Washington National Guard is now on scene. The number of missing is still unknown. This morning, Keb and I will be deploying with Guy and his wife, June. Tall and slender like Guy, with a short haircut showing her natural gray, June shares Guy's lifelong commitment to hiking and mountaineering. I trust her no-nonsense personality: she says what she means, and she's become an important confidant as we face challenges growing our K9 team. We've been instructed to attend a briefing at the Oso Fire Station at 7 a.m. sharp. As we pull up, the parking area is overflowing with people milling around: emergency workers, SAR volunteers, firefighters, law enforcement, and family members. Oso Fire Chief Willy Harper leads the briefing, and all are heartened by his warmth and professionalism. I try to imagine what it's like to see your home community devastated, wonder how many friends or acquaintances you may have lost, and yet continue to lead such a complex disaster response.

As Chief Harper winds down the briefing, I look around at the sixty-plus volunteers, wearing a hodgepodge of SAR uniforms, police and fire insignia, and logger overalls—all of us packed shoulder to shoulder in the cold fire station bay. Some faces are attentive; some show the fatigue from multiple days of searching; all show a determination that would make our nation proud. I'm struck with the realization that Keb and I are now part of something much larger than ourselves, something that will change us in ways we can't predict.

All the living people rescued from the slide were found on the first day before K9s were deployed; we are now into the seventh day. Chief Harper ends the briefing with an emphasis on safety guidance for search teams. "I want to stress for everyone that we will not be risking life or limb to find those already dead." Invisible and silent, a wave of emotions flows across the assembled searchers. Many of the volunteers have friends or neighbors among the missing. For all of us—SAR, fire department, civilian volunteers, and the families of the missing—it's becoming painfully clear that the Oso Mission is now a recovery, not a rescue. Human remains detection dogs will be increasingly important in the effort ahead of us. We are searching for the dead.

Sometimes conflict drops upon us from the sky. Sometimes people carry it with them into the room. As we head toward the door, a K9 handler from another county approaches me from behind, angrily shoves a glass jar under my nose, and with flaring nostrils growls, "This must belong to you!" I reel back from the foul-smelling jar, which contains decaying human tissue. The jar (an HRD training aid) is not mine and is quickly claimed by its rightful owner, who apologizes for having lost sight of it momentarily. Why that person brought such a thing into the briefing room defies explanation.

I don't engage with the rude K9 handler and instead walk away silently. My stomach is hardening. What the hell caused this outburst of hostility? Is the stress of the disaster making tempers flare? It's a good idea to remind my teammates to give others some slack the next few days and not get hung up on the little things. All of us need to understand that stress-driven emotions may be roiling just below the surface. Later I learn this sort of outburst is simply the style and *modus operandi* of this particular person, and I'm just thankful she's not on my team. We have enough drama already.

This may shock some, but in order to search for the dead, we have to train our dogs with the real stuff. Our friends and family have become used to strange requests: "Did you just have a nosebleed? Any chance I could have that bloody hanky? Can I have the tooth you just had pulled? Anybody planning any surgeries? We would love to get your kneecap or hip joint. Any body fluids? Oh, you are pregnant? What are your plans for the placenta?" I vividly remember my hairdresser looking at me with incredulity when I explained my interest. But bless her heart, she subsequently asked permission from the hospital to donate her daughter's placenta. Her daughter is now seven and proud to have been an important part of Keb's early training. Both have been supporting our HRD search career ever since. A few years ago, Scott had a nasty fall in the bathroom, with blood spurting from a deep scalp cut. He still jokes about my lack of compassion when my face brightened up in a smile at the sight of all the gooey red on the floor. "Oh cool, can we use this for our HRD training?"

Years ago, in a fit of SAR exuberance, Scott and I decorated our Toyota 4Runner. Colorful twenty-inch insignias adorn the driver and passenger doors: "Mountain Rescue" on the right, "K9 SAR" on the left. As Guy, June, and I leave the Oso Fire Station parking area, a young woman spots our decals, rushes up to my car window, and urgently gestures for me to roll it down. Her face is drawn and pale as she holds something out to us. "I brought some clothes for your dog to smell." Her voice and hands tremble. "Will you please search for my niece?"

June and I exchange a sad glance. We know this is an act of desperation, but we don't want to crush this woman's hopes. Gently, June reaches to take the clothes from her. "Thank you, we'll do our best." Fearing those words will be all the comfort we can give to her; we continue our drive toward the slide and our assigned search area.

Arriving at the west edge of the slide, Guy, June, and I pause to scan the scene. We see a firefighter sunk down to his hip. It takes two rescuers to pull him out, leaving one boot behind in the deep sucking mud. We also see half a dozen SAR dog teams from neighboring counties, including King County Search Dogs, Kitsap County Search Dogs, and Northwest Disaster Search Dogs. Many of them are from K9 teams we know, and it's a comfort to see their familiar faces.

Guy and I will assume leadership for coordinating the west side K9 effort today; after all, we're in our home county. We put together a plan for deploying K9s and share it with the west side operations chief. While interviewing

Suzanne and Keb amid a sea of devastation. Despite looking weary, Keb continued to search well each time we deployed.

all arriving dog teams to assess their experience, certifications, and physical stamina, we're surprised to meet resistance from one or two K9 handlers. One refuses her planned assignment and hisses that she and her dog "will be searching for the baby" that is missing. It's clear to us that her emotions have taken over. We silently wonder if it is an appropriate assignment for her but decide against arguing, which would just use up a lot of needed energy. Shortly thereafter, we all start moving out onto the slide plain.

As we work our way into our assigned search segment, we see that volunteers have created a makeshift walkway by laying four-by-eight sections of plywood over the ooze. These allow us to make progress into the slide, but many of the boards are smeared with mud and made slick by rain showers passing overhead. June slips and falls a couple of times. I see chagrin on her face as she wipes mud from the seat of her pants while sighing heavily. We then approach a man wearing a faded shirt and muddy jeans. He's wandering forlornly in small circles. We notice he's collected little kids' clothes and toys in bleak piles. He grabs me by my elbow and rasps, "Can your dog find my little boy?"

I'm not prepared for this. Never in our experience have we searched alongside family members. I really don't know how to reply but tell him we will give it our best try, as I gently squeeze his hand. I decide to have Keb search here for a while before moving on to our assigned area. She shows some interest around a tree stump—probably "crittering" (following animal scent) I think. When I tell the man that my dog has found nothing, he just shakes his head slightly and gives me a blank look. As we continue on our way, we run in to another K9 search team and ask them to doublecheck, just to be sure. Later in the day, they let us know there was a small dead animal near the stump. Good girl, Keb. It's a good thing we regularly "proof" off animal carcasses—hours of training for Keb, in which she gets rewarded for reporting the scent of dead humans but not the scent of dead animals.

Soon we leave behind the slick plywood boards and watch as Keb maneuvers across the mud fields without sinking in. I'm not sure how she does this. In the meantime, the rest of us sink in and get stuck with every misstep we make. "*Förbannat!*" I fret about what hazards Keb may be exposed to. I see her exploring around a demolished car lying wheels-up in the mud. It looks like we're next to what is left of someone's garage. The puddles of rainwater show faint oil slicks. "June, watch Keb closely, that might be antifreeze fluid or something else that might poison her! Don't let her drink anything!" We continue to stumble through mud; Keb continues to walk on water.

Large backhoe machines rumble and clank nearby. We come upon a group of volunteers working alongside the excavators in a large debris pit. A fireman calls out, "Can you have your dog search down here?" We stay for quite a while, sending Keb down every so often as the excavators gradually enlarge the hole. She's now definitely interested, but there's no hint of her trained alert. Kebbie girl, what does your nose say? Everybody is staring at

We were shocked to find our assigned search area was a sea of mud. I was envious of Keb's ability to move across the soggy terrain.

me with intense expectation. I peer into the fifteen-foot-deep hole filled with broken boards and sharp edges, and reluctantly announce I will go down to take a look. Once at the bottom with Keb, it becomes crystal clear what her interest is all about. We're standing in the middle of someone's demolished kitchen. I can see crushed food cartons and smell all the spices.

Now it makes sense why June had spotted a bag of raisin bread some time earlier. All around me are perishables from a refrigerator, along with everything else you would find in a pantry. The smell of curry is pervasive and creates a jarring someone-lived-here sensory experience. From down in the hole, I call up and explain what we found to the rescue crews.

Inwardly, I'm relieved that Keb did not give her *I smell dead people* alert. Our dogs, even well-trained ones, may alert for a variety of reasons, and as handlers we need to understand why. It's well understood that dogs can easily detect unspoken cues, unconscious gestures, or even glances from humans, such as a ring of firefighters staring down at us. As a relatively inexperienced HRD handler, the last thing I want to do is to divert search resources with a false K9 alert. Before climbing up and out of the hole, I take a second to whisper praise. "Good girl, Kebbie, you passed an important test."

No dog is 100 percent reliable, and we're now working in an extremely stressful environment: more complex and physically demanding than we've ever experienced. I've heard many seasoned K9 trainers tell me that on a real mission your dog will *not* behave exactly as during training. For that reason, you have to spend hundreds of hours learning to interpret your dog's changes of behavior. You need to observe the minute details that predict a real find. What is Keb's tail doing? What about her ears? What is her overall posture? What's her energy level?

As we continue to search through the smeared wreckage of homes, I find myself worrying about shit—literally. Will Keb alert on shit? Stories come to my mind told by experienced HRD K9 handlers who have been deployed on previous disasters—about dogs giving alerts on latrines, old bathroom sites, and toilets. Will Keb indicate on anything that comes *out of* a human? Have I proofed her off feces? Will she alert on sewers, port-a-potties, toilets, or latrines? Like many rural areas in our state, Steelhead Haven relied on septic tanks for sewage disposal. How many of these tanks were ruptured and spread across the slide?

A week ago, when my first day of deployment on the Oso Landslide ended, Keb and I loaded up in my car and drove home covered in mud, and who knows what else, from toe to head. By contrast, as this deployment day winds down, we wearily trudge back to the makeshift search operations base to find a decontamination station of sorts has been set up. All of us, including Keb, are gently rinsed off by a friendly firefighter using a hose from a fire truck. We humans appreciate getting our legs and boots hosed off. Poor Kebbie is less than enthusiastic about the experience, but she perks up when we finally get back to my car.

"You're looking pleased with yourself, little girlie," I say while lifting her sixty wet pounds up into the backseat. I rigorously rub her down with a towel. Even though I'm exhausted, I muster up energy for a full body check-over to make sure she is not injured. She patiently lets me check her out and gives me a hopeful glance as she slowly rolls over on her back to see if she perhaps can get a tummy rub as part of the deal. I methodically work myself down to her nether regions. This is routine for Keb, and she cooperates with a full-body stretch and a big yawn. All is looking good. A tummy rub and a scrumptious meal will be forthcoming this evening, maybe for both of us. Hours later after arriving home, I shed my filthy boots in the garage, we both walk directly into the downstairs shower, me with most of my clothes on. Keb enjoys her warm shower tremendously and shows her appreciation by vigorously shaking water all over the bathroom floor.

Convicts and Marsh Masters

Our Marsh Master is sinking. Guy, Keb, and I nervously eyeball a slowly increasing lean to our port side as our amphibious tractor heads back toward dry land at its full speed of just over one mile per hour. Well, OK, Keb has not noticed and is hanging her nose over the side, simply enjoying the ride and the water scents as we float by. Ben, our trusty captain, seems as unconcerned as Keb. The Marsh Masters, looking like small tanks, have been commandeered from the Washington State Department of Natural Resources. Their metal treads allow you to just smash through low brush and also serve as "paddle wheels" to propel the vehicle when the water gets deep enough to float. We'd never seen or even heard of these things until we arrived for this day's Oso Landslide deployment. Here on the eastern side of the slide, the blocked waters of the North Fork of the Stillaguamish River have flooded houses and fields for several miles. Nearer to the foot of the slide, where the community of Steelhead Haven was, nothing is left but piles of mud and clay, separated here and there by muddy streams and brown ponds. Somehow, they must be searched, and the assignment will be given to our K9 teams.

Today, nine days after the slide descended on Steelhead Haven, I'm glad to see I'll be deployed with Guy as my field support partner. County and state resources are better organized now that the first frantic days have passed. We hear that the small staff at the Snohomish County Medical Examiner's Office has stepped up to the overwhelming mass-casualty challenge and has taken responsibility for identification of slide victims. At the end of each day, they provide the official report on the number of persons found and identified. The total number of missing has finally been confirmed at forty-three, and to date, only twenty slide victims have been found. There is one terrible unifying fact that haunts families and rescuers alike: because of the forces involved, identification of victims is, well, hard to think about.

Each day the number of victims found increases by one, or two, or three. And this is a good thing, because our daunting but uniting goal now is to find all those lost. Is it possible that some may never be found?

> *The main challenge was the scale of the site. Think about 9/11. That was around 16 acres and it took them more than six months to get to native soil, down to the foundation of the World Trade Center. [At Oso] we were dealing with 800 acres. A vastly larger scale with a small number of people we were looking for.*

> —*USAR Task Force Leader Thomas Richardson*

Three miles west of Darrington, the grounds of the Blue Grass Music Park now look like a small military encampment. This is our staging area. Four huge brown canvas Quonset huts are lined up along one side of the parking lot, accompanied by a neat row of two-dozen blue port-a-potties just across the muddy lane. The east side of the park grounds is packed with SAR vehicles of all types. FEMA incident command personnel are now managing all search efforts, and they have commandeered two of the canvas huts to serve as the Incident Command Post. There are still no FEMA dog teams on scene, but a large number of SAR volunteer K9 teams are here from Washington State counties, neighboring states, and even Canada.

We pull into the huge grass parking lot at 6 a.m. and are worried we're going to be late for the scheduled briefing. Guy quickly hops out, locates the FEMA incident command tent, and is relieved to find out that the briefing is not until 7 a.m. Dan, Guy, and I then wander the encampment, and are amazed to find a huge tent where a full breakfast is being served by oddly dressed volunteers. A hot food line with fresh scrambled eggs, fried potatoes, and stacked pancakes has been set up. Nearby picnic tables are populated with fire, rescue, police, FEMA, and SAR personnel, all enjoying a warm meal before getting their assignments. We proceed eagerly to the breakfast line, and savor mouth-watering steam rising from the warming dishes. All of our attention is on selecting our bacon, eggs, and potatoes, and we're slow to realize that our "volunteer" servers are all wearing orange jumpsuits. Gradually, it dawns on me: "Guy," I whisper, "these are work-release prisoners!" We thank them for their help and proceed to look for ketchup for our eggs.

At 6:30 a.m. we return to the cold of the parking lot to organize our gear prior to the FEMA briefing, only to find I've locked my keys inside the 4Runner. OK, what now? We're on the biggest search of our lives, and our gear is locked inside my car. Seconds pass while I'm totally flustered and Guy fumes with ill-concealed exasperation. Then, "Wait, wait! Scott told me he's hidden a spare key inside the tow hitch thingy!"

Guy bends down, "The damn tow hitch cover is rusted shut!" Crap. Dan, Carter, and Guy all take turns pulling and pounding on the tow hitch cap, and finally they wrench it loose to reveal the extra key. Saved by teamwork.

"Suzanne," Guy says sternly, "zip your keys into a vest pocket and leave them there!" My shoulders slump.

Once the key crisis is resolved, Guy, Carter, and Dan disappear into a tent where a FEMA search manager has started giving out assignments. Carter emerges from the tent twenty minutes later and calls our team together. We have our orders now! We climb into our vehicles and convoy to our assigned search area. I'm struck by how different the scenery is from the west side of the slide. Everything is flooded here: the highway, the driveways, and the fields. Water stretches almost as far as we can see. We park our vehicles next to fire and rescue trucks along the shoulders of the closed-off highway. Carter, as usual, has done a superb job of preorganization for our four K9 teams and soon has assignments and gear all ready. Two of our teams will deploy via boat, while Carter, Dan, Guy, and I, along with K9s Mav and Keb, will deploy via the Marsh Masters parked and ready on the shoulder. I look at my teammates and my heart just fills. I want to hug them, but I don't—they would only be embarrassed.

Before loading onto the Marsh Master, I have to make sure Keb has taken care of business. This is part of our ritual before starting any assignment and ensures that she remains optimally focused on searching once deployed. The last thing I want is for her to inadvertently relieve herself near any human remains we encounter. I lead Keb over to a "safe" area along the shoulder of the road. She has this habit of relieving herself and violently kicking up the dirt with her hind legs after the deed is done. If you are standing within five feet behind her, you are most likely showered with rocks, dirt, or grass. She's trained to do her thing on command, and even when there is no pressing need, she will make valiant efforts. "Go potty!" She almost instantly squats down in the grass and empties her bowels followed by a quick pee. "Brilliant! What a good dog you are!" I reach for a baggie to get rid of the evidence. Now that we've taken care of that, we can focus on the task at hand.

Keb's gait seems just a bit lighter now, but as I return to Dan, Guy, and Carter, I find them in a worried huddle. Crap, what now? Life vests: we didn't know until this morning that our assignment was over water. For safety reasons, deploying without life vests is out of the question, and we don't have any. Damn, stuck again. Carter craftily approaches the volunteer who will be piloting a twelve-foot skiff as our safety boat. Yes, he has some extra life vests he is willing to lend us, but with bushy eyebrows drawing together, he tells us we need to be sure he gets them back at the end of the day. We gratefully receive the vests, which fit uncomfortably over our radio harnesses but perhaps will keep us from drowning. Finally, we're ready to go. To this day, I have no idea whether the life vests were ever returned to their generous owner.

Upfront in each Marsh Master are narrow seats for a driver and passenger. In the back bed, it's even more cramped, just large enough for two people, two mission packs, and a wiggling, slightly smelly dog. After checking radios and gear, we carefully clamber up into the Marsh Masters and load the dogs into the back beds. Kebbie jumps right up as if she does this every day. Mav just sits and barks until Carter lifts him up into the bed. Engines fire up, metal tank tracks turn, and we lurch forward. We hang on to the frame with one hand and to the dogs with the other, as our dull yellow Marsh Master crashes off into low brush on the side of the road. Soon water is halfway up the treads, and shortly afterward I can feel us rocking side to side. I can't get over being amazed that these things actually float. The treads churn brown froth, as we pass drifting branches, logs, and debris. With Dan, Carter, and Mav in the Marsh Master just ahead of us, we make a turn to the west, and soon are passing a house that is submerged up to the roof but still flying an American flag. Were these houses occupied when the slide came down? Will we have to wait until the water recedes to search inside them?

We see a line of fence posts in the surprisingly clear water below us. Suddenly, our Marsh Master groans, slows, and veers to the right. We look off the stern and can see that we've been snagged by an old coil of barbed wire still attached to the fence. Guy glances over with a grin, "Well, it looks like we're swimming from here!"—a pronouncement I don't find very comforting. Kebbie, as usual, appears unconcerned; I expect she would actually love a quick swim. To our relief, driver Ben manages to reach back with a long pole and push the barbed wire out of the way. We are free again and under way.

After another twenty minutes of thrumming slowly across expanses of brown water and occasional muddy mounds, our Marsh Master crawls up the foot of a small mountain of dirt and lurches to a halt. We can see the lead Marsh Master beached not far from us, looking like something out of the Normandy Invasion. "This must be our stop!" Guy never misses an opportunity for questionable humor.

As we clamber out of the Marsh Master and look around, it dawns on me that what at first seemed to be a fairly simple deployment will be anything but. Houses, trees, or landmarks that might have been here before have been simply scoured away. All around us we see a wasteland of shallow pools and

We held our breath as our Marsh Master lurched up to land at the base of the Oso Slide. Keb, as usual, was unfazed.

mudflows, weaving through mountains of loose brown dirt. Our two teams are far from the main search efforts and alone somewhere at the foot of this huge slide. Closing my eyes momentarily, I ponder that getting stuck and requesting assistance would make us a huge liability for the mission.

As I look around, I'm not sure where we are heading, but I trust that Guy and Carter know what they're doing. They scan the slide terrain, check their GPS maps, and make a decision. Carter, Dan, and K9 Mav will work their way west, while Keb, Guy, and I will search toward the northeast, moving even closer to the base of the slide. Our main task will be to mark any areas where our K9s show interest, leaving small flags and recording the location on our handheld GPS units. We are the advance scouts for rescue teams that will be digging in the days to come.

For the next several hours we carefully wind our way around small streams and big pools of quicksand-like mud. Dead ends often force us to backtrack. For better footing, we quickly learn to stick to firmer, light-gray clay deposits that hold our weight better. My sweet Kebbie is searching diligently, every now and then stopping to sniff something. After we've been searching for some time, I catch her drinking water out of a puddle. "Leave it, Keb!" Hollering does not seem to deter her. "*Faan!*" I say out loud. Has she become dehydrated? Now she is probably ingesting toxic substances I don't even want to think about. I approach her in a sprint and grab her snout gently. "Stop drinking that stuff. It will give you diarrhea!" Keb has learned to drink directly from the sip tube on my mission pack and soon is happily lapping the small stream of water from my hydration bag. "Good girl, doesn't that taste better?"

Around noon, we find a downed western red cedar, 3 feet across, 100 feet long, and split lengthwise as if ripped apart by a giant. We take a break sitting inside the split tree, enveloped by the smell of drying mud and fresh shredded cedar. We're thankful it's not raining today, and the overcast sky occasionally opens to let bits of sunlight play upon us. Here on the northern area of the slide it's quiet and strangely peaceful, but off in the distance we hear the drone of chainsaws. In the midst of death and devastation, we are at peace for a moment.

While we munch on dried jack cheese, Wheat Thins™, and carrots, Keb sits by patiently and is rewarded with a small carrot to chomp. Guy opens up a Ziploc™ bag with homemade chocolate chip cookies that June baked, and I gratefully accept the shared cookies. Keb looks on hopefully but does not get a cookie. Chocolate and dogs don't mix well. One of the secrets of search and rescue is this: when we are searching for the lost, when we are rescuing the injured, usually we're having a pretty good time. We're out with SAR friends; we're having an adventure; we're trying to save the world (or at least a small part of it). And yet, at the same time, we reflect that every mission may be a life-changing tragedy for families left behind.

Over the next several hours, we place a few flags where Keb shows interest, but nothing tangible materializes. At one point, Carter calls over the radio, "We may have found . . . something!" Carter and K9 Mav are not certified in HRD, but Mav is getting close to attempting certification. "It might be part of a dead mountain beaver but can't tell." Their find is bagged carefully and brought back to base. I don't want to even ask how they carried this in someone's pack. We never learn if this find was animal or human. This is a small reflection of what searchers are dealing with throughout the Oso Landslide search area, where humans and animals were exposed to the same forces that split trees in half.

Six weary hours later, the radio wakes up, "Teams 5 and 6, report your status, and begin returning to your pick-up points." We look at each other with relief and begin to trudge our way back to the Marsh Master beachhead. Guy can see this as a waypoint on his GPS map screen and uses that to navigate back across a terrain where every mound, every stream, and every mud pond looks exactly like the last one. Tired and muddy, we load ourselves and our even muddier dogs into the Marsh Masters. Kebbie crawls into my lap, and snoozes in comfort during the hour-long churn back to where our vehicles are parked.

Once back at advance base, we're pleased to find that procedures have evolved significantly. The National Guard has set up a two-station decontamination process. At an intake station, a guardsman washes mud off of our boots and gaiters with a soap-water spray. We strip off our gaiters, then walk into a second station where yet another guardsman rinses off our boots and muddy pants. They can't help grinning as they gently wash our wiggling dogs with a warm water hose. We're grateful for this care and thank them profusely. One guardsman hesitates, then reaches to gently squeeze my shoulder. I'm surprised when my eyes suddenly brim with tears.

The Chicken Chase

On our next return to the Oso Landslide, Guy, Keb, and I are assigned to search a new and oddly different area. In the center of the slide, the wave of fast-moving debris flow split east and west around a forested peninsula of evergreen trees on high ground. Planners speculate that the force of the slide may have literally blown victims up into this area, and it needs to be searched. While the ground teams will perform grid-searching in formal line patterns, we'll be following Keb's nose through these woods on the southern side of the valley.

A deputy escorts us down a winding dirt driveway, past a run-down house with even more run-down chicken coops in the back. From the side of the house, we can climb up the nose of the knoll to access our assigned search area. We're hiking slowly around the edge of the property when suddenly, Keb (no doubt bored during the three-hour drive up) decides to be a *bad dog*.

She hops a low wire fence, and to my horror, starts barking, while gleefully chasing chickens in tight circles around the yard. This is embarrassing beyond belief, and I look around quickly to see if there are any witnesses to such a transgression. Fortunately, no one is in sight. After repeated, and increasingly stern calls—"Keb, come here, right now!"—and shrill whistles, Keb decides she has had enough of this grand adventure and hops back over the fence to happily rejoin us with an expression that seems to say, "What? I wasn't supposed to chase those chickens?" No chicken feathers (nor slightest traces of remorse) are in evidence, and we proceed hastily toward our assigned search segment.

As we climb east over the nose of the knoll, we see on our left a steep slope dropping to the mud fields below. On our right rises an undamaged Northwest forest of fir, hemlock, and vine maples, dressed with dark green Salal ground cover. Keb is on her "search for the smell of dead" command and begins traversing happily through the woods. This is exactly the type of wilderness terrain she trains in week after week. Keb typically will range some 100 to 500 feet away from me, sometimes within eyesight, sometimes not. This behavior, combined with her sensitive nose, creates a potential detection zone dramatically larger than that of any human searcher. She is wearing a GPS collar, which transmits her location to my handheld GPS unit. As we work our way through thick brush, this allows me to see her position on my small map screen, even when she is out of sight.

After forty-five minutes, we've crossed the main knoll and descend the east side to the edge of the mud. Above us on the hillside, searchers are struggling to maintain their grid spacing as they thrash their way through knee-high ferns and prickly salmonberry shrubs. Wearing helmets, gloves, and eye-protecting goggles, they move forward slowly, call out to each other to adjust the line, and then move forward again. Because Keb is on her "search for the dead command," she will not alert on these searchers, although she might do a drive-by for some quick pets. As we continue along the east side of the knoll, we're blocked by a downed tree. I watch as Guy easily swings his long legs over one at a time, while Kebbie simply scoots underneath. Sighing, I wriggle one hip up, then awkwardly roll over the log with all the grace of a sack of potatoes.

Thirty minutes later, as we are working our way uphill, we hear on Guy's VHF radio that one of the ground teams calls in a find! "Team 12 to Command. We need a deputy at our location to examine possible evidence." We're just uphill from their location, so we move down to check it out. The ground team members are pretty excited, and the younger members look to us expectantly. While I'm amazed the team was able to find *anything* on the ground amid the thick ferns, as we look closer at a flattened mass of fur and bones, it quickly becomes evident that this is a small animal, perhaps a raccoon or a possum?

"Don't touch it," Guy adds somewhat gratuitously, grinning at me. I lead Keb closer for a sniff, but she shows no interest, which confirms our conclusions. To be triple sure, a Snohomish County detective will later come up to review the remains and rule them not human.

Over the next two hours, we work our way back west across the top of the forested knoll. Keb ranges in loops ahead of us, while we walk through thick ferns, forest duff, and more downed tree branches. She is having a grand time sniffing and searching, but we get no indications of human decomp odor from her. Soon we can see on my GPS map screen that we're approaching our starting point: the site of the Chicken Incident. Finally, we break out of the woods and can see the dirt road ahead of us. A sheriff's deputy has escorted family members down the road to view the slide area from this high point. I put Keb back on leash, and we put on serious expressions. The family ignores us. Perhaps seeing a search team is just too painful of a reminder of the loved ones lost out here, something we understand and feel deeply about.

The Final Days

Who among us wants our bodies to be left out in a field after we die, to slowly decompose at the predation of weather, insects, and bacteria? Many of us would shudder at the thought: it's a fate we would curse upon our enemies. Surprisingly and thankfully, there are rare individuals who make a noble contribution by choosing exactly this fate. The decay of their donated bodies brings enlightenment to scientists, to criminal investigators, and to those who search for human remains.

Five months after the Oso Landslide, Keb and I had an opportunity to go to the Forensic Anthropology Research Facility (FARF) run by Texas State University, near San Marcos, Texas. FARF is a carefully controlled twenty-six-acre outdoor research laboratory used by forensic scientists and law enforcement personnel to learn about the postmortem decomposition processes under various environmental and climate conditions. Since opening in 2008, research at FARF has been conducted on hundreds of sets of donated human remains. Select members of the K9 SAR community are invited a couple of times annually to expose their dogs to full bodies in various stages of decomposition. For Keb and me, this was an invaluable HRD training experience.

At FARF, Keb was exposed to a human corpse that had been out in the open (in a cage to prevent vultures and other animal disturbance) for two weeks. As she circled the cage over and over at a very slow pace, she crouched low, almost as if she were stalking the body. Then she finally turned around, looked straight at me, and slowly sat down: her trained final indication for human remains. Ben Alexander, who coordinates FARF K9 trainings, reassured me Keb's reaction was not unusual. In a rush of memory, I was back in the mud debris of the Oso Landslide watching Keb signal her first find. My mind replayed Keb's behavior in slow motion; her response was strikingly similar. Observing this "response to a full human body" behavior several times at FARF was a critical learning moment for me, and on a dark night years later, it helped us find a person who had died from exposure.

We're now on our ninth deployment to the Oso Landslide, and almost a month has passed since disaster descended upon the community. Each time we return to search, the situation and environment is starkly different, darker and more depressing. In the first days, we were searching through wet mud and fresh rubble, still hoping against hope to find the living. Now in the final days of the search, we work side by side with excavators, earthmovers, and safety spotters. Every foot of dirt has been turned over by machines and lined out with grid markers. K9 handlers feel their dogs are less and less effective. The odor of death has been spread everywhere; our dogs are alerting all over with no remains evident. Despite this, the fire/rescue crews, our sheriff's deputies, and K9 teams continue to return day after day with the shared goal of finding every last victim.

Today, Guy and I are sitting in the "Blue Tent," a collection of large plastic shelters set up by FEMA. These are fifty yards from active searching sites and serve as a forward staging base for SAR K9 teams. Our shelter is large enough to hold five to six people; it's open on one side, and a blue plastic floor has been laid down to keep us out of the mud. Along the south wall of our shelter, a row of four portable K9 kennels serves as the remaining décor. Heavy rain showers continue to move through, and we sit on uncomfortable folding chairs with our boots in rapidly growing puddles. Near the open side of the tent, it's cold and drafty, and we pull on extra down layers to try to stay warm. K9 teams are being sent out occasionally, when there is a bit of undisturbed earth to be inspected, but most of our deployment today has been spent sitting in or around the Blue Tent.

During a break between rain showers, Guy succumbs to boredom and wanders over to a large canvas tent adjacent to us. He reappears moments later smiling broadly below his ever-present cap embroidered with an image of Mount Adams. "Guess what's right next door?" He doesn't stop for my guess. "There's this huge warm comfy dry tent with a heater in it, and the sign on the door reads 'K9s Only.' I met the FEMA veterinarian inside, and her assignment is just to care for any dogs that need attention. If we were dogs, we'd have it made! Plus, the vet is sort of cute." For those readers keeping score at this point, let me summarize:

Humans: Cold, drafty, open wet tent with puddles on the floor.
K9s: Warm, enclosed, dry, comfy quarters, with attention from friendly FEMA vet.
Guy's Spirit: Irrepressible.

But for me, this is a depressing time to deploy. Everything in the environment is brown and dirty; any early hope we felt is now long gone. Only a small number of K9 teams are being deployed: all are certified in human remains detection, and all are searching for the dead. The majority of our time is spent waiting for short windows of deployment, mostly moving into the areas being dug out by large excavators. We spend hours just watching the excavator teams. Spotters carefully observe each shovel load, and occasionally small pieces of remains are found. Our talking is muted, our faces are drawn and tired, and our dogs look bored and bedraggled.

The waiting at times feels unbearable. Keb also seems subdued. Is she feeling depressed from the experience? Is my dark mood being transferred through the leash? Poor Kebbie is covered in dirt from head to toe; the daily decontamination process has made her fur look dull. Emotion wells inside me, and I sit down next to her on the damp earth and hold her tight. Our unbreakable bond has somehow strengthened as we've shared this experience together.

A few days later, Guy, Keb, and I are once again assigned to the Blue Tent, along with two FEMA K9 teams. This Easter Sunday has dawned to a clear blue sky, and we hear the soft whistle of a varied thrush trilling in the quiet morning. For the family members of the Oso Landslide victims, there is little comfort. For rescuers though, time and routine have soothed our initial reactions of shock and dismay. We think there are four victims yet to be found and determined search efforts continue. Unseen by us, our SAR deputies Charles Thayer and George Kirby have been returning day after day after day to identify and search new areas.

Later in the morning, we hear the sounds of earth-moving equipment, and occasionally a K9 team will be requested for a short inspection of newly turned earth. But for the most part, today we sit and get much-needed rest. It's about 11 a.m. when Guy spots someone approaching on the dirt road that leads up to the Blue Tent. "Look, it's the Easter Bunny!" Up walks a six-foot-tall disaster relief volunteer dressed in a bright pink bunny suit with tall rabbit ears and wearing heavy boots and a warm smile. We can't help but grin and walk over to say hello. Keb just stares at this apparition, somewhat astounded. The Easter Bunny is handing out small candy treats from an Easter basket, and I eagerly pick out a small bar of Hershey's chocolate. This is totally incongruous with such a postdisaster environment—an absolutely lunatic idea that somehow brings smiles and comfort to all of us at the advance staging area.

Just before 2 p.m. we hear sudden radio chatter on both SAR and FEMA frequencies. Two bodies have been found! We hear a call for 4 x 4 transport vehicles and see them begin to move in the distance. A tradition has arisen here on the plains of the Oso Landslide. When found victims are transported out of the slide zone, a single long horn wails across the valley. All work stops, and rescuers stand in respect for those who have perished. Guy and I walk down the dirt road to where we can see the black medical examiner's truck arriving on scene. A single horn sounds across the slide. We stand and remove our helmets in respect. All is quiet as the procession goes by. Two blasts sound on the horn. Rescuers return to their searching.

Our days at the Blue Tent finally come to an end. One week later, we hear that Charles and George helped locate the last two Oso Landslide Disaster victims, found in slowly receding waters on the far east boundary of the slide zone. Their unwavering dedication, and the perseverance of all involved, allowed every one of the forty-three Oso Landslide victims to be found, recovered, and identified.

Mission Debrief

Guy

During the Oso Landslide, we simply responded when called and went where we were told. As we slogged through mud and debris, Keb's nose and our eyes focused only on each small area assigned to us. We helped match K9 teams to assignments each day; we helped coordinate deployment of K9 teams from all across the northwest. But we were searchers, not planners. We were only dimly aware that somewhere in the midst of chaos, someone was crafting pieces of a larger search strategy and weaving them into a master plan.

And on a cold morning, as I shortcut through an empty FEMA tent, I encountered this planning for the first time and began to realize that answering the question "Where should we search?" might become a larger part of my SAR career. My eyes were drawn to a three-by-four poster taped on the hut wall on which planners had marked a location for each victim found to date. Then, as victims were found and identified, planners added another mark for the location of their house and drew a line between the two points. You could clearly see that when the slide swept through Steelhead Haven, it swept debris and victims ahead of it in a fan-shaped pattern that split into two streams. This was the pattern planners were using to predict where to search for those still missing! This is how they were figuring where to assign our dog teams!

Looking Back

Suzanne

Searches that continue day after day are characterized by "operational periods," the SAR equivalent of twelve- to twenty-four-hour work shifts. Keb and I were deployed on ten operational periods over the month-long duration of the Oso Landslide search. We were there the first day K9s were used, and we were the very last K9 team to be deployed. Throughout the mission, we worked in environments ranging from rubble and collapsed houses, to forested wilderness, to mud and water, where searching was conducted by amphibious vehicles, hovercraft, and small rescue boats. We look back, and are proud of what we and the rest of our team were able to contribute. Our own team's experience of the emergency response to the disaster was but a small bit of a huge effort. But we know that our dogs helped on the ground and also, in an important way, showed our community its own strength and resilience.

For Keb and for me, our relationship experienced new heights. I was able to empathize in a different way with what her experience was like. While my world was focused on what I was seeing, Keb's world was all nose, and I wonder what strange mélange of odors filled her nasal cavity. She encountered smells different and more overwhelming than anything she had experienced before. The notion that dogs can smell emotion such as fear and sadness from people in distress became more real in my mind. People were found in the debris: people whose last moments, no doubt, had been in panic and fear. What did she smell those first few days when she was alerting on piles of rubble and wood? This is a part of Keb's world that I may never know.

Of those involved in the months-long Oso Disaster Search, I often think of the many that we did not see. We didn't see the civilian volunteers who built the urgently needed bypass road on the south side of the slide. We didn't see the FEMA staff who set up tents and provided incident command logistics. We didn't see the community members who cooked and delivered warm food to searchers. We didn't see the hardware store owners who emptied their shelves to deliver shovels, gloves, and flashlights to the Darrington and Oso fire stations. We didn't see the medical examiner's staff who worked so hard to identify victims. We didn't see the helicopter support crews who provided gas, service, and maintenance to keep them flying. We didn't see the girl scout troop that prepared and delivered baskets of treats and toys for our dogs.

We look back on our successes proudly. We wince at our failures and mistakes. Soon after the Oso Landslide, we realized we had allowed a brand-new team member to join us on her first-ever SAR mission. She was unprepared for the stress, she was unprepared to move across the rough terrain, and she was unprepared to face the emotional impact of widespread death. We should never have deployed her under those circumstances.

Even some of our experienced members struggled to cope with the Oso Disaster. My dear friend Brenda had years of experience as a SAR volunteer. Upon her arrival at Oso, she was thrown into supporting incident command, where she worked to hand out K9 assignments. Later during the day, teams began returning, bringing with them wallets, diaries, photos, and other personal items left behind by slide victims. As she carefully bagged and labeled these items, Brenda was overcome by waves of sadness. She feared what she would see out on the debris plains and imagined fields strewn with bodies and remains. She didn't think she would be able to handle finding a body or parts of a body. During our critical incident stress debriefing, Brenda shared her feelings of guilt for not deploying into the field.

The Oso Landslide changed us forever. It broadened our understanding of community and service, and it expanded our view of the role of our K9 team. The passion for our mission as a K9 team bloomed. Our shared experience allowed our vision to mature, our culture to solidify, and our commitment to high standards to evolve. Our K9 team's engagement, then and in the years to come, was evidenced by a second-to-none mission response rate and a commitment to training higher than any other specialty team in our county's larger SAR organization.

Following this tragedy, our Snohomish County K9 team took a leadership role in Washington State to strengthen regional partnering between SAR K9 teams, with an increased focus on what we could do to be prepared for disasters. It was the beginning of new friendships and a newfound level of regional collaboration, as diverse K9 teams came together in the pursuit of one single mission. We started training regularly with dedicated local K9 disaster search teams and sought out national disaster training opportunities at places like Camp Atterbury in Indiana and Crisis City in Kansas. I'm proud that Keb and I were first in the Pacific Northwest to certify in the National Search Dog Alliance (NSDA) First Responder Disaster Certification as it was adopted in 2016. While we hope to never be needed for a disaster again, we are better prepared when and if the unthinkable happens.

We returned to the Oso Landslide time after time during the weeks of searching, but its prominence in our lives gradually faded as we moved on to other missions, to our routine of almost constant training, and to a renewed focus on growing our K9 team and becoming the very best we could be. We had no way of knowing that our future would bring us back to the community of Oso, where Keb, Guy, and I would search in the shadow of evil.

4
Finding Bigfoot

In Which Keb Makes a Breakthrough

"What you experience while conducting an HRD search
may haunt you for the rest of your life.
It may not affect you on the first search or the first dozen searches, but there
will come a time when it affects you."

—C. JUDAH AND T. SARGENT,

HOW TO TRAIN A HUMAN REMAINS DETECTION DOG

K9 Keb can sense my nervousness; I'm hoping the detectives standing nearby cannot. I've been a search and rescue K9 handler for over ten years of "lost person in the woods" searches, but we're still early in our career of searching for human remains—a highly specialized discipline in which my yellow Labrador retriever Keb and I have only recently been certified. When our SAR sergeant Charles Thayer called me directly this morning, and personally asked if Keb and I would deploy on an HRD mission, I said, "Yes!" hung up, and suddenly realized I had signed up for another important test in our SAR career.

What I'd heard from Charles was not a surprise. In our region of the Pacific Northwest, highways provide quick access to forest service roads that snake their way up green mountainsides and lead to remote, secluded areas. So if you've just murdered someone and need a fast way to hide the body, we've got the perfect environment. Our Cascade mountains hide very real but seldom seen predators, such as bears and mountain lions. And sometimes in the dark shadows, our forests conceal the remains of murder and mystery.

Charles had briefed me that a logging crew in the deep woods of eastern Snohomish County had been clear-cutting a steep slope when they took a mid-morning break. Amid the devastation, a small island of trees had been spared, possibly to prevent the dirt logging road above from sliding into the small valley below. Walking into this preserved area, a logger had glanced down and seen something that looked odd. He reached low, picked it up, and to his horror realized it was a partial human skull.

The Search

Guy gets my call around 11 a.m. "Charles just called me to go on a human remains detection assignment! Are you available?" I hold my breath momentarily.

Guy understands the importance of this call, and to my relief, agrees right away to be my field support for the mission. "OK, how soon do we need to leave? Want to take your rig and go together?" Guy does not like any dog hair in his new Land Rover. Even though he does not own a dog (sometimes I wonder if he even likes dogs), Guy has been a member of our K9 Team for six years now. He is organized and capable, and exactly the person I need to back me up, especially on searches in rough wilderness areas. We've partnered on many searches in the past, and I know I can count on him.

Guy also knows that Charles calling me directly was a *big deal*. For some time now, I've felt I've been struggling against political resistance within our SAR organization to build credibility as an HRD K9 handler. "Political resistance" is a phrase encompassing two concepts that are unfortunately common in the K9 world: "My dog's better than your dog," and "My K9 training method is the only training method in the known universe that works." If those concepts seem childish to you, well, you're not alone.

My struggles with internal county SAR politics are not new. Ten years ago, our K9 team exploded in a cloud of anger and animosity, fueled by a couple of toxic personalities. Our team's salvation came in the form of my dear friend Bob Fuller, whose calm approach and soft tones might initially be misinterpreted as slowness but reflected deep thought and caring. As the new K9 team coordinator, Bob became the front face of our efforts to resurrect our team from shambles. Bob and I worked together in this effort, but for years I remained in the shadows as much as possible, leading from behind to avoid drawing fire from members unhappy about the direction of the team.

Keb races back and forth between the kitchen and the garage as I hurriedly load gear into my truck. While Keb and I are still rookies when it comes to searching for human remains, she has been performing rock solid on HRD trainings for some time now, both because I've become a better trainer and because she was carefully selected for her working lines. I was introduced to Keb when she was just six weeks old. The breeder had invited me to meet the litter, and that day is still vivid in my memory. She was the feisty one, crawling on top of the other pups, running with fervor and gusto after the furry toy animal thrown at random in the grass. Her otter tail was rapidly swishing back and forth. She was so, so blond, with a black nose and eyes as dark as wells. With eyelashes blinking seductively, she bounced across the lawn and into my lap to give me an enthusiastic greeting. Me, she is choosing me, I remember thinking. As she wiggled out of my embrace after a few furtive licks of my chin, I knew the decision had been made.

Keb has the high hunt-and-prey drive every SAR handler looks for, and we quickly become a natural team. She has good work ethic, nerve strength, and focus, and not an ounce of aggressiveness toward either humans or other dogs. She has an independent streak I value, but she can also be irritatingly stubborn and blow me off at times. She's a dog that needs a job and wants to partner with me in accomplishing the tasks we are given. When searching, Keb moves in a methodical and precise way, which is my preference when we are engaged in human remains detection. A very fast dog can move too quickly and, in my opinion, may run a larger risk of missing something. Oh, yes, Keb also has a wild, fun side to her and can get the "zoomies" in the right environment. And she is ball crazy!

My "career" as a SAR K9 handler flourished in a complex ecology that was hidden from most outsiders. In Snohomish County, as in many other places, the leadership structure was very much modeled after military "command and control" top-down management. At the top sat the Snohomish County Sheriff's Office (SCSO), whose division chiefs seldom were involved in day-to-day SAR operations, unless questions of costs, resources, or politics raised their heads. The sheriff's office was extremely happy to have volunteers who would do the hard work that county deputies couldn't do (such as technical rope rescue) or (in the case of clearing brush for a hands-and-knees evidence search) didn't want to do. At the same time, they had good reason to think of their small army of SAR volunteers as a herd of trained cats, at times a source of worry and exasperation.

The SCSO appointed a SAR sergeant to direct search and rescue operations; he was seen as a demigod by many SAR volunteers and often served as Incident Commander (IC) for missions. Throughout most of our SAR careers, our SAR sergeant was Charles Thayer, who also served on the helicopter rescue team and was well respected throughout Washington State for his many years of SAR leadership. Charles came from a background on the SWAT team, and in general brooked no nonsense while herding cats or SAR volunteers during missions.

Don't get the wrong idea when I say "career." Oh sure, we spend thousands of hours each year training, deploying on missions, and then training even more to maintain our professional readiness, but we're unpaid volunteers. I've got a full-time job as a business executive coach, which is useful to pay for all the search gear, special training, dog expenses, and gas that we don't get reimbursed for. Guy? He's retired and is continually recommending it to me. As we arrive at our rendezvous with the deputy sheriff, and begin to pull on our boots and gear, Guy reflects on this: "Honestly, Suzanne, I don't know how you manage both careers." Grinning now, "which is why I cut you some slack when you forget your radio . . . or compass, or glasses, or map." I just roll my eyes as we throw our gear into the sheriff's truck.

After a short, bumpy ride farther up the rutted dirt logging road, we carefully unload from the bed of the sheriff's 4 x 4 pickup: ourselves, our search packs, and four-year-old K9 Keb. She immediately begins her inspection of the surroundings, which includes three Snohomish County sheriff deputies. Thankfully, they don't seem to mind as Keb quickly sniffs each one in turn before returning to my side. She's exploring the world the way she knows best, with her nose.

Förbannat! Damn, I left my VHF radio back in my car. Thankfully, Guy has his (along with a handheld FRS radio and a GPS) in his chest harness, so we'll be able to communicate with the deputies using our primary SAR radio channel. Gathered over a truck hood, which today serves as our incident command post (ICP), we confer briefly with the deputies. Then, as we pull on packs, helmets, and gloves, Detective Bernard Simms points over the steep side of the road. "The partial skull was found about 200 feet downhill from where we stand. We've got two detectives from the Snohomish County Major Crimes Unit waiting down there for you." He looks straight into my eyes as I nod and try to exude confidence.

Our immediate obstacle is a treacherous pile of logs that we must clamber over before descending the hillside. Guy and I have years of climbing and mountaineering experience, and our bodies have learned how to move in steep and awkward terrain. Nowadays, we are no longer doing fierce climbs, but muscle memory helps with the careful movements that allow us to descend safely through the log pile. By contrast, Keb is eager to get going and fearlessly leaps through the logs without an ounce of hesitation. We follow at a much more cautious pace. On Guy's handheld GPS, he has started to record an electronic track. We can use this as we travel to see our position and can use this track, after we return, to review our search pattern on a map. The hunt is on, and I recognize the familiar burst of adrenaline as we clamber down through the log pile trying to look as graceful as possible.

Once over the logs, I call Keb to my side, and command her to "sit," while softly stroking her head to let her feel my presence. Seemingly confident about the task ahead, she leans into my thigh. When she is sitting and focused, I say, "*Sök!*," which is Keb's special command to search for the odor of human remains. We spot the detectives far below and begin a gradual descent down the steep hillside, while gaining a feel for our surroundings and the terrain. In this unlogged island, hemlocks stand sixty feet high, shading a very light underbrush. Outside the island we can see the terrain is a wreckage of downed trees and branches, fragrant with the smell of fresh-cut wood and turned earth. Using hiking poles for the descent, we're moving slowly and carefully. Within minutes we spot a deer lower jawbone, studded with ivory-colored teeth. "Kebbie, check it!" She takes a deep sniff, filling her snout with scent before ignoring it as nonhuman, exactly as she has been trained. "Good girl!"

HRD K9s like Keb (also known as cadaver dogs) are especially trained to detect chemical compounds that result from the decomposition of human tissue. After death, the human body goes through four stages of unsightly and odorous, but perfectly natural, processes: *autolysis*, in which our own enzymes start digesting cells from the inside out; *bloat*, in which internal gases cause discoloration and inflation of the body; *active decay*, in which soft tissues gradually liquefy and dissolve; and *skeletonization*, after which all that remains are bones. All of the above stages are aided by insects, birds, and animals in ways that are left to the reader's uncomfortable imagination and best not contemplated while eating a spaghetti dinner. Unless, as Scott often points out, you are an HRD handler, who after years of doing this line of work has become tone deaf to what constitutes appropriate boundaries and appetizing dinner conversation.

We arrive near the bottom of the forested area and meet our two detectives, a man and a woman, sitting on a log. We carefully introduce ourselves: "We've been assigned by Detective Simms to link up with you." They look up as they continue to nibble on what we assume is a late lunch. The female detective folds her arms in front of her, while skeptically giving us another once-over. "This is my dog Keb," I say by way of introduction. "She's been trained to alert and communicate to me when she smells human remains. Am I correct that, based on the fact that you already found a skull, your primary focus for us is to search for bones?"

Kebbie immediately goes over to them to sniff, make friends, and shame-lessly solicit a few pets. The detectives point out the cranium (the top part of the skull) several yards away. "Would it be possible for Keb to take a quick whiff?" I ask. My thinking is that by smelling the skull, her nose-brain will lock in on bones more readily. I carefully lead Keb over to where we can see the top of the cranium, partially buried in the dirt. Keb sniffs several times and then sits: her trained indication for human remains. I reward her by throwing her favorite orange ball, the ball she only gets when she indicates on the odor of human remains or has found a live human. She is obsessed with that ball, and we allow her to play chase and fetch for a few minutes.

"Lassie! Go find Timmy!" Many people think search dogs are motivated by a heart-warming, tear-inspiring desire to save lost humans. That is not quite true. Most search dogs are motivated by a desire to play with their Most Favorite Toy in the World, the magic toy that *only* appears after they have led their handler to a lost person. This is the Search Game taught to search dogs throughout the world and responsible for saving hundreds of lives every year. While search dogs are always happy to find a new human (and practice what some of our volunteer hiders call the Rescue Face Lick), most are driven by playing the Search Game for the Most Favorite Toy in the World.

The wind is light now, gently wafting up from the valley below us. This is good. The air currents will carry scent to Keb, which expands her range of detection. I turn to the detectives, who still seem unimpressed by our presence. "We're going to begin by ranging back and forth across the forest slope. That will best expose my dog to any scent." The afternoon is starting to cool, and we're guessing that we have only about two hours of remaining daylight. Why do they always wait until late in the day to call us out? We fig-ure we'll be able to cover only about an acre an hour given the terrain. As we move away to start searching, the detectives are sitting and chatting. They're friendly enough, but they don't seem to hold much expectation that we'll find

Keb disappears into the impenetrable Pacific Northwest rainforest. Often, we know her location only when we can hear the bell on her collar.

anything. "*Sök!*" I send Kebbie out again on her "search for dead" command, and she begins ranging ahead of us with her large black nose eagerly sniffing ground and air.

While Keb ranges, I watch her behavior like a hawk (well, OK, like a hawk that needs to avoid tripping over that next tree root). When closing in on a source of scent (a live human, or perhaps a whole body), our dogs will often follow a "scent cone" to find its source. Picture a lost little boy in thick brush just 200 yards ahead of you. You can't see the child, but Keb has already begun to detect his scent particles in the light wind blowing toward us. Keb has learned the simple tactic of moving toward where the scent is stronger. If she moves off to the left or right, the scent plume will be weaker, so she moves toward the center again. If she moves directly toward the child, the scent steadily becomes stronger. In the field or even looking at Keb's track on my handheld GPS, I may see a narrowing zigzig travel pattern that indicates that she is working her way to the tip of the scent cone where the lost person is located.

As my field support on an HRD search, Guy knows that our main sensor is Keb's nose, but he can serve as an extra set of eyes while also handling radio communications and navigation. While my attention is focused on watching Keb closely for any changes in behavior, Guy flanks several yards to the side and scans the ground for anything that looks out of place or unusual. It's not quite dusk yet, but we turn on our 500-lumen helmet headlamps to add a bit more light on the ground before us. While the upper slope just below the road was steep and hazardous, we're pleased to find that lower down, the terrain is less steep and not difficult to traverse.

Guy is about five yards away when we find the jawbone. My heart leaps while Keb's bottom sinks. She sits: her trained alert for human remains. Keb calmly looks up at me expectantly. *Well, where's my ball?* I am not calm as I shout "Guy, you need to come over here right now!" He is at my side in seconds. We both just stare down at the mandible, not quite believing. The detectives told us they believe the skull found was from a female. The jawbone and teeth on the mandible at our feet seem just huge.

"Jesus," Guy says, "this looks like it's from Bigfoot. How could this be from a human female?" I'm pretty sure that Keb would not indicate on Bigfoot bones, but one or two hairs begin to rise on my neck. Keb's tail is now swinging wildly from side to side. She is still sitting, but she has stopped staring at what's on the ground. Her pink tongue is lolling out and her eyes are now intently staring at my pocket. Oh yes, she has earned her favorite ball!

One thing we learn early in SAR is to be very careful on the radio. Even though our SAR frequencies are not listed publicly, we know they can be monitored by the sneaky media or by the curious. Broadcasting "We Found a Body!" to the world has the potential to ignite a media storm and, more importantly, to cause unnecessary anguish to the family of the lost. So most SAR incident commanders will prearrange a distinct but neutral, secret code phrase:

> "Team 4 to Command!" (usually somewhat breathlessly)
>
> "This is Command, go ahead Team 4" (usually in a slightly bored tone)
>
> "John has a long mustache!"
>
> Command (usually after a stunned pause): "Team 4, can you repeat that transmission?"
>
> "John has a long mustache!!!" (much more urgently now)
>
> "Command to Team 4, please secure the area, radio your UTM coordinates, and we will be sending a deputy to rendezvous at your location."

In our case, the two detectives are sitting only about fifty yards away, so Guy cups his hands around his mouth and shouts out our own secret code phrase: "Hey guys! I think we've got something here!" They look at each other in surprise, immediately leap up, and begin scrambling over branches and bushes to join us.

We continue to just stare at the mandible. It is obviously weathered, and peering closely, we believe we can see some animal bite marks. "Don't touch it!" says Guy grinning, and I roll my eyes and just give him an exasperated look. We both know to be extremely careful not to touch or disturb the bone, as we're trained to treat it as evidence in a criminal case. Still, I'm about to burst with excitement and silently count my blessings for having spent so much time and effort making sure Keb has been exposed to a variety of human bones of different ages, and also that we've done a lot of proofing, so that she won't respond to animal bones. Although I confess, I don't know if Keb would consider a Bigfoot bone human or animal.

At home I take special precautions with the bones I use for training Keb. Animal bones are kept in a different part of my garage, totally isolated from any human remains, or "source" as we HRD handlers call it. I don't want any scent contamination that might lead Keb to alert on nonhuman bones. K9 noses are so sensitive that we constantly worry about mixing other scents. If you let a training bone develop mold, for example, you run the risk of having your K9 only alert on bones with mold. Storing human bones in paper bags or glass jars is one recommended method, as this helps prevent moisture from building up. I've also been told that some dogs have been known to *not alert* on bones that have been out in the wild long enough to have other environmental scents blend in. When that happens, your dog may decide it's not the same scent picture that they get rewarded for during training. Regardless, today the gods were smiling at us. I quickly lead Kebbie away for a well-deserved romp with her ball, while the detectives carefully pick their way to us across the forest slope.

They are with us in minutes and are equally pleased and surprised with our find. They photograph the mandible in place before pulling on blue nitrile gloves and carefully lifting it up to examine it. They had carried the cranium over in what Guy is now referring to as an Official Major Crimes

Evidence Container (a paper bag), and gingerly show us how the mandible was a perfect fit. So, I guess Guy's Bigfoot Theory is out. From his handheld GPS, Guy reads the UTM coordinates to the detectives, who record them in their notebooks. Soon, they are on the radio to the deputies above at the trucks, and the news is then relayed to the Snohomish County medical examiner.

Our detectives gently place our mandible in the Official Major Crimes Evidence Container and start trudging back up the steep hill to the parked trucks. We still have maybe thirty minutes of light left, so I put Keb back on search; Guy and I will grid back and forth a bit while we climb up the hill at a slower pace. You never know, it's possible we might find more human bones. It's almost dark when we reach the deputies and detectives gathered at the trucks, and they greet us with broad smiles and thanks. "Good job today. That pooch of yours knows what she's doing!" Inside, I'm singing with excitement. I'm thrilled that we've made a good impression and just might be called upon again when the next opportunity arises. We load our gear, Kebbie, and ourselves into the sheriff's pickup bed for another short, bumpy ride back down to where my vehicle is parked.

After pulling off muddy boots, and transferring gear, packs, and Keb to my truck, we all convoy slowly down the logging road: three Snohomish sheriff department trucks, followed by my aged Toyota 4Runner. We're all in high spirits, until we reach the gate to find that someone has locked us inside the logging area. We try to hide our laughter, while the deputies swarm out like irritated bees to examine the gate and make angry radio calls. They are not swearing in Swedish, "What kind of idiot would lock the gate on us. Does anyone have bolt cutters?" Our sheriff deputies seldom have much patience with locked gates.

During the wait, I call our SAR sergeant, Charles Thayer, to give him the good news. "Say that again. You found what? That's great, Suzanne!" He

Keb searches inside a huge hollow stump. "Nothing here, Mom!"

sounds surprised but is pleased, and his hard-won congratulations are welcome to my ears.

My relationship with Charles, though anchored in mutual respect, was always complex. Over time, Guy and Charles would develop a close working partnership. I liked Charles as a person and respected his competency, but at times I struggled with what seemed to me like organizational lack of transparency in decisions, as well as a style of leadership probably common in law enforcement but very different from my own experience in the world of business. I approached leadership from a cooperative perspective, via engagement and open communications. Charles operated within the quasi-military hierarchy of the sheriff's department, in a culture that appeared to discourage asking questions. Many of us who volunteered within that hierarchy often failed to understand why certain things took place and how decisions were made.

Mission Debrief

Guy

Mandibles hold teeth. Teeth are described in dental records. Dental records provide the Snohomish County medical examiner with an identification.

The mandible Keb found leads to a major breakthrough in the case of a missing woman who disappeared *nine years* prior to our search. Nine years! And while there is not enough evidence to reveal the cause and manner of her death, major crimes detectives now have information critical to begin pursuing a homicide investigation. How did her remains end up in the forest? We know that there was a logging road nearby at the time of her disappearance. We know that no abandoned vehicle was found, which implies she did not drive herself to that location. One can easily envision the dark path along which this speculation leads.

As a K9 team, however, we are not part of this continuing investigation. During a search, our interest in the case surges, our curiosity is piqued, and we are thrilled when we find evidence. Then the door of the case is slammed shut before us. Subsequent facts and findings are kept confidential until and unless they are revealed during public court proceedings. We understand the reason for this but always wish we could peek behind that door. When human remains are found, there is sometimes talk of closure for families of the lost. At the most, our finds provide some sought-after information (where is my loved one?) and remove some uncertainty (what happened to my loved one?). For those of us who find and those who have lost family, there is seldom any real closure.

Looking Back

Suzanne

Relief and happiness fill me, as I reach into the backseat to give Kebbie a hug. She responds by leaning forward to lick Guy's ear. Once the gate is opened, we're on the road for less than five minutes when I glance in the mirror to check on Keb in the backseat. She is sleeping soundly with an occasional twitch of her paws, as she dreams of her Most Favorite Toy in the World.

My own thoughts circle again and again. We've once again proven ourselves as a Human Remains Detection team. We've passed our test; we've passed our test.

5
Lost on Mount Rainier

In Which We Face Past Fears

"Our real journey had now commenced . . .
Now we were about to encounter unknown and fearful dangers."

—JULES VERNE

On the two-hour drive south toward Mount Rainier and a search for an over-due hiker, I share my apprehension with Guy: "The last time I was deployed on Rainier, we were up on the Muir Snowfield, and I was coordinating the deployment of half a dozen search dog teams from three counties." Swallowing hard while pushing the hair out of my face to glance at Guy, I can tell he is listening, as he's making a quiet *hmm* noise. "It was hard work, but on terrain I had traveled before, and the fact that we worked close by other K9 teams made me feel a bit safer. You know, today it's going to be just Keb, you, and me, and we don't know where they are going to send us." My mind is racing through scary possibilities. Guy, ever the introvert, usually doesn't talk much unless I prompt him or he gets excited about something. I know his brain is constantly working, but I have little clue about what his thoughts are. Honestly, sometimes I have better conversations with Keb.

Guy seems unconcerned by my fretting, but I feel uneasy about my stamina. Will my daily conditioning support whatever is thrown our way today? We know we'll be searching for a missing hiker, but don't know where rangers will deploy us—it could be steep forest or high snowfields. Granted, I've done a fair amount of climbing both in the Pacific Northwest and abroad, but I'm increasingly steering away from highly technical missions. I fear I'll become a liability and not be able to keep up with mountain rescue members a decade or two younger than I am. Guy and I are well paced together: we are slow and steady, and neither one of us wants to get in over our heads.

The story of our missing hiker has already been on the Seattle evening news. Local mountain rescue teams have also received a more detailed incident description from park rangers. Two days ago, sixty-four-year-old Edwin Birch and his son set out on a "key exchange" hike of the challenging eighteen-mile segment of the Wonderland Trail between Box Canyon and Fryingpan Creek. Edwin dropped his son off at the Fryingpan Creek Trailhead and then drove around the mountain to start his hike from the south at Box Canyon. Their plan was to meet at the midpoint, where Edwin would hand over the car keys to his son, who would then hike down to Box Canyon, drive to Fryingpan Creek, and meet his father at the north end of the trail.

Edwin's son reported that he met his father at around 3:30 p.m. at 6,600 feet, just south of Panhandle Gap. His son recalled that Edwin seemed well but looked a bit tired. From this Point Last Seen (PLS), the two parted: the son continued hiking south; the father continued his slow trudge north toward Panhandle Gap. It took the son another eight hours to hike out to the Box Canyon Trailhead, where he picked up their car and drove north back around the mountain to meet his father on the White River side.

Panhandle Gap is a high-point on the ninety-three-mile Wonderland Trail that encircles Mount Rainier. This world-renowned backpacking circuit travels through some of the most beautiful wilderness in the world. Fit hikers with strong legs can complete this arduous circuit in eight to ten days, typically climbing and then losing over 2,000 feet in elevation each and every day as the trail meanders up over one ridge, down across the next river valley, then up the next ridge. In recent years, the trail has become so popular that a lottery system is now in place for reserving campsites along the trail. But despite this popularity, the Wonderland Trail deserves its reputation as a mountain wilderness area, with stunning beauty around every corner and hazards both seen and unseen.

Edwin Birch did not arrive as planned at the Fryingpan Creek Trailhead. His son waited until well after dark, then alerted rangers at the White River Ranger Station. The national park deployed search teams at 7 a.m. Tuesday morning, and ten ground searchers aided by one helicopter performed initial "hasty" searches of the entire trail and adjacent areas. Early expectations were that Edwin was simply delayed on the trail or perhaps spent the night at the Summerland high camp. But by the end of the first search day, no signs of him were seen.

On Monday, the search effort expanded as park rangers called in volunteers from Portland Mountain Rescue (PMR) from their home base in Oregon. A four-person PMR team, deployed by an Army Chinook helicopter, was transported high into the Ohanapecosh Park area, southeast of Panhandle Gap. After searching this area, rangers asked the team to search cross-country down the Ohanapecosh drainage: an assignment that required an overnight bivouac—sheltering in the wilderness with minimal gear—and desperate bushwhacking all the next day. After over twenty-four hours on the mountain, the exhausted search team made it out to the White River Road at 8:30 p.m. They had seen no trace of Edwin Birch.

Late Tuesday night, the Mount Rainier National Park Service (NPS) incident manager contacted the Washington State Emergency Management Division with a request for additional mountain rescue resources to search the next day. This request was transmitted to volunteer teams throughout the Puget Sound area, and members from Tacoma Mountain Rescue, Seattle Mountain Rescue, Olympic Mountain Rescue, and our own Everett Mountain Rescue responded. Mountain-capable K9 teams had also been called out. Edwin Birch had now been missing for over two days; a large, urgent search mission was spinning up.

The Search

At 6:30 a.m. we arrive at the White River Ranger Station on the east side of the mountain and pull in to park between trucks from Tacoma, Seattle, and Olympic Mountain Rescue. For Mount Rainier, as in other large national parks, overdue hikers are a regular occurrence, and SAR incidents are well practiced. At the command post, park rangers serving as incident command staff have things well organized, with a check-in station for volunteers, a gear cache, a communications station, and an operational assignment station. We greet and chat happily with mountain rescue volunteers that we know from other counties.

The mountain rescue turnout is impressive: we see about fifty searchers getting ready to go into the field. One of the lead park rangers assembles us for a quick briefing, and as he describes how Edwin Birch was last seen just south of Panhandle Gap, I see a flash of recognition on Guy's face. He gives me a look to get my attention but remains silent as the incident commander continues to describe search plans. As the briefing ends, there is some concern that not all teams will have radios with the frequencies and repeater channels used by the park service. Steve from Olympic Mountain Rescue calls out, "Anyone need a radio programmed with park repeater channels? We've got extras here!" This is a small thing but so typical of the camaraderie in our search and rescue community.

Guy and I wait patiently while most other teams are given their assignments and depart the staging area. Nearby, we hear two younger searchers wondering how a person could possibly get lost on a well-traveled hiking trail. Now Guy leans close to whisper quietly, "I know exactly how. Suzanne, I know that route!" It's easy to tell when Guy is excited—his hands trace circles and shapes in the air. "Ten years ago, I was on a solo backpacking trip in the same regions of Panhandle Gap that Edwin attempted to traverse. My route was *exactly* the one planned by Edwin and his son! On my second day, it started to snow in the morning and never stopped. I was trying to follow tracks of hikers who had left thirty minutes before me but finally realized that their tracks were going the wrong way. They had lost the trail! I eventually managed to find my way over the pass, but I'll never forget how relieved I was to get on a recognizable trail. Believe me, I know how easy it would be for Edwin to make a wrong turn on those snowfields." My confidence level, already a bit shaky this morning, is taking another dive. I worriedly bite my lower lip.

For mountain rescue operations such as the search for Edwin, we'll carry twenty-four-hour mission packs, heavy with gear, clothing layers, food, and emergency equipment we may need should we be forced to bivouac overnight high on the mountain. We'll also carry with us unseen, the training, successes—and fears—from our past experiences in the wilderness. These provide us with the judgment needed to move across hazardous terrain. These also provide us with personal challenges that need to be overcome. On the mission today, Guy carries with him the memories of the several times he's hiked this remote trail between Fryingpan Creek and Box Canyon, along with the unsettling memory of the time he was lost in a snowstorm as he crossed Panhandle Gap. I carry with me memories of personal mountain tragedies, along with the hard-won inner confidence that comes from conquering past fears. In a reversal of our usual roles, Guy has shared his own past of fears and failure. This morning, I'm keeping my innermost thoughts and fears to myself.

Sitting on round granite boulders outside the White River Ranger Station, we put thoughts of the mission aside for a few minutes and discuss positive developments in our K9 team. Back home our K9 team is thriving, but not without aggravating challenges. Our leadership team has expanded, and we've added elected positions to increase membership representation. Our membership numbers are growing by leaps and bounds as a result of our recruitment efforts, and we are working hard to find ways to integrate one small subset of members, who stubbornly resist our efforts to expand and integrate the team.

On the positive side, as a team we're gradually being recognized as a mountain rescue K9 asset, as evidenced by our deployment today. Both Carter with K9 Mav, and I with Keb, have recently acquired national-level avalanche certifications. Our dogs have demonstrated they can locate humans buried under snow and are trained to start digging where the scent is strongest. In

Guy carries with him a full SAR pack, along with memories of when he almost got lost crossing Panhandle Gap.

recent years our team has also started offering regional K9 snow and ava-lanche training, both at Mount Rainier National Park (which required special permission from the park superintendent) and at Stevens Pass (in collabora-tion with the Ski Patrol).

Keb has a good foundation working in snow. Her snow training started when she was just a pup, when we were invited to participate in the biannual Stevens Pass Ski Resort K9 Avalanche Training. I remember the thrill of hav-ing to ski double-diamond terrain through four feet of new snow with puppy Keb gleefully bounding along beside me. Our trainers, Marcel and Chriegel, were Swiss Alpine Rescue guides. They were a hoot, and in the evenings after training, they would down copious amounts of schnapps and serenade us with their melodious yodeling. Laughing, I tell Guy how Marcel would insist on using only sausages to reward the dogs as they dug us out of snow holes used to simulate avalanche burials. "First mit der sausage in der hole, then der dog in der hole!" Dutifully, the volunteers would tuck sausage into their jackets, then crawl into the snow hole to await being found and dug out by the dogs.

Now the operations chief calls us over to brief our assignment, and we're surprised (and secretly thrilled!) as it becomes clear the plan is to insert us via helo to get a K9 team high up into the Panhandle Gap area. Guy explains to the operations chief that he has hiked in that area before and knows the terrain. He somehow omits the fact that he got lost up there. We're told to drive fourteen miles up to the Sunrise Visitor Center where a helispot, a temporary landing zone, has been established at an elevation of 6,000 feet. Right before departing the staging area, we're given a SPOT satellite locator beacon, with instructions to turn it on as soon as we are in our assigned search area. This will allow park rangers at search base to track our position as we search high on the mountain.

Thirty minutes later, we arrive at the helispot, a wide area on a closed-off dirt service road, staffed by two NPS rangers and four helicopter techs. The helo techs hand us bulky flight helmets, along with jumpsuits made out of Nomex material designed to withstand fire. We awkwardly pull these on over our hiking clothes and boots, and immediately look totally unstylish: Guy in orange and I in blue. The helo crew gives us a detailed safety briefing, and then we see and hear the helo approaching in the distance. Soon the Hughes MD530, looking like the world's tiniest helicopter, sends up a cloud of dust as it descends upon the road.

Once the MD530 has landed, the helo techs patiently walk us through cold loads: a rehearsal of entering and exiting while the engine is off and the rotors are still. Again and again, they repeat the cardinal rule: exit in a crouch; do not walk to the rear of the helo. Outside a small helo like ours, the main rotor could easily dip and lop off your head. And if you walk too close, the

Keb loading into the world's smallest helicopter.

tail rotor is waiting to shred you. The techs are also worried about loading a K9—the last thing you want in a helicopter is a dog going crazy with fear. I reassure them that Keb has been exposed to helicopters in the past. "She is cool as a cucumber in helos."

Keb, Guy, and I will be crammed together in a backseat smaller than you would find in a Volkswagen Beetle. The helo tech looks at our mountain packs and then hesitates. "OK, well, we're gonna ferry you up in two trips to keep the weight down. Packs will go on the first flight, then we'll come back for the three of you." Guy and I exchange a look and hope that this is routine. We also hope that hungry marmots won't break into our packs between flights. During our cold loads, Keb, bless her little heart, seems totally unconcerned and happily climbs in and out of the helicopter like she does it every day.

Before we know it, it's time for takeoff. The MD530 (did I mention how tiny it was?) returns from ferrying our packs; we load up and are airborne. As we lift off, I realize with a jolt that the helo crew has removed the doors to reduce aircraft weight. The weather is sunny and clear as we rise quickly above Sunrise Park then head south: over Winthrop Glacier, then over Goat Island Mountain, then on to Panhandle Gap. Guy, peering out the doorless sides, is enjoying a stunning aerial view of areas that he has hiked for years. We're both grateful for the seatbelts we're wearing. We've snugged them up as tightly as we can get them.

The impact does not fully strike me until we've been in the air a few minutes and I look down: thousands of feet of air and then snow-covered fields, with nothing between me and earth, only air. I'm grateful that Keb and I have had the opportunity to train with helos before. I know she won't be rattled by the noise and wind. I've secured her to the floor with a strong nylon leash, but it's clear I don't need to worry. Taking in the landscape as if she is sightseeing, she's sitting next to the open door, with no concerns whatsoever. It's just another car ride for Kebbie; if I let her, she'd probably hang her head out the side to get her nose in the breeze!

During the ten-minute flight, my mind drifts back several decades, and it dawns on me how much I've changed. Twenty years ago, it would have been impossible for me to sit through this helicopter ride with a drop-off that looks like thousands of feet below me. Why? As a result of a horrific event in California's Sierra Nevada the year I moved from Sweden to the United States, I had developed an intense, irrational fear of heights, which lasted decades. That nightmare remains vivid in my memory.

Our friend Staffan had been visiting my then boyfriend, now husband, Scott and me at his parents' property just outside Yosemite National Park. Staffan was an amazing young man practicing as a psychiatrist in Lund, Sweden. He had a sense of adventure and was excited that morning to be hiking and scrambling with us in the awe-inspiring nature surrounding Yosemite. The property had several waterfalls along Gertrude and Whiskey Creeks; one of them was six stories tall with an expansive, glacially polished rock slope above and a large pool below. On that hot summer day while we were reclining against a boulder, Staffan got up and walked thirty feet out onto the granite shelf and lay down in the trickle of water to cool himself. I remember cautioning him, "Be careful, the rock over there is much slicker than it looks!"

To my horror, moments later, I remember hearing a wet thud and glancing over to see he had slipped and fallen on the slime under the thin sheen of water where he had been sitting. He was sliding, as if in slow motion, toward the drop-off thirty feet away. The slope was not steep, but the angle was just enough to keep him sliding, and the moist expanse was wide enough and slippery enough to prevent him from escaping his fate. Burned into my memory are the images of him grasping for something, *anything*, to hold on to as he slid slowly but inevitably over slick rock toward the edge. Worst of all is the memory, forever etched in my mind, of him looking back at me, desperate and helpless as he soundlessly disappeared. The replay is always the same, always in slow motion, and always includes searching for him—it seemed like forever—and finally noticing that one of the side pools at the bottom of the falls was tinted red. I shudder every time I recall Scott scrambling down the rocks over to the side of the pool, where he grabbed a hand barely visible below the water's surface, pulled it and gingerly cradled Staffan's head as he coaxed the body over to the side of the pool. For years, I had awakened from dreams in which I was sliding slowly toward that same terrifying edge.

My memories recede as our helo floats down carefully to land on a small heather patch amid high snowfields. We do a hot unload: carefully departing the MD530 with engine running and rotor blades slicing air above our heads. As each one of us exits the helo door, we're led away in a low crouch by the helo tech, to kneel in a safe position twenty yards away. I hold Keb (who doesn't need to crouch) closely on her leash, and the three of us hunker low by our packs, as the helo revs up and drifts away into the blue mountain sky.

Within seconds all is quiet. We're on a high shoulder on the east side of Mount Rainier, looking across rolling terrain dotted with large snowfields, barren rock, and occasional patches of heather. Below us to the east, rolling subalpine forests and smaller peaks spread as far as we can see. Now on our own, we purposefully take a moment to settle ourselves and have a quick snack of almonds and cheese to help us focus for the many hours of searching before us. In priority order, our objectives are (1) stay safe and (2) find Edwin.

We also take a few minutes to orient ourselves to our location and our assignment. It's vitally important that we have a clear mental image of not only where we are on the mountain but in what compass direction we are heading. Guy turns to me: "Suzanne, look here on my map. We're at an altitude of about 6,500 feet, about a mile south of Panhandle Gap. We're almost *exactly* where Edwin was last seen by his son." Keb is resting calmly beside us, clearly enjoying the sweet smell of high mountains and snow—and fondly remembering the chunk of cheese that Guy shared with her.

Guy points to the map again. "See that cliff band below us and to the east? We'll need to keep Keb away from that. I think we should generally follow the Wonderland Trail north toward Panhandle Gap, but we need to look for and check out any places where Edwin might have lost the trail in the snow." In the direction we need to search, we see broad white snowfields punctuated with dark rock outcroppings. In short sections we can see the trail on bare earth, but it's mostly covered by snow and hard to follow. "Suzanne, this is exactly what it was like on my solo hike ten years ago. It's easy to see how Edwin could have lost the trail."

Unlike Guy's experience those years ago, the weather for our search today is gorgeous: blue mountain sky with high, white, cumulus clouds. While we haven't forgotten the seriousness of our mission, we're both taken in with the beauty of what we are seeing and with the opportunity to spend a day in this wilderness together doing something meaningful. "Guy, I think this is what my friend Andy meant when he described search and rescue as an opportunity to hike with a purpose." Ever the untalkative one, he merely nods in agreement as I continue. "We're pretty lucky we get to do this together. Let's just hope we find Edwin today. I'd love to bring some news to the family."

For the next several hours, we search across high snowfields, with Keb ranging enthusiastically for up to 100 yards around us. She's having a blast traversing across the snowfields, but I fear for the dangers that might be lurking below. Be careful, Kebbie girl. We cautiously listen and look for snow bridges that might conceal water running beneath our feet. One of the possible scenarios we've discussed is that Edwin fell through a snow bridge and was carried away by a stream under the snow.

I flash back on an image from our climb of Mount Kebnekaise in Sweden a few years ago: a father with his two little kids had been crossing a snow bridge above a huge river. As Scott and I watched in horror from below, what we could see and they could not was a dark, gaping hole hiding a raging glacial torrent immediately below them. The family was halfway across, and we just stared and held our breath. We knew that if that snow bridge failed, we could have done nothing to save them. Oddly, it was only after we saw the family cross safely that my whole body shuddered. In our SAR experiences here in the United States, we're aware of the fatal consequences for hikers and skiers that plunge into swift water when hard packed snow collapses below them. These incidents happen at Mount Rainier every year or so. There is no real warning: one moment you are walking on top of snow, the next you are being dragged in the water along narrow icy tunnels carved by the water under the snow.

"Go find!" Keb is now searching independently on a "find live humans" command. Full of energy and thrilled to be on snow, she ranges far away from me as she searches for human scent. But she remains within my control and lopes back happily to join us for a quick pat on the head each time I whistle or call "Kebbie come!" With extra vigilance, I'm now paying attention to where we are hiking and where Keb is ranging. I'm glad Guy is with me: he knows what he's doing and is keenly aware of the need to stay safe. So far, the snowfield looks relatively benign; we can't see any obvious hazards. The snow conditions are excellent: just enough give on the surface for our mountain boots to get traction. We're using our hiking poles to cross the snowfields, but thankfully we won't be needing the ice axes and crampons strapped to our packs.

I intermittently check Keb's paws to make sure ice crystals have not formed between her toes, because snow can be quite abrasive and might rub her paws raw. I have dog booties in my pack just in case. Keb doesn't like these booties but will tolerate them. "It would not have been a bad idea to spray some Pam™ on her paws," I remark to Guy, "or bring Musher's Secret™—the special sled dog lotion I have for this very reason."

Guy lights up at the words Musher's Secret™ and spends the next several minutes not-quite-correctly reciting poetry from Robert Service: "Strange things are done, 'neath the midnight sun, by the men who toil for gold. And the arctic trails have their tales, that would make your blood run cold." Neither Keb nor I are impressed by this. Fortunately, Guy's recollection fails about halfway through, and we're spared the remainder of "The Cremation of Sam McGee."

As we search across the snowfields, I can see Guy scanning for "decision points": places where a tired or distracted hiker might miss a turn or take a wrong one. Park rangers know that the Panhandle Gap trail section has many such decision points, and almost every year hikers get in trouble up here. Guy pauses again to show me his map. "Can you see where the trail ahead gets covered by that long snow patch?" he points, which gets Keb's attention, hoping perhaps for another bit of cheese. "Right there the trail jogs up and left, but it's obscured with snow. Now, see that broad natural alley that leads downhill and to the right? That would be perfect inviting terrain to misdirect Edwin and lead him toward steep cliffs below." My eyes follow where he points. Before us is a crazy quilt of green heather, pale snow, and brown dirt. If Edwin was already tired at this point, it's easy to imagine him choosing that wrong path. For thirty minutes, we detour down this wrong-turn alley. Keb ranges happily ahead of us, until I call her back from the cliff edge. She pauses, then ambles happily back to my side. The wind is rising gently from below, and I'm confident that Keb would have alerted on any human scent below the cliff band. She shows no interest whatsoever, so we turn to climb back up to the main trail.

We've been searching for about three hours when suddenly Keb takes off, almost disappearing in the distance across an expansive snowfield. Wondering what has caught her interest, we squint and see two small points moving way off in the distance above us: she's caught the scent of backpackers hundreds of yards uphill. Guy gives me a big grin: "Wow, Keb's nose caught their scent when we could barely see them!" We stop to watch her run all the way up to the two puzzled hikers, pause to solicit pets, then race back to us. Her tail whirls in excitement. I found someone! I found someone!

Out comes her favorite orange ball for a quick playtime in the snow. "Good girl, Kebbie!" With boundless energy she manages to chase her ball around, while simultaneously having a glorious time rolling in the snow. I let her enjoy her reward while Guy and I take a brief standing rest. Soon, however, we continue our search for Edwin. "OK, Keb, find another!" She looks up at me almost grinning and dashes off again, eagerly continuing her quest. She's having the time of her life out here, and my heart just glows.

Keb is still relatively young, and so while I feel she is under my control, I'm not comfortable with her working close to some of the very scary drop-offs we are encountering today. I keep calling her off the edges, but what if our subject actually walked off the cliff; might it be safer to search from below? I momentarily reflect back on Staffan's fate. This tragic event left me with an irrational fear of standing near cliffs, drop-offs, or waterfalls, and it tainted our experience as a family on hikes and backpacking trips in the Pacific Northwest for many years. I was always trying, but not always succeeding, to hide my panic any time we were faced with exposure to heights. Somewhere along the journey, I found some consolation in reading that the fear of falling is the only fear we are born with. But that little piece of knowledge didn't address the cost for me personally and others around me. It took many years for me to break through. As I reflect on this today, it also dawns on me that in some way Staffan's tragic fall years ago prepared me for what we are doing now, but I don't share that private thought with Guy. Over the years, I've rarely shared that story beyond immediate family.

The day is wearing on as our search for Edwin continues. I sense Keb's energy and ears are beginning to droop a bit—ours too. We reach within spitting distance of Panhandle Gap, then reverse our course to traverse a higher route as we work our way back to our helo insertion point. We pause for a break and snacks, and Keb takes the opportunity for another cooling roll in the snow, which she thoroughly enjoys before coming back to sit beside us. Guy opens his pack to pull out cheese, crackers, and dark-chocolate-covered almonds, and—discovers the SPOT satellite locator beacon. "Damn. I forgot to turn the SPOT beacon on, and here we've been searching for hours. How embarrassing." We wonder if search managers are worried about us, but we later find out that while they had not entirely forgotten about us, they weren't at all concerned about not seeing our SPOT signal.

Over the next several hours, as we continue searching back toward the southeast, Guy starts scheming. "You know, Suzanne, from here we could descend the Wonderland Trail about two miles down to the Indian Bar Shelter. It's in one of the prettiest remote valleys in the park and this would be a rare opportunity to get there. It's also possible that Edwin may have returned down there, and we could have Keb check it out." After futzing with radio channels for a few minutes, Guy finally hits the correct park radio repeater channel and is able to communicate with the command post. We relay our plan and ask if a helo pickup down near Indian Bar would be feasible.

Incident command responds the way command always responds: "Stand by." So Guy and I stand by anxiously while they think on it. Keb stands by as well, but she seems much less interested in their decision. Minutes later we hear back from command. "Um, yeah, Team 10, the helo pilots say they can land near Indian Bar, but they're on another assignment and won't be able to pick you guys up for at least three hours."

Let's see: if it takes us two hours to hike down to Indian Bar, we would be forced to relax in the sun for another hour. We quickly decide we could survive such a cruel ordeal and confirm with command via the radio. As we work our way down the trail, Keb continues to range, and we scan the landscape, because one possible scenario is that Edwin got lost while attempting to return to Indian Bar, where Guy took shelter on his solo hike years ago.

Hiking with a purpose: we descend to Indian Bar through fields of mountain heather and Bear Grass.

We reach the valley floor, and the trail leads us through reeds and marsh along the northern edge of the Ohanapecosh River. As we move downstream, Guy suddenly stops on the trail, blocking our path. "Suzanne, just up ahead there's a really scary bridge over a gorge. It's short but very narrow with open wood railings. If Keb fell off the bridge, well, it would be all over." I call Keb to my side, and she reluctantly allows me to clip on her leash. As she pulls me across the tiny wooden bridge, I glance down and just shudder at the roaring death below me.

We arrive at Indian Bar and hike up the path to the small shelter: three stone walls and a wooden roof. I sit on the stone steps, overwhelmed by colors. Nearby, fields of green are dotted by blue lupine, pink heather, and white valerian. High above us at the end of the valley, we see cloud-white edges of the Ohanapecosh Glacier. Thin waterfalls plunge down to form the headwaters of the Ohanapecosh River, which flow and gurgle through emerald heather meadows past the mountain hut. Our grand plan is that the helo will arrive in about an hour, but we realize it's possible we will get stuck here overnight. As I check my bivouac gear, Guy tells me of the night years ago that he spent inside this hut, with wind and rain blowing outside and the mice scurrying around inside. Hmm . . . Keb might think this an interesting distraction. We're tired from a long day of searching, and as we sit snacking on the hut steps, two backpackers arrive. They're very interested in hearing about our search and enjoy visiting with Keb, who shamelessly solicits pets and attention.

Lying down in the field of wildflowers, I take in the beauty of our surroundings, while Keb decides to do some exploration in the nearby heather fields, often stopping in her tracks to inhale the scent of some morsel invisible to me. Finally tired, she plops down by my side and proceeds to give me big, sloppy kisses and snuggles up, her back against my stomach, our heads side by side. We languorously stretch out alongside each other. As I lie there looking up to the sky, I see the massive granite walls above us and hear the roar of streams nearby: for a moment we are one. The silence is speaking a million words of love and peace.

As Keb, Guy, and I searched through hazardous terrain earlier that day, there were times when I had to leave the rational, logical part of my brain and simply let myself be in the flow of the here and now. When working with my four-legged partner in mountain terrain, I have to find that space within myself, a space that allows Keb and me to engage in an intricate, intimate, and almost beautiful dance together in the moment: a space that allows us both to push our limits and master new challenges.

Suddenly the radio squawks with incident command advising us that our helo is inbound and will be at our location in twenty minutes. We're instructed to move up the valley about 200 yards to an open area where the MD530 can land. Guy and I look at each other grinning—it's great when a plan comes together—especially when we don't need to hike another eight to ten miles to extract ourselves, or have to spend the night in a mouse-infested mountain hut. While we didn't find Edwin today, we accomplished our search objective: to provide a highly trained air scent K9 search of a remote mountain pass, an important part of the entire search effort. And in different, but combining ways, the memories we carried with us made us a stronger search team.

Mission Debrief

Guy

Almost a year later to the day, mountaineers hiking off-trail above Panhandle Gap are shocked to stumble upon human remains. They hike for hours down to the White River Ranger Station where they breathlessly report their find. The next day, NPS climbing rangers are able to mount a recovery operation.

The Pierce County medical examiner is able to confirm the body is that of Edwin Birch but reports the cause of his death as "undetermined."

When a lost person is not found during the search but remains are found at a later date, all search teams anxiously ask the Big Question: "Was the person found in the area we were assigned to search?" You can just imagine the pain and guilt hanging on this question. Suzanne and I quickly consult the park service press releases and news media reports; we carefully review the map of areas that we searched, along with our GPS tracks. To our relief we see that Edwin's remains were located near the Fryingpan Glacier: higher on the mountain and well outside of our assigned search area.

Did other search teams pass nearby and miss Edwin? It's possible, but it's more likely that teams were not assigned to such a remote area. Searching high mountain areas is one of the most difficult challenges we can face, both as search planners and as searchers on the ground. We know that Edwin had wandered way off the trail, but we'll never know exactly what happened. When I was lost years ago on that same high pass, did I refind the trail due to my wilderness skills, or had I simply been lucky? Did Edwin encounter the same decision points that I had? And if so, what choices did he make? Perhaps he just met with a slip of misfortune in the game of chance.

Looking Back

Suzanne

As I rested in the grass on Mount Rainier with my loyal K9 partner by my side and Guy dozing some feet away, I could see in sharp relief how that tragic day near Yosemite importantly shaped me as a person. For many years it would limit me. Later it would allow me to feel the success of stepping into my fear, embracing it, and using it to propel me forward. When I first joined SAR and mountain rescue, it wasn't clear to me that my experience as a volunteer would allow me to once and for all break through my fear of heights and falling. Taking the Mountaineers climbing course led to climbs in different parts of the world, summitting a nontraditional route of 19,400-foot Kilimanjaro in Tanzania, 17,000-foot Nevado DeToluca in Mexico, multiple fourteeners in Colorado, and many peaks in the Pacific Northwest.

My experience and skills pale in comparison to those of the world-class climbers and skiers on my mountain rescue team, but given the fearful place I came from, I give myself credit for having done what I've done and continue to do in the mountains. Of the many moments of conquering fears on the journey, the one that stands out was my first technical rock climb on The Tooth, in the Washington Cascades. The day had started out in the most horrible of ways, with rain making the rocks slippery and hazardous. In hindsight, the climb probably should have been canceled at the get-go because of the conditions, but our climb leader, a seasoned mountaineer with an impressive climbing portfolio, was known for his penchant for climbing regardless of the weather. At the outset I spent ten minutes just trying to find a way to get up and over the first damned boulder. "Hey, Brian, this may not work out. I can't reach any grips or footholds to even get up. This rock is slicker than snot on a doorknob. Plus, I'm simply too short to reach." The climb leader peered down from a rocky perch thirty feet above, and simply ignored my whining.

Finally, sheer determination got me over the boulder to the place where the real climbing started. I knew this was my big test, and a strange calm came over me as I continued to climb, one hand, one foot at a time. Images of Staffan kept flickering in front of my eyes, and then I was in the flow. I was doing it, almost without thinking! There was a moment of hesitation when I came to the crux of the climb, the infamous "catwalk": a scary step over an abyss to reach a small ledge. And then it happened: in the blink of a moment, I just took that one big step.

Brian looked at me curiously with a faint smile. "That's the spot where novice climbers usually get stuck in their own fear for quite a while, not being able to commit. You just did it!" At that moment I had stepped into my fear without blinking, a step that symbolized letting go of decades of my fear of falling. To overcome my fear, I had to stop resisting it. I had to face it directly. In a sense, I had to embrace fear, make it my friend, and have faith that I would get through in one piece on the other side: I had to take that *one big step* onto the ledge.

6
Abandoned Car, Lost Soul
In Which the Demons Win

"Who lives? Who dies?
What went wrong? What was done right?"

—ROBERT J. KOESTER, *LOST PERSON BEHAVIOR*

I'm in the middle of an important client meeting, when suddenly I hear *woof,* *woof, woof* from my pocket. *Damn.* In a moment of enthusiasm last week, I set my smartphone to make the sound of a barking dog for a SAR call-out text message. This may not have been one of my best ideas. Looking around in embarrassment and hoping that no one else has heard, I quickly switch the phone to vibrate. It's been a while since we've had a search, and I'm itching to go, but this client organization is critically important to my career. I can't just walk out of this meeting, and I also have yet another one lined up shortly after. There are times my dreams of being independently wealthy or retired have great appeal. When am I going to win that lotto?

As an executive coach, my niche is to work with high-potential, but sometimes slightly flawed, senior executives. Although there may be some work needed to get them to their full potential, these are leaders the organization does not want to lose. One of my CEO clients today is superb at getting the work done but leaves a trail of corpses in his wake: he needs his emotional intelligence tuned up. Another client is being groomed for a senior VP position and quickly needs to gain depth as a strategic thinker. Good thing I love my work. But it's *seriously distracting* to feel my iPhone having a grand vibration party in my pocket. *Jävlar Anamma!* What am I missing out on?

Finally, I'm out of the meetings and able to check. It's a voicemail from Guy. "Heads up, Suzanne. I just got a call from our SAR deputy Stan, for a search in Wildwood, right close to us. It's a missing woman. Stan's asked me to be PLANS chief, so I can't be field support for you. Looks like Rob is going to be OPS chief. I'm going to be planning and printing maps for the next thirty minutes, then will head down there."

I'm dying to call him for more details, but I don't because I know he's under a huge amount of time pressure to get planning and mapping done. One of the cruel paradoxes in SAR is this: the more urgent the search, the less time Guy has to do the vitally important planning. If a logger stumbles over a human skull and we need to search for more remains, he has all the time in the world to plan. If an endangered child is lost in wilderness, he has almost no time to plan.

Tonight, our search is urgent, and Guy is faced with two fiercely opposing needs: (1) to get our dog teams searching in the neighborhood as quickly as possible; and (2) to get enough planning done so that our K9 searching is as effective as possible. If he screws up his planning and sends our dogs into the wrong areas, it's a waste of limited search resources and a risk to the life of our missing person. I've seen Guy, who is usually friendly and outgoing, react to this pressure, shocking others by swearing in the command van when the equipment repeatedly fails.

Soon I'm heading from Seattle to my home in Edmonds, fifteen miles to the north. We moved here over thirty years ago and love the proximity of Puget Sound, the small-town feel, and the "artsy" flavor. Plus, Scott is an avid scuba diver and instructor, and he can get to supreme dive locations within a few minutes of our house. Finally, I give in and call Guy on my hands-free. "Hey, what have we got?"

His voice is rushed, and I hear his printer whirring in the background. "OK, here's what I've heard from Stan. Two nights ago, Wildwood PD got called for a report of an abandoned car in someone's driveway. The homeowners didn't recognize the car, so they got concerned that a stranger might be wandering their property. The police searched around the house for the driver, and attempted to contact the car's registered owner, but they didn't find anyone. So, they just filed a report and then had the car towed. This was, wait, let's see, Tuesday night, and it was late, around midnight. Remember how rainy it was? Then this morning, Seattle PD gets a call from a worried family that a thirty-five-year-old woman, Eileen Graham, is missing under mysterious circumstances. She hasn't shown up at her workplace. There was no sign of her at her apartment. Apparently, she hasn't called, emailed, or texted for two days. And here's the thing, the police just matched the plates of that abandoned vehicle to Graham. That's why Wildwood PD called SAR in for a search."

Once home, I quickly change into warm upper layers and waterproof pants, and load an excited Keb into the car. She knows from my SAR clothes, and from my frantic packing of gear into my Toyota 4Runner, that a new Search Game is starting. Darkness is falling, and I'm getting mentally prepared for a night search. As we back out of our driveway, I feel a cool nose poking into the back of my neck, while Keb's tail thumps enthusiastically on the backseat.

The Night Search

Arriving on scene twenty minutes later, I see SAR volunteer vehicles crammed along the narrow shoulder of a quiet street lined by huge houses. I park on a thin grass strip, trying not to block any driveway. I follow flashing lights to find our command van parked in an expansive circular drive in front of a small mansion. The out-of-town owner has given us permission to set up our command post here. I greet Deputy Stan, who, as usual, is reserved but friendly, and Guy, who, as usual, is a blur of energy as the mission spins up. Waiting for maps to be printed in the command van would delay search teams for an hour, so I'm relieved to see that Guy has brought maps he printed at home.

"Can I get K9 handlers and team leads over here for a minute?" Guy calls us over to the side of our command van to review maps and plans. "Our search tonight is based on 'reflex tasking'—we are going to start by searching areas close to where the subject's car was located. You can see on this aerial map that we've got a neighborhood of widely spaced houses surrounded by these huge, parklike estates." Guy pauses and grins at the group. "Once I get all my SAR back pay, I'm going to move here."

I'm standing at the back of the crowd, and it's hard to see as Guy's hand traces a large rectangle over the map, which is illuminated only by slashes of light from our headlamps. "Our highest probability area is inside this huge block. You can see it's bounded by residential roads on all sides, and it's about one-quarter mile long and one-quarter mile wide. Here, here, and here, you'll see that I've divided this block into three segments: east, middle, and west. We don't have any search area outlines to download to your GPS units, you guys are just going to have to navigate through people's yards as best as you can."

As we're waiting for individual assignments, I see detectives gesture to Stan, Guy, and Rob and lead them away. The waving beams of their flashlights disappear around the back of the house. Something's up, but they're not telling the search teams yet. Minutes later, they return. Stan and Rob hop up into the command van and Guy silently signals me over to the side where we can talk in private.

"Suzanne, we've really got something here. The police found a pile of the subject's clothes on the back porch of that house."

My ears perk up at this. "She took off *all* her clothes?"

"Well, I didn't get to dig through the pile, but it looked like most of them. The important thing is that we now have a Last Known Point; we can start man trackers and K9 trailing teams from the pile of clothes. This LKP is going to become the center of the universe for my search planning."

Keb is fussing at her leash by my side. She's not interested in this private briefing; she wants to start searching right now! I give her a firm "sit" command, which she reluctantly obeys. Guy looks around to make sure no one can overhear. "We also know something else, and it's not good. It's a safe bet that our missing woman was not in a normal mental state at this location. Taking off her clothes, especially in this cold weather, indicates intoxication, or hypothermia, or both, and that's a life-threatening combination." My mood shifts as I realize the situation has become more serious.

In search management classes, we're taught the Search Imperative: "Every search is an emergency." Formal determination of search urgency is usually done by asking a few critical questions: (1) What is the age of the subject? (2) Is the subject alone or with a group? (3) Does the subject have a mental or physical condition that puts them at risk? (4) Is the subject experienced and familiar with the area? (5) Are weather conditions a threat to survival? (6) Does the subject have the clothing and equipment to survive in current conditions?

You add up the points for "at risk" answers and get an urgency rating of high, medium, or low. It's not rocket science, but it gives you a mental place to start. Tonight, we have a missing woman who removed clothing in cold, wet weather. The woman has been missing for two days now, and we're faced with a lot of unknowns. Is she in someone's house? Is she alone or with companions? How could you hide in a residential neighborhood for two days and not be noticed? Is she even in the neighborhood, or has she left the area entirely? She could be in peril; she could be at a friend's house sipping tea. Our sense of urgency is clouded by the demons of uncertainty.

Guy and I have fallen into the habit of conferring on the best tactics for deploying our K9 teams. "Suzanne, what I want to do first is to assign man-tracker teams to start from where the woman's clothes were found behind the house. After that, we'll deploy our K9 teams."

I nod in agreement. Trackers are highly skilled men and women who can see "sign" (traces of human travel) that is invisible to us normal humans. Their tracking abilities, hard-earned through many hours of training, can provide us with a "direction of travel," and sometimes can lead searchers directly to a lost person. When combined correctly, the talents of man trackers and search dogs can direct search efforts to the right areas and provide sensitive K9 noses in those same areas.

Guy walks me back to the map taped to the side of the command van, where I suggest ways to deploy our K9 teams. Tonight, as we start searching, we don't know if our missing woman is alive or dead, so we're applying all the K9 resources we can get, and fortunately, we've had a good turnout. "We should start our trailing teams from where the clothes were found, and then maybe assign them to fan out along the northern boundary of our search area, along the road where her car was found. Our air scent teams can be assigned to larger areas in the neighborhood that you've already outlined. With her HRD certification, Keb may also be able to detect a deceased subject."

Guy nods, and scribbles on his notepad, as I start by specifying air scent team assignments. "In the western search segment, I want Janiece and K9 Roxie searching along with Nick and K9 Lobo. Keb and I will be covering the middle search segment, along with Rolf and K9 Magnum. Carter and K9 Mav are an experienced team, so we can assign them to cover the entire eastern segment. There's that restricted watershed area immediately to the south, let's send Deputy Samuels and K9 Justice to search that."

In all, we deploy three German shepherds, two Labs, one border collie, and three other "DoKDs" (Dogs of Kaleidoscopic DNA) into the dark neighborhood. All our hard work to grow our Snohomish County K9 team is paying off, and we are increasingly getting recognized within our SAR organization for our high response rate. I pull in a deep breath while enjoying a moment of pride at what we've accomplished.

Guy rejoins Stan and Rob in the command van to review the maps and finalize assignments. Search management is an exercise in organized chaos, and it's a struggle to keep both distractions and emotions well under control. More SAR teams are arriving now, and some folks are beginning to crowd around the back doors of the command van, eager to learn what's going on

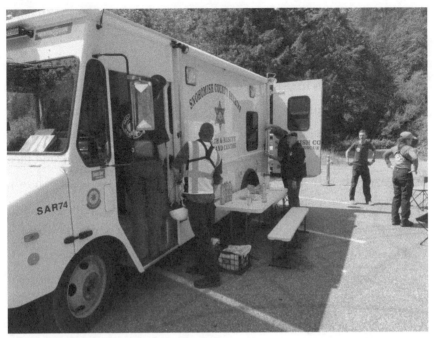
Our somewhat-reliable command van.

and to get deployed. I look up and can tell this is irritating Guy, who I'm afraid has developed a reputation of being a bit caustic when asking our volunteers to keep the area clear.

Peek into our command van this night. You'll see an old 1980s delivery truck about thirty feet long. Outside it's decorated with search and rescue banners, along with dents and scrapes from unfortunate episodes on not-quite-wide-enough logging roads. Inside, a narrow alley separates three cramped workstations: radio communications and mapping on the right, and documentation on the left. The documentation station is next to a printer and a copier, which serve the mission-critical purpose of producing maps for our search teams. These work reliably—as long as the network cable is plugged in, the hidden network adapter switch has been set correctly, the hidden circuit breakers have not tripped, and the AC inverter does not drain down the aging truck battery—and someone has remembered to load spare paper and spare ink cartridges.

Guy frequently complains that the workflow inside our command van would make human factors experts roll their eyes in dismay. Radio traffic on at least two channels is heard throughout the interior, as the communications operator tries to keep up with multiple calls. The documentation person (maintaining the mission activity log) and mapping person (adding clues and team positions to the mission map) sit immediately across from each other, attempting to do their own jobs while helping to translate faint radio messages for the hard-of-hearing radio operator. Mapping is done at a tiny desk on an underpowered laptop computer, which works reliably—as long as the mapping software licenses have been kept up-to-date, the cordless mouse does not fail, the correct maps have been installed, the flaky wireless connection to the printer works, and Microsoft Windows does not try to install a major operating system upgrade during the middle of the mission. This explains why Guy occasionally swears and throws pens out the door.

As more SAR volunteers arrive on scene, they assemble at the entrance of the circular drive and do what SAR volunteers do. They greet friends; they catch up on the latest K9 training news; and they speculate about the search they are about to embark on. Local news media people also show up and do what they *should not* do. They use telephoto lenses and long-range microphones to spy on our SAR volunteers, seeking mission information that should be kept confidential.

So what happens is that on the TV news the very next night, we see a video clip of Ruth, one of our SAR volunteers, doing something perfectly human: she's telling a story about how she slipped and fell "right on my butt" on her last wilderness training, and the group is laughing with her sympathetically. Any of us who've done wilderness searching have slipped on our butts more than once. And while the TV news headline that night is not "SAR

Volunteers Laugh and Joke while on Life and Death Search," the damage has been done: it looks like we're having a jolly time while a lost person is in peril. The next day the Snohomish County Sheriff's Public Information Officer calls the TV station and reads them the riot act.

By 7 p.m. Rob, Stan, and Guy are standing outside the back of the command van briefing K9 team leads one at a time on their specific assignments. I hear Guy assigning a team to Search Segment K, when Deputy Stan takes a quick phone call and looks over while rolling his eyes. "Hey Guy, we need to watch out for the owner of the house on the northwest corner of that segment. Wildwood PD tells me he may be armed and has a history of violence and craziness." Overhearing this, the searchers widen their eyes and look anxiously at each other. One of them is new to search and rescue and nervously looks at the map. Our sheriff's department is pretty sensitive about protecting their SAR volunteers, so this is a no-brainer for Stan. He quickly inserts himself into the briefing. "OK guys, listen up. Let me make it clear that you are *not to approach that property* unless escorted by a police officer." Or maybe two or three, I think to myself.

My field support person tonight will be Sven, a valued team member who is a veterinarian in his day job. Tall, and with a slightly uneven gait, Sven is training his young German shepherd, Shuksan, in the wilderness air scent discipline, and they are growing into a strong team. Keb, Sven, and I are soon heading into the darkness behind the house where our missing person's clothes were found. Keb is jerking on the leash, testing my patience with her impatience. "Hey, girlie, calm down. We're on our way now." We've been assigned to the northern half of the middle segment: about ten acres containing two stately houses with huge wooded yards.

It's disorienting to work in the dark: we can't see around corners; we can't see through the dense shrubs in the estate landscaping; I can't see Keb as she searches off-leash in the shadows. There are fences and tall hedges that block our travel, adding to a weird claustrophobic atmosphere. Nearby in the darkness, we occasionally hear other teams moving around, calling their dogs, or talking on their radios. Our narrow headlamp beams pierce the black as they play over lawns, compost piles, and other mysterious shapes.

Searching in the dark is hard, especially for us mere humans. The critical tasks of navigating a search pattern, keeping a close watch on our dogs, and visually scanning for clues are seriously impaired while we stumble over unseen objects and try to keep ourselves oriented. We turn our heads and visual references disappear. Our world is restricted to small cones of light beaming out from our headlamps, and a large portion of my attention is focused on not tripping over the next hidden fence or low hedge. We pause briefly in the shadows. "Sven, my night vision is not as good as it used to be," I complain. Growing older is hell, I commiserate with myself. "That means I really rely on you to let me know if you see any changes in behavior from Keb."

"No problem, Suzanne, I can see like a hawk. I've got your back." His response is reassuring, and I feel confident moving into the darkness. Keb and I are now in our sixth year of training in human remains. We regularly train in dark conditions, and she is in her prime. I think I am too, except for my night vision. Keb's scent radar works just fine in darkness, and she is thrilled with the cool temperature, the wonderful new smells, and the pure adventure of searching through strange yards at night.

We've been searching less than fifteen minutes when I notice Keb acting differently. She's slowed down, is tasting the vegetation, and exhibiting all the signs suggesting she's detected the odor of human remains. "Sven, pay close attention to Keb now!" I keep checking my GPS map screen, which is linked to a transmitter on Keb's collar. I see she's moved about twenty yards away from us; I can't even see her illuminated collar through the dense underbrush. Then, out of the dark, she comes bounding back and jumps on me: her signal for a live find! I'm puzzled and confused. Did she jump on me because she can smell other searchers moving around and talking to each other behind a nearby fence? Why has she alerted in this way?

But now she's moving slowly again, almost crouching or stalking. I grab Sven's arm to stop him. "I think Keb's onto something. I've seen this behavior before—it was when Keb encountered dead humans at the body farm in Texas just last year!" Using a simple SAR trick to increase illumination, we both aim our headlamps to play over Keb. We now see she has her nose to a tall chain-link fence and is roving back and forth along it. We need to move in the direction she keeps taking us, but there's no way we're going to get over that fence." Now what?

Sven quickly sorts things out. "Suzanne, we're gonna have to go back to the command post and get law enforcement to request permission from that homeowner so we can explore the property beyond that fence." I cringe with frustration for a moment, then reluctantly agree. After calling Keb to me, we start tramping back to where the command van is parked.

Just as we breathlessly report to the OPS chief that we've seen clear changes of Keb's behavior, we're stunned to hear that the search is being shut down for the evening! Damn! We're going to have to wait until tomorrow to find out what Keb is telling us!

Stan suspends the search just before 9:30 p.m. Police have been getting calls from residents, concerned about seeing strange people, strange lights, and strange dogs roaming their yards. Stan also knows from experience that searching at night, while often necessary, is just not as effective as searching in daylight. The dogs are OK, but humans are poor at finding subjects and seeing hazards in the dark. It's for this reason that another Search Imperative is "When you resume searching the next morning, *always* search again the areas that you searched in the dark."

I arrive home around 10 p.m. I'm tired, but I can't sleep as I think about tonight's search. Everything I saw tonight, and everything I know about my dog, tells me that Keb was communicating something important to us. Scott is sleeping soundly beside me as I lie awake, with my mind still swirling with the thought that Keb may have found something out there. I want to make sure we get to pick up that assignment right where we left off. Quietly I rise and pad downstairs to my laptop on the kitchen table. Keb leaves her warm couch to join me in the dark, nuzzle my knee, and help compose an email to Guy and Rob.

> Keb and I did not complete the assignment we had last night. Keb wanted to get in behind the fence on the property to the right of where search base was. It was decided we would finish the assignment in daylight after permission is received from the homeowner. It would be great if we could do that assignment first thing this a.m.—should not take very long.

The Search Imperative

The next morning, we show up early, eager to deploy. But to my dismay, we're not getting the assignment I asked for. Rob has instead assigned Janiece, with her certified air scent dog Roxie, to search in the area where Keb showed her distinct changes of behavior last night. *Byxfisare!* It's an unwritten expectation on our missions that you simply do what you are told. But this morning, I'm not going to accept this.

I grab Guy's elbow while planting my feet in a wide stance and pull him over to the side. "What's going on? Didn't you get my email?" He pauses for a moment, then shakes his head, but I can't tell if it's a "yes" or a "no."

"Suzanne, I just dropped the ball on this one. I got home around 11 p.m. last night, then spent over an hour preparing maps and assignments for this morning. I've been here at command since 6 a.m., so not much sleep last night. I got your email, but I guess it went into one tired brain cell and right out the next one. It's a good thing that Rob remembered, but you're right, he hasn't matched the right K9 team to this assignment. If there's a chance our subject is deceased, we need a team certified in both air scent and HRD."

We call Rob over, and after a few more minutes of making my case, all agree that Keb and I will be completing the assignment I requested. Where others might fuss and fume, Janiece is a true team player and has no problem being reassigned. She is one of those handlers who can hold up the mirror, see her own limitations as a team, and focus on what actually serves the mission best. In her typical unassuming manner, she adapts to the new plan. "Roxie's not certified on human remains, and I don't feel confident I'd be able to read her body language if she comes across a dead person."

I thank Janiece with my eyes, adding, "I really have a strong hunch that Keb was onto something last night." I can feel myself getting excited as my hands are tingling in anticipation. Keb has picked up on my vibes and is starting to tug on her leash. Mom, let's go right now!

With detective Bernard Simms in tow and adrenalin pumping through my body, I lead Keb down a narrow path that winds between head-high rhododendrons behind the house and toward the fence that blocked us last night. Detective Simms doesn't know much about search dogs, but he is a friendly guy and seems excited to be on this assignment with us. I've briefly scanned his physique, and he looks like he's in decent shape. Good to have someone that can keep up with us. I'm pleased to see that Keb is in full-on search mode, following the trail and enthusiastically making short excursions in and out of bushes and trees. You're making me proud, girl. I love watching her weave fluidly through the challenging terrain. She now has a single purpose, to find the odor that will provide her Most Favorite Toy in the World.

Shortly after we start traversing the woods, we spot something glimmering in the leaves and moss. The detective and I both lean down and peer at the ground. My heart gives an extra thump. It's a pair of glasses! They look clean and new, like someone took them off just minutes ago. Our eyes meet,

I look down at Keb wearing her SAR harness and GPS collar and wonder what's going through her mind.

knowing we may have found an important clue. While Detective Simms radios the find to incident command, I tell him, "I'm going to take Keb away from the scene until they've determined if the glasses are significant. If this is fresh evidence, we don't want the scene disturbed more than necessary." For another fifteen minutes Keb and I search toward the fenced area where we had been the night before. We then return to the detective and get the go-ahead to continue searching the vicinity near the glasses.

Searching together sometimes resembles an intricate dance, with Keb and me working off each other's subtle signals. I muse to myself, is Keb having my experience now? Is she feeling in sync, marveling at the well-oiled piece of machinery we have become? Keb abruptly takes off with a burst of speed, and while I'm crashing through shrubbery trying to keep up, I see her steadily moving off to my right, head held high. Then it looks like she's lingering in a small clearing, and suddenly I see her sit, turn around, and give me The

Look. I get goose pimples all over my arms. She's about fifty feet away, and from that distance, I can't see anything out of the ordinary near her. I hurry over, and it's only when I am almost right on top of Keb that I see a depression in the ground and something lying there. My mind is spinning. What's a mannequin doing out here? And then it strikes me. *It's not a mannequin, it's the body of a dead woman!*

Most SAR volunteers have not, and will never, encounter a dead body. It's an experience totally outside normal everyday civilian experience, and even outside our normal mission experience. We find lost children in the woods. We locate confused elders wandering neighborhoods. We rescue injured hikers from rough terrain. And so when faced with the unfamiliar, our eye-brain system will often change what we see into the more familiar. "What's a mannequin doing out here?" In hindsight, I realize my first reaction was a normal one. Guy would later assure me, by relating that our team leader Carter had the same reaction when they came upon a body on a previous search.

"Can you please come over here!" I yell loudly to Detective Simms, who is still examining the glasses we found, while I put Keb on her sit/stay. Someone rushes up. I point to the body on the ground, and he looks back up to me in shock. Keb is getting impatient, so I put her on leash, holding on firmly as we slowly back out the same way we came in to protect what might be a crime scene. When at a safe distance, I stop, mentally collect myself, and give Keb some quiet praise. Her usual reward involves an enthusiastic chase of her ball, but when on a somber scene like this with others close by, a few words whispered into her ear will make do. "Good girl, Kebbie; you're my sweet girl."

I know some handlers in the K9 SAR community believe their dogs will be forever ruined if they are not profusely rewarded every single time they have a find, whether on trainings or real missions. But this has never been a problem for Keb, and I believe most of our four-legged partners aren't harmed by intermittent rewards. A few times of not being rewarded is a nonissue for

Keb. "You really are more resilient than we give you credit for, aren't you, Kebbie?" She jams her nose hopefully in my pocket, but quickly accepts that there will be no ball this morning. She can sense I'm happy with her.

Gazing into her eyes leaves me wondering if Keb is self-aware, or if perhaps I'm just projecting human traits onto her. I sometimes wonder, does Keb understand death? I have no answer, but I know for sure that she perceives and smells a lifeless body. We've all read stories about dogs seemingly crying while lying next to the caskets of their deceased owners. I vividly remember the intense coaxing it took me and my first search dog, Bosse, to get a little dog named Shotgun to leave his owner who had died falling off a cliff in a remote part of the Cascade mountains. Shotgun had been sitting for days by his dead master in the snow. Starved and exceedingly cold, he refused to leave his owner until the presence of another dog finally persuaded him to return with us, and to a tearful reunion with the victim's wife. For her, Shotgun was the last bit of living connection with her husband, and I remember her grateful tears that the little dog had been rescued.

As we start slowly walking back to the command post, my emotions cycle from high to low over and over again. A woman has died. We found her, but not in time. My sadness is tempered with thoughts that we will have provided some resolution to a family. Even though the outcome is sad, for us this mission is now a success. Our skills and training have resolved a mystery and revealed a tragedy. The scene is no longer ours; it now belongs to law enforcement and medical examiner staff. We've done our part. We've delivered a lost soul into good hands.

I know we'll be back at our command van within minutes, but I can't help calling Guy breathlessly to share my news. "Guy! We found her! She was right where Keb had changes of behavior last night! We found her! We found a body! Keb found her!" I guess it's a good thing that the sneaky media can't monitor our cell phones.

As Keb and I approach the command van, someone with an inflated sense of importance scolds me for not staying on the scene where the body was found. I listen, decide to not engage, and instead ask if I can complete an incident report, something we always do after each search assignment. I also remember in contrast, the kindness of another teammate, "How are you doing? Are you OK?" and me reassuring her that I was OK, even after finding a dead person. Most of us who have done this for a long time have learned how to compartmentalize, much like healthcare professionals probably do. Emotions may well up later on, but I know how to deal with them at the appropriate time and place.

A universal characteristic of successful SAR missions is that many will search but only a few will be involved in actually finding the lost person. The reality is that many dedicated volunteers will spend their entire SAR careers training constantly and regularly responding, yet *never* be on the team that locates and rescues a lost subject. On our K9 team we've always de-emphasized praising individuals when they find a subject. It's all about the larger team success, and we acknowledge the teams that played an equally important role by "clearing" all the other areas where the subject was *not* located. But the private truth is that it's a gratifying, special occasion to be on the team that actually finds a lost person.

Why didn't Keb take us to the subject the first evening? Well, for one, the subject was behind a fence some distance away, and we needed to get permission to enter another neighbor's backyard. Command staff decided to wait until the next morning, but had we been granted permission that evening, I feel in my heart that Keb would have led us to her on that first night.

I reflect on how yesterday Keb came running back to me doing a "live find" jump alert. Had she actually reached the body but was unable to lead us back because of the fence? We'll never know. What I do know is that we spend hours and hours to hone our ability to "read" our dogs. Many seasoned HRD K9 handlers will tell you that when finding a real human body, the behavior you see from your dog may *not* be the trained final response that you get on normal trainings. Only a small number of handlers can obtain the money and permissions to train at "body farms" where Keb and I have trained. Realistically, most will never be able to train their dogs on full bodies. The first time your K9 encounters a dead person, the scent pool may be so overpoweringly different than anything they've trained on, that expected behaviors, including the normal trained final response, will fly out the window.

As I sit in the back of the cramped command van, quietly debriefing with Stan and Rob, I see small clusters of K9 team members and other searchers in conversations nearby. In the aftermath of every mission, there's often much discussion, second-guessing, and armchair quarterbacking by people who simply don't have the whole picture or don't understand how our dogs work. Some in the K9 SAR community can be cruel, and not everyone is happy on your behalf when you have a mission find. While the vast majority of my colleagues will celebrate with me and rejoice in team success, others inside our team will come up with negative spins. It's the nature of the beast and a common source of friction and jealousy in many K9 teams.

As the postdeployment debriefings wind down, I see our trailing team handlers standing alongside the command van. Tonight, I'm pleased that despite the continuing internal friction in our K9 team, the trailing team members have shown up for this mission. To their credit, they do regularly respond when called, as do the rest of us. And we all perform and act professionally when on missions—well, most of the time. If that would only carry over to other team interactions, I commiserate with myself. Outside of missions, our team is increasingly being consumed with a steady stream of petty issues and acrimonious squabbles.

My thoughts return to tonight's search. My self-confidence gets a huge boost from this mission, and for the moment, my worries about internal K9 team strife fade into the background. I remembered how Keb would slow down and literally stalk human remains at the "body farm," mesmerized while circling a body over and over before eventually sitting in her trained final response. I recognized that *same behavior* in the dark on our first night of searching. I trusted my gut and my dog, put my reputation on the line, and requested to complete the assignment. I stood my ground, and Keb and I found the missing woman.

People often ask if our dogs feel emotions. There's been much written, for example, about dogs that searched after the 9/11 disaster becoming depressed. Did they have a reaction to the physical reality and discomforts of the environment? Yes. Did they have a reaction to the state of mind of their handlers? Undoubtedly, yes. But depressed, grieving the dead? No, not in my opinion. As we drive home from the Wildwood Search, Keb seems back to her normal self while enthusiastically rearranging her blankets in the backseat. I don't think she is having a traumatic day because she found a dead body. I bet if I stop the car and throw the ball, you would jump and play as happily as ever. Am I right, girl? You sure showed what you can do today, filmstar girl! I reach back with my right hand and gingerly scratch her back. Wiggles of contentment ensue.

After arriving home tired and dirty, I share a private dinner celebration and a bottle of wine with Scott. Keb enjoys a juicy steak, cooked medium-rare to her liking. She probably has no idea why she hit the jackpot, but she chows down with enthusiasm before hopping up on the couch cushions and closing her eyes for a well-deserved snooze. I say good night to her with gentle strokes to her head. Good girl, Kebbie.

Mission Debrief

Guy

When safety experts began to study the chaos of airplane disasters, they discovered something profound and unexpected: that most incidents are caused not by a single catastrophic failure, but by a constellation of smaller factors, aligned by misfortune to result in death and destruction. In our personal lives, events can combine in similar ways: a misstep here, a wrong turn there, a brief mental lapse. In an instant, these forces can conspire to produce life-threatening consequences and drive desperate searches.

And every search is a battle between wizards and demons for the life of a lost soul. The wizards, our search planners, cast spells of probability and take up weapons of mapping and terrain analysis. They send out familiars with special search powers, sometimes in human form, sometimes in the shape of search dogs. Arrayed against the planning wizards are three powerful demons: Time, Weather, and Mystery.

Time hides footprints, conceals clues, and allows our subjects to wander ever farther from us. Weather in the Pacific Northwest comes from systems that sweep inland from the Pacific Ocean. For search teams, the rain and cold from these systems mean temporary discomfort. For lost subjects, weather can bring a dangerous killer: hypothermia. Mystery is the most powerful demon we face. What happened? We don't know. What decisions did she make? We don't know. What route did she take? We don't know. Where is she now? We just don't know.

Against the demons of mystery, we array imperfect searchers and fatigued planners, supported by gear that would be the envy of any army surplus store. With luck and investigation, evidence builds to fully characterize the lost person, along with their intents and behavior. With thoughtful planning and diligent searching, clues can be found that add to our constellation of knowledge and can be used to focus our efforts on specific areas or directions. Tonight we prevailed, but that's not always the case.

Looking Back

Suzanne

What ghosts visit us in the night, stealing our sleep with uncertainty and fear? What is every searcher's nightmare? Whether K9 handlers or search planners, our looming fear is that the demons of mystery will win, and we'll miss finding a subject that could have been found. And no one wants to be on that team that missed finding a living person or walked right by human remains. That being said, it does happen, and it can be emotionally devastating. As I contemplate our success, I realize how near to failure we came.

"Guy, I just can't get over that Keb found our missing woman less than 200 yards from where she left her clothes in the back of that house. Less than 200 yards! I am grabbing the sides of my head in disbelief. "Why didn't the police find her three nights ago when investigating the abandoned car? Why didn't the SAR man-tracking team find her?"

"I know, I know. All reasonable questions, Suzanne, but I think each question has multiple reasonable answers. Even under good conditions, the eyes, noses, and brains of our human or K9 searchers are imperfect. They miss things; all of us miss things. Then pile on stress, darkness, weather, and fatigue, and our search effectiveness drops even more." Guy pauses momentarily with eyes squinting to see if I'm listening. "I know this kind of outcome opens the door wide for criticism of the police, but really, I think it's unwarranted. They're not perfect. And it's pretty clear we're not perfect. Remember, I blew it when I forgot about your email requesting to be assigned back to the same area."

Our trust level has evolved over the years and now makes it easy to candidly debrief after missions. I appreciate that Guy is fessing up to having "ignored" my e-mail, but I also know that he was under a lot of pressure. "I understand that, Guy," I take a deep breath. "But it's going to become an issue in our team that our trailing K9s were unable to acquire a scent trail that might have led them directly from the pile of clothes to the missing woman. They're going to be defensive about this for the next six months."

"Well, that's sort of just tough twinkies," his response is unsympathetic. "We'll need to remind the whole team that on some missions, our air scent K9s will find the subject when the trailing K9s do not. On other missions, our trailing K9s will find the subject when the air scent K9s do not. We've got to realize that during missions, the larger demons of mystery and environment can easily outweigh the skills of any particular searcher or K9 team. I just hope people get that."

I hear him, but a heaviness in my stomach tells me that logic only goes so far with some of our team members. "Hmm, I hope you are right."

"Remember, Suzanne, thanks to *your* perseverance and Keb's nose, we found our missing woman on this search. The man trackers were unable to follow her traces. The trailing K9s weren't able to follow a trail from her abandoned clothes. Command staff almost dropped the ball and failed to adequately follow up on reported K9 interest. You and Keb made the difference on this one."

A week after the Wildwood search, Guy and I hear from the Snohomish County medical examiner that our lost woman died of exposure, with drugs or alcohol possibly playing a contributing role. It's likely she died of hypothermia in the cold rain on that first night, overcome by demons even before we started our searching. But we will never know.

7
Where Coyotes Wail
In Which Bones Move at Night

"It is common for canids to scatter or remove
skeletal elements from their original location.
Elements are often scattered along game trails,
away from human activity,
and toward areas of visual cover."

—Sincerbox and DiGangi, *Forensic Taphonomy*
and Ecology of North American Scavengers

"Come on in!" our SAR sergeant, Charles, smiles and looks up from his computer screen. His cramped office in one corner of our search and rescue hangar has just enough room for a worn chair and a gray government surplus desk in front of a huge map of Snohomish County. Unlike some of his sheriff colleagues, Charles is a staunch liberal, and someone has teased him by placing a six-foot-high Hillary Clinton cutout figure in the corner of the room. "How are things going?"

I engage in some small talk, but at the earliest opportunity blurt out my good news. "Keb and I just certified with NAPWDA and now have two national HRD certifications!"

Months earlier, our sheriff's department had stipulated that to deploy on HRD missions, Snohomish County K9 teams would need to be certified by a national law enforcement–led organization. To meet this requirement, on my own time and on my own $2,000, I had taken a week off from work and flew with Keb to Denver, Colorado, where we completed our first NAPWDA (North American Police Work Dog Association) HRD Certification, under the careful evaluation of Lead Master Trainer Matt Devaney. Returning as a proud team member with *two national HRD certifications in hand* (and the first on our K9 team to reach this level of certification), I am eager to share the news with Charles.

The atmosphere in the office suddenly shifts. I'm surprised to see that Charles does not seem to be equally excited about the news. After some hemming and hawing on his part, I'm stunned to hear, "Suzanne, we've decided to deploy only single-discipline dogs on HRD missions."

My face starts to flush, and I have to bite back a surge of anger. I suspect this requirement is based on the bias that K9s previously certified to find live persons are less effective in finding human bodies or remains. It would mean that no matter *how many* nationally recognized certifications Keb has, we would not be deployed on HRD missions because she had previously certified as an air scent K9. "But Charles, I've just taken a week off from my business, costing me almost $2,000 to meet the requirements set just last month!"

"Suzanne," Charles says, trying but failing to mollify me, "You and Keb are a good team, but I really need to stay out of this decision. George is the deputy in charge of law enforcement K9 work, and this is his call."

My head is now hanging in seething dejection, and I realize what may have happened. George is a nice enough guy but seems to be under the sway of the "My-Way-of-Training-Search-Dogs-Is-the-Only-Way-in-the-Universe" woman, who I think still harbors a personal animosity toward me. It appears that she's using her influence to shape county policies to exclude Keb and me. Welcome to the world of personal grudges and petty power struggles in K9 SAR. In our county's SAR culture, you do not question things. You do as you are told and bite your tongue, even when things appear to make no sense. Not doing so can have severe consequences. I'm now going to try to explain to Scott that the thousands of dollars spent meeting law enforcement certification requirements ultimately resulted in nothing.

On the drive home, instead of brooding in silence, I discuss my ongoing frustrations with my backseat passenger. "Kebbie, why are people being such butts, when all we're doing is trying to improve HRD search capabilities within our county?" Keb leans forward to nuzzle the back of my neck in sympathy. "We're one of the first teams in our whole county to be nationally certified in HRD. What do you think about that?" Vigorous tail thumps from the backseat. "I just can't understand why they are making it so hard for us. Why? People are so hard to figure out, and all we want is to do some good, don't we, little girl? Why do we keep getting the short end of the stick, no matter what we do?" I am having a bit of a pity party. Keb expresses her solidarity with a wet lick to my ear.

A pattern clarifies for me as I recall another recent policy change: "No personal vehicles can have SAR insignia larger than six inches high." At the time, out of over 100 volunteer vehicles, only 3 had large SAR decals: mine, Guy's, and Carter's. Was this another policy missile, aimed right at me and my close friends on the air scent team?

By the time I arrive home, I've decided I'm not going to accept the new HRD policy without pushing back. The unfairness and the lack of respect for my time, money, and dedication to K9 SAR fuel my fire, and I spend several weeks doing a survey of some of the most highly recognized HRD trainers and handlers in the nation. My goal is not to advocate for a black-and-white answer, but to lay out the pros and cons of the "single discipline versus cross-trained HRD K9" debate, because in my mind, the science on the issue is inconclusive. My personal experience and training tell me that the reliability of dog teams has less to do with whether they are trained in several disciplines (as Keb is) and more with the innate characteristics of a particular dog, the quality of training she receives, and the level of handler skills. Keb, I know, has no issue with distinguishing between her different commands: "Find a live person!" versus "Find the dead!"

With a small flare of satisfaction, I summarize the survey results and email them to our SAR deputies. In the months that follow the submission of my survey to the Sheriff's Department, I don't hear anything official, but then to my surprise I detect a change. Charles has started to call on us for HRD missions! Historical conflict and egos continue to color how HRD K9s are deployed for years, but a door has now opened, one that leads to life-changing opportunities for Keb, my teammates, and me.

The Search

I'm in my home office preparing for an upcoming executive roundtable meeting, when I'm thrilled to get a call from our SAR sergeant, Charles Thayer, notifying us of an opportunity to participate in a human remains search. My curiosity is definitely piqued, and I grab a pen to start taking notes. Charles talks fast and does not like repeating himself. "Suzanne, this is going to be a mixed jurisdiction search. It's in our county, up on the Tulalip Tribal Reservation, but it's related to a murder case in neighboring Salish County. Detective Eric Watson, who's also the SAR deputy from that county, will be incident commander for the search, and we're going to call in certified HRD K9 teams from all over the region."

After a long and painful history of being left on the sidelines, Keb and I are being called for HRD missions! Coolness! The nice thing about this kind of mission is that it's planned in advance, so we don't have to rush out the door in the middle of the night in the rain, sleet, and wind. I hear from Charles that the mission is scheduled for the upcoming weekend, which is great news as my schedule is open. Fortunately, Keb's business calendar is clear as well.

On Saturday morning, Guy and I arrive on scene. We locate a large dirt parking lot that serves as the staging area and pull in alongside sheriff's department trucks and several vehicles marked Tulalip Tribal Police. The Tulalip Reservation lies thirty miles north of Seattle and is bounded on the west and south by twenty miles of Puget Sound coastline, and on the east by busy Interstate 5. The reservation covers almost forty square miles of mostly forested terrain, dotted with small clusters of residential housing. Like other sparsely populated areas in our state, the woods provide concealment for drug deals, for crime, and sometimes for human remains.

Guy and I smile and shake hands with Snohomish County Detectives Ambrose Barry and Bernard Simms, who remember us from earlier searches. "Hi Suzanne, did you bring your dog today?" I smile in reply and point at my rig, where Keb is leaning her head out the window, intensely observing our conversation. Looking around, I see that someone has had the presence of mind to order a port-a-potty, which is a bonus for female SAR volunteers.

It's been discreetly stationed right in the middle of the gravel lot and provides a special ambience to the area where teams receive their instructions
and assignments.

Shortly after we sign in, Eric Watson, the detective in charge, briefs our
small gathering of HRD handlers: "As I think you've heard, we're following
up on a homicide case." Eric is tall and ruggedly handsome, with silver streak-
ing his short, spiky hair. In addition to being a detective, he's one of the most
experienced SAR coordinators in Washington State. He pauses, grins, and
looks around for effect. "One body has been found in a shallow clandestine
grave nearby, which we've designated as the DRT point." He can see us all
exchanging puzzled glances. We have lots of acronyms in SAR, but DRT is
not one of them. Eric's grin widens. "Dead Right There."

Eric rolls a large map across the hood of his truck, and we gather around
as he points with his finger. "While I can't comment on our information
sources, we've got strong suspicions there's a second body buried somewhere
in the wooded area just west of us. I can't share many details of the case, but I
want all teams to be especially alert for black plastic bags." Eric pauses again,
scanning our group. "Everybody got that? Black plastic bags."

Guy and I exchange a quick glance. Plastic bags? Maybe the first body
was wrapped in one? We often don't get a lot of detail about the crime itself,
and we understand the reasons for this. On evidence searches such as this one,
law enforcement will try to tell us what we need to accomplish our search, but
they must often withhold details of active criminal investigations. They don't
want the bad guys to know what the detectives know, and they don't want to
weaken the case for prosecutors.

Eric continues, "I'll give you a heads up right now that those woods
on the west contain homeless camps. The tribal police tell me they've been
cleared recently, but they will be escorting you. You'll need to proceed with
caution." Eric then puts his finger down on the map again. "We also need

these fields to the east of us to be searched. It's looks like maybe 100 acres of open space, then, let's see—looks like more woods on the other side. It's possible that bones from our case have been scattered over in those areas."

We learn that our first assignment will be in what Guy is now calling Homeless Camp Woods. As I'm unloading gear, Keb immediately jumps out of the car door, which I've forgotten to close, and tears around the scene as if she has been locked up for days. "She is ready to go to work!" I exclaim, hoping that none of the deputies has noticed. "More than ready," I mumble under my breath. After getting briefed on our assignment, I put Kebbie's search vest on her, and she settles down, knowing it's time to work.

Keb has an entourage today. We're being led by a Tulalip tribal officer and followed by detectives Barry and Simms. The tribal officer has a striking weathered face with a light brown complexion. He points to a beaten trail leading from our feet into the woods. "You can see this is a regular travel path for homeless folks. They use these woods for encampments and drug deals."

This is a huge red warning sign for us. We're concerned that our dogs (and ourselves) might be exposed to used drug needles and other nasty hazards. My mind winces at the image of Keb's paw being pierced by an old needle, but we need to help if we can. Keb doesn't get to vote about where she is deployed, and sometimes I feel guilty about that. As her spiritual guardian, I often have to weigh the risk for Keb against the human needs driving a search. Where's the balance point when we are searching for a lost child? What hazards are justified when we are looking for what might be just bones? Keb doesn't worry about this; she just happily romps off searching when I ask her. Keb has had minor injuries on past searches. It's something that keeps me up at night.

We agree to proceed cautiously. From the road, we're led down a wide, beaten dirt path that winds through low woods of Big Leaf Maple dotted with occasional stands of evergreen cedar. Along the sides of the path, the green sword ferns are over Keb's head, and the forest floor is covered with downed branches of all sizes. We arrive at the location of one of the camps to find discarded clothes, ripped old tents, rusted cans, and shredded plastic tarps strewn about. Guy and I scan the ground carefully for sharp objects and discarded needles.

A Smell of Death

After our initial checkout, I let Keb off her leash, and send her out on a search command. She begins ranging with her nose continuously moving from air to ground and back, while Guy and I follow. We leave the encampment behind and follow Keb's intentional wandering south through the woods, thrashing occasionally through thick blackberry thorns that have filled in where old road clearings allow the sun in. As she enthusiastically searches along the soft, gravelly edges of a small stream, Detective Barry suddenly calls out from twenty yards away. He's found an empty black plastic bag, and he wants us to lead our dogs down a steep embankment to check out the area.

Instantly upon arrival at the stream bank, we're assaulted by a strong, rancid scent of something dead wafting up from below. Our noses cringe and our stomachs wince, while our hopes of finding something soar. I pause to remove Kebbie's vest so that she won't get caught up in tangled branches in the stream bed. "Sök!" I restart Kebbie on her "search for dead" command, using the Swedish word for "search." I watch her as she starts ranging across the stream bed as we move downstream. But something is odd. Sometimes we can smell the foul odor and sometimes we can't. Keb seems to be having a hard time too. She circles around but apparently can't locate where the scent of death is coming from. I can sense her frustration building. What's going on here? Keb's got the nose, but I've got the brain: it's my responsibility as the handler to help her sort through the mysterious scent flows that can be caused by wind, temperature, or terrain.

"Sök!" I restart Kebbie on her "search for dead" command.

Keb suddenly does a full body shake. Yellow fur, skin, floppy ears, and otter tail become a blur as every body part whirls in rapid movement. A body shake often follows a find, and she now has my full attention. It's as if she is telegraphing a change in her emotional state: I am done with this task and now I am ready for my magic ball to appear! At other times a body shake might suggest frustration and uncertainty. This time the shake is not followed by a sit, which is her trained indication for a find.

This is puzzling. "Kebbie girl, are you smelling something, but you can't pinpoint the source? What are you trying to tell me?" This is when we engage in a search dance together. I take out my Professional K9 Scent Direction Device (a jar of soap bubbles from Toys R Us) and determine what direction the wind is coming from by watching where my bubbles go. I study the terrain to visualize how drainages, trees, or thick ferns might impact how scent is weaving and flowing. I try to see the world from Keb's perspective—she is all nose—and little by little a search strategy emerges. After a few minutes we start doing concentric circles together—maybe my girl and I can figure this out together?

I'm growing more nervous by the minute. Keb is getting frustrated, and I'm afraid I'll start cueing a false response by leading her over the same area again and again. Lo and behold, suddenly she sits, giving her "trained final response" smack in the middle of the small stream, where it's obvious to all that there aren't any bodies to be seen. Detectives Barry and Simms are standing on the gravel bank directly above, looking at us intensely. Sweat starts to warm my armpits. Now what?

"Well, we're at a bit of a loss about what has just happened with my dog. Is it possible to bring down another seasoned HRD K9 team to get a second opinion?" Within a few minutes, I'm relieved to see Penny with her beautiful white shepherd, Snowflake, clamber down the embankment toward our location. Penny and her husband Bryce have a long, successful career in K9 search and rescue. They know their stuff. Sure enough, it doesn't take long for her to find a very rotten salmon carcass only 100 feet upstream from where Keb gave her alert.

A fish! I wince inside, as my face flushes with embarrassment. It dawns on me that I've never proofed Keb off dead fish! Penny kindly reassures me that she has had the same experience with SAR dogs she has trained. "Don't worry, Suzanne; it's all good." I hear her saying the words, but I am anything but good. It's frickin' humiliating. This will get the rumor mill going for sure, I whine to myself.

Detective Eric Watson, the SAR sergeant for this mission, has overheard the radio report about the black plastic bag and has hurried to the scene. He's a former police K9 handler, and a colorful personality—jovial and easy to talk to. He has seen my dogs and me on quite a few missions over the years and now approaches with a teasing smirk. "A fish, eh?" In the years since, the "fish find" has become a part of our signature greeting. "Hey, Suzanne, had any good fish for dinner lately? Caught a fish today?"

Not long after this mission, I placed a salmon on the wood pile by our garage, with the intention of letting the carcass rot for a few months. When Scott started complaining about a mysterious stench that kept getting worse and worse, I fretted that the neighbors would turn us into our homeowner's association. To my dismay the fish eventually slumped down behind the woodpile where I couldn't reach it, *Djävlans helvete!* I chose to just stay quiet, wondering with Scott, "What in the world is that stench?" He wasn't amused when months later, I confessed what had happened, and we had to disassemble the wood pile piece by piece. But my mission was accomplished, and now when Keb runs in to a dead fish, she'll hopefully just check it out and move on. "Good girl, Kebbie."

For our afternoon assignment, Eric directs us to the expanse of fields and woods on the east side. My ears are still burning about the salmon, but Guy and Keb have apparently already forgotten our embarrassment. Picture a rolling, 100 acres of tall grass, spotted here and there with low brush and an occasional scrubby oak tree. To our left, on the east side of this field, we see a wooded area of low evergreens. Our assignment is based upon the "coyote scenario"—that additional bones may have been carried away from the initial body location and transported across the grassy field or into the woods beyond. In rural searches for human remains in western Washington, coyotes are on top of the list of "usual suspects" for scattering bones. But many people don't realize that domestic dogs also scatter human remains, and there are classic stories of Fido bringing home an unwelcome surprise, "What's that ya got there, boy? What ya got? *What the hell!?*"

Our first task is to orient our search map to the landscape before us; it's important to align our brains with north, east, south, and west. When starting an assignment, it's easy to let adrenaline take over. Guy and I have learned from embarrassing experience that it's quite possible to dash off in the wrong direction when not carefully oriented. From where our vehicles are parked, we start by moving east into the field, and I allow Keb to range freely. "If she shows interest, we'll follow her lead. If not, we'll guide her across the field, then into the woods over there on our left." With a quick nod, Guy agrees with this tactic, which will expose us to a light wind from the east—sweeping scent from that direction to Keb's sensitive nose. Silently, I'm grateful for a support person who gets this right away. As we work our way through the grass and shrubs, I keep an eye on Keb, while wondering if there are any coyotes lurking in the woods ahead of us.

On this assignment we're looking for human bones, and I secretly wonder if Keb has been sufficiently "proofed" off animal remains and bones. I remember when early in my HRD career, I had been riding to a training session in another K9 member's truck. Suddenly he slammed on the brakes, came to a screeching halt, and excitedly announced, "Roadkill!" With wide eyes, I watched him get out of the rig with a huge Rambo knife in hand and carefully cut off the paw of a dead rabbit. He returned to the car, mumbling something about "proofing off of animals." As he reentered the car with paw in hand, his wife, a seasoned HRD handler, acted like this was the most normal thing in the world. At that time, I had just started training my first SAR dog, Bosse, in HRD, and had little idea of what would be involved and what proofing was all about. That day was just a teaser of some of the bizarre training techniques yet to come.

Over time, I came to realize that proofing your dog to *not* alert on any odor, animal remains, or bones that are nonhuman is essential. What should I proof my dog on? Live animals, dead animals, animal bones, dead fish, people, garbage, glass jars, gloves, plastic, fresh food, rotten food, excrements, and the list goes on. In other words, I need to include all these items and others when I set up training problems in controlled environments to make sure Keb understands that they are *not* what she is supposed to be looking for. You might ask, "Why glass jars?" Well, we often store and put out human remains in glass jars, so unless we proof our dogs on the jar, how do we know that they are actually alerting on the odor of human remains and not the glass? So, we place clean jars, clean gloves, rotten chicken, sardines, and a bunch of other stuff in our training scenarios to make sure that our dogs only get rewarded when alerting to the odor of decomposing human remains.

At home I have a cupboard full of animal bones, carefully wrapped in acid-free tissue paper, and stored in paper bags, away from human bones and other "source," to prevent cross contamination of scent. Human remains for training (referred to as "source" in the HRD K9 world) are locked up and kept separately in hermetically sealed boxes, and even stored in different parts of my car as they are transported to trainings. HRD handlers are a strange bunch. In addition to roadkill, you will find them proofing their dogs on things like chicken, pork chops, fish, and more—all in various stages of decomposition. I would love to hear my neighbors' conversations behind drawn curtains when they see me throwing pork chops and other rotten food distractions in our yard. "We suspected Suzanne has more than one screw loose, but she's for sure gone off the deep edge now!"

Proofing is frankly a pain in the butt, and often tests the patience of handlers and our dogs alike. But it's an essential and important example of the nuanced and complex training required for a successful HRD K9. Imagine the false alarms and wasted time if on missions our dogs alerted on discarded meat in dumpsters or on the myriad animal bones scattered in the Pacific Northwest wilderness. We'd never get our assignments completed, and law enforcement simply would not trust our dogs to find human remains. We proof our K9s effectively by setting up proper training assignments and helping our dogs understand what alerts they are rewarded for, "Good girl, Kebbie"; what alerts are mistakes, "No, leave it"; and how to make those judgments in the field. And hold onto your hats and stomachs now, we also have to train our dogs not to eat or chew on what they find! I'll leave the implications of that to your imagination.

Keb, Guy, and I spend tedious hours searching back and forth across what Guy is now calling "Coyote Acres Regional Park." His humor is often sharp and dark, and seldom appropriate for a search base where family members or media might be present. We progress steadily toward the wooded area on the far side—it would be normal coyote behavior to carry remains across the open field and into the protection of those woods. I'm certain that Keb can smell the coyotes that live and hunt in this area, but I don't see any signs of nervousness from her. We finally reach the edge of the forest, climb over a low wire fence, and start searching in the trees. Keb is still full of energy, and I see her sniffing something white, partially covered by leaves. As I draw near, I can see a small pile of pale, finger-sized bones, but their shape and size are unfamiliar, and I can't tell if they're human or animal.

Now is when I really have to trust that Keb is solid enough to give me a correct answer. I walk up to the bones and point down at the earth. "Kebbie! Check it!" Nothing. No bark, no alert. She looks at me like I'm a crazy woman and saunters off in search of something more interesting. After conferring, Guy and I decide we still should have one of the forensic investigators come check the bones. "Team 3 to Command, we have evidence that needs to be evaluated."

We're back on our hands and knees peering at the bones, when "*oohweeee, oohweee,*" the sharp yips and eerie wails of coyotes erupt out of the nearby woods. It sounds like they're only ten feet away! I look up nervously to see Keb resting on a patch of dry moss, looking totally noncerned. Guy is just grinning. "If we don't bother them, I guess they won't bother us." His attempt at humorous advice is less than comforting, and I call Keb in closer, just in case. My eyes continue to scan the brush around us as the wailing gradually

Our postcard from Coyote Acres Regional Park.

fades. Were they complaining about our intrusion? Were they warning us to stay away from their dens? Keb may know, but she's not telling.

Shortly thereafter, two investigators from the medical examiner's office show up, kneel down, and quickly determine we have found animal bones. They thank us and assure us it's important to get a double-check. At times like this, I always wish I had more training distinguishing between animal and human bones, and in the years following, I have taken multiple classes to learn just that. And while I am better trained now, I still prefer having the experts decide what bones are relevant and which ones are not. Smartphones have become very helpful tools, as we can take photos of bones we find in the field, text them to the experts, and quickly get determinations in almost real time.

Keb has an unmistakable and distinct personality: always gentle, always hungry, always ball crazy. She's eager to please but her independence can occasionally surface in a stubborn streak, and she'll blow me off by becoming deaf. "Keb, come here." "Keb, this way!" Sharp whistling. "Damn it, Keb, *come!*" Not an eye nor an ear is twitching; she is very intent on sniffing something invisible to me, most likely dog pee. *I do not hear you; I do not hear you.* Times like that can be infuriating, but I know it's usually a sign that she is either physically tired, has run out of "nosetime" (scenting takes a lot of mental and physical energy), or she is picking up on my stress. That's when I have to put on my big girl pants and find a way to replace my irritation with becoming a good and compassionate handler who makes difficult decisions. During a mission, that may show up as "It's time to pull my dog from this assignment," hard words to say out loud. Ouch, it hurts, but it happens to all of us handlers at one time or another.

By midafternoon, I can see Keb's energy level winding down. We've been searching for hours; she has detected nothing that tells her that her Most Favorite Toy in the World is forthcoming. All of us are getting tired. As we work our way out of the woods and cross the field heading back toward our cars, I am elated to run into two of my favorite people from Kitsap County

Search Dogs: Sally Olsen and her dog, Skye, and Katherine Murphy with K9 Hooligan. I am extremely fond of both these strong, dedicated women. It doesn't hurt that they also have great dogs. Sally greets us with hugs. "I'm so glad to see you!"

Keb immediately perks up when she sees Skye. Over the years Sally and I have done road trips to K9 trainings all over the western United States, and our dogs enjoyed spending time together. "Skye is on her search command and is all business right now," Sally says, as Keb bends on her forelegs, let's her tongue loll out of the mouth, puts her butt up in the air while her tail whips up a storm: Let's play! Keb is actually very picky about whom she plays with, and this is behavior saved for only a select few. If given a choice, she vastly prefers to play with me, not with other dogs. As SAR handlers, we actually want to be the best thing in the whole world for our dogs; we need to be the center of their universe. Yes, we let our dogs engage in play and run off some excess energy and stress at the end of trainings occasionally, but you would not typically find Keb and me in a dog park, more likely we would be just outside, playing fetch with distractions.

Guy and I eagerly share with them whatever tidbits of information we have gleaned throughout the day. We give them the lay of the land and point out the woods where we've been searching, while mentioning our close encounter of the coyote kind. By now Keb has figured out that her attempts to play with Skye are failing. "Let's get going, girl. Want to get some snacks in the rig?" She seems to like that idea—Guy and I think we see a faint K9 smile—and we continue on our way. With their K9s bounding ahead, Sally and Kathy continue east across "Coyote Acres Regional Park" to double cover what we've already searched.

As we traverse fields on our return to the staging area, I take pride in the fact that we have nurtured a solid relationship with Sally, Kathy, and their team, Kitsap County Search Dogs. "Wouldn't it be great if they were actually on our team?" I say. "They play straight, and I never worry about secret agendas when I am around them. They would fit right in with our culture." Guy, being the killjoy he can sometimes be, points out that while the vast majority of our team indeed is rallying around the culture, vision, and initiatives we've generated over the last several years, we continue to spend a disproportionate amount of time trying to manage our small clique of malcontents. I'm more optimistic by nature. In spite of these challenges, our leadership team is doing a great job staying consistent and advancing new, progressive directions.

Where Bones Grow in Trees

The three of us are soon back at base taking a break. Keb slurps up a bowl of water, then proceeds to wolf down handfuls of high-protein kibble. We're chatting with Eric (who continues to tease me about the salmon), when he takes a call on his cell phone. "What? OK." He quickly calls Guy over for his pen and notepad. "Give me those coordinates again. OK. Put flagging around the bones and don't let anyone touch them. I'll start the detectives on the way. Send one team member out to the road to flag them down and lead them in."

Eric looks up with a wide grin, "We may have found our second body already!"

Thirty minutes later, our hopes are not dashed completely, but they get beat up rather badly. The detectives have located and examined the bones. Detective Simms calls Eric directly, "Well, they're definitely human bones," he pauses, "but it's definitely not our guy." Eric, Guy, and I are a bit stunned to hear this. Bernard continues, "The bones are way too old for our case. It's sort of weird looking. A fast-growing alder tree has actually grown through one of the bones and lifted it six feet above the ground."

Well, well—we don't know what to think. This is sort of bad news and sort of good news. The medical examiner is called in to assess the mystery bones, and we return to our continued searching. *Jävlar i helvete!* Are there bones all over these woods?

Human SAR volunteers are taught a concept called the "Searcher's Cube," a reminder to look in *all* directions (up, down, left, right, forward, back) when searching for clues, and to avoid the natural tendency to just look forward on the ground. While people can intellectualize this concept of searching in three dimensions, our dogs can't. So, part of training our HRD dogs actually includes training them that they may need to look *up* to find the source of scent. I've purposefully designed training assignments for Keb in which the HRD source has been hung in trees above her head. Why such esoteric training? One reason is that we're called to search for despondent subjects, who are sometimes found hanging from trees. Another reason here in the Pacific Northwest is that cougars are known to carry deer carcasses high up into trees. They could easily do this with human remains.

It's Raining Bones

A week later, I get another call from Charles and discover that my involvement with the mystery bones is not yet over. "Do you guys remember where the mystery skeleton was found on the Tulalip crime scene search?" he asks. "Well, those remains were identified as a known missing person and his family was notified, but now there's a problem. The family has started to return to that area on a regular basis to look for more bones. Each time they find another bone, the family shows up at the ME's office, bone in hand. The medical examiner wants this to stop."

The very next day, we make arrangements to meet with HRD handler Hattie and her K9, Gavel. We pack up gear and dogs, and drive north to meet up with Elisa Henricksen, the lead forensic investigator from the Snohomish County medical examiner's office. She's waiting for us at the edge of the woods and gives a brief overview of what's planned for today. "I've been working with my forensic team, excavating the area adjacent to the human bones found by the K9 team a couple of weeks ago. We want to make sure *every single bone* has been found and removed from the site, and we believe we have located most. But we want you to deploy your dogs to make sure we haven't missed anything." Elisa is eyeing our two dogs, and she continues with more than a hint of exasperation in her voice. "We've been digging here all morning and *really* don't want the family to keep bringing any more bones to our office. Really." Guy and I force ourselves to keep our expressions serious.

Elisa and I have recently rekindled a relationship that began in the aftermath of the Oso Landslide, one aimed at developing a stronger cooperation between the Medical Examiner's Office and Snohomish County Search and Rescue. In our discussions to date, Guy and I have focused on how we could help meet the medical examiner's needs while at the same time providing the K9 team and other SAR members with educational and training opportunities. One of the ideas we've jointly explored is that of establishing a SAR specialty team consisting of planners, K9 teams, man trackers, and ground searchers who'd be willing to be called on short notice to help medical examiner office staff excavate, dig, and help explore cases like this.

Elisa's request will be an important test for us. It's an opportunity to develop more credibility with both our law enforcement officers and the medical examiner's staff. They'll all be observing us, and I can feel my nerve endings tingle a bit. We all follow Elisa a short distance into the forest and are greeted by a handful of dirt-smudged medical examiner staff, looking tired and bedraggled. They've been digging on their hands and knees all morning long.

The forest of widely spaced hemlock trees and sparse shrub cover looks exactly like where we searched weeks ago. My mind has started imagining that bones are buried everywhere. Before us I see an area of about ten by thirty feet that has been thoroughly dug up. It looks like a brown wound surrounded by the typical rough undergrowth and greenery of the Pacific Northwest. Elisa turns to me and says, "Can you have your dogs search for bones in the area we just excavated? We'll just stay here and watch if it's OK with you," Elisa adds innocently, taking her smartphone out to snap photos.

In the excitement of the moment, Hattie, I, and both our dogs nod our agreement and immediately start getting ready to deploy. Damn. When it's already too late, I realize that Hattie and I should have consulted with each other and decided on a plan. Instead, we deploy both dogs at the same time in this confined area. Fortunately, they work well together, though in hindsight, it would have been a much better idea to have our K9s work separately to avoid unintentionally cueing each other—the things we miss when stressed.

Hattie and I lead our dogs in. Within minutes, we agree that both Keb and Gavel are showing a noticeable change in behavior right next to a little stump. Keb puts her nose right down on the roots, before sitting and turning her head toward me.

"Elisa!" I call out, "They're both alerting right around this stump." Elisa breaks into a broad grin and looks very pleased. "We actually planted a very small bone right under that stump to see what your dogs would do!" *What a sneak!* But I'm relieved that, so far, our dogs have done well. Shortly thereafter, Gavel finds another little bone hidden under some dirt, one that the medical examiner staff missed while doing their own sifting. *Good job, Gavel!*

We continue to search for another hour, with our dogs wandering back and forth. Their energy level is good, but we see no signs of interest. Thirty minutes later, Kebbie, Guy, and I are working the perimeter of the site when Keb suddenly sits right next to an old hat, giving her trained indication for the odor of human remains. Elisa is right there taking photos and exclaims, "That's probably the hat that belonged to the victim, and it may have come in contact with remains. I think your dog has made a good call!"

I decide to praise Keb who is still sitting by the hat with her nose pointed right at its peak. "Good girl, good girl! Let's go find another one." Since I do not know for sure she is correct—there is no visible proof—the magic ball will not come out at this time. Keb seems no worse for wear and knows that "find another one" means that the hunt will continue for more. We keep doing increasingly larger circles around the excavated site for the next hour or two, but nothing else is found. We're all tired, and we declare the assignment complete. I walk alongside Elisa as we leave. "Thank you so much for letting us help you out today. We don't take it for granted. We train hard and really appreciate the opportunity to use our dogs."

I'm hoping Elisa is pleased with what she has seen, and I feel reassured when she replies, "I really learned a lot about your dogs today and took a bunch of photos that I'll send to you." A smile lights up my face as she continues, "I look forward to working together in the future."

We head back to our cars and get ready to leave after a day of hard but rewarding work. Before taking off, I take the opportunity to remind Elisa that we have a joint workshop in a couple of weeks. "We'll be bringing all our HRD K9 teams to the medical examiner office. I think we'll have a dozen or so K9 teams attend, including Detective Jack Samuels with his K9 Justice, another HRD team working directly with him, as well as field support and our two new SAR sergeants." As she affirmatively nods her head, I continue "I know everybody is interested in the presentation your staff has been preparing."

In spite of a tiring day, I'm excited about this upcoming event. It really feels like a breakthrough in our relationship and the beginning of a joint venture that many K9 teams in other parts of the country would envy. We're talking about doing joint scenario-based trainings with forensic investigators, man trackers, ground searchers, and, of course, our HRD-trained K9s supporting medical examiner staff. We already have several bone identification classes lined up for next spring, one for general SAR personnel and another one specifically for K9 teams and man trackers. "So many exciting things ahead," I whisper to Keb as we are rolling down the freeway. Keb lounges comfortably on her backseat blankets, while I relish the thought of holding a glass of wine and lowering my aching body into our bubbling hot tub.

Mission Debrief

Guy

The very first time I set out HRD source (human remains) during a training session for Suzanne and Keb, I was trying to be helpful but didn't quite know what I was doing. She had asked me to set out three jars of source (yuck), spaced at about 100-yard intervals, just off of a forest road. As I drove carefully about one-half mile from our search training base, I nervously eyed the plastic carry box on the floor in front of the passenger seat and was thankful for my WeatherTech floormats. The carry box contained the jars of source: donated human anatomical tissue. Even though the box was pretty well sealed, I worried about, you know, *dead person molecules* that might be wafting in the air inside my car. I rolled down all the windows. I opened my sunroof.

After carefully following instructions to bury the three glass jars about six inches below loose soil, I called Suzanne on the radio and let her know we were all set to go. Within ten minutes she joined me, and I showed her where the test zone started. Keb's task was to walk the edge of the dirt road and locate the three HRD jars hidden not far off of the road in the adjacent woods. I followed along, not to give directions or hints, but to provide feedback when Suzanne thought Keb had located one of the HRD source jars. Keb started sniffing down the road, poking here and there, following her nose. I remember Suzanne commenting worriedly that Keb appeared to be having a hard time. After about thirty minutes, though, Keb had correctly located all of the hidden HRD jars and, at each, had given her trained response of sitting, and looking eagerly to Suzanne to see if her special ball would appear.

As I got ready to pick up the jars at the end of the training session, Suzanne turned to me and said, "Make sure that you put the upper lids back on the jars to double seal them before you put them back in the box."

I had paused before responding: "Umm, you mean I was supposed to take off the upper lids?"

Looking Back

Last week, as we were packing to leave what Guy is now calling "the salmon search," Eric walked over and offered all remaining HRD K9 teams an opportunity to expose our dogs to the shallow grave where the first body was found. What a fantastic training opportunity! The body was long gone, but there would still be large amounts of decomposition fluids ("decomp" in the jargon of forensic anthropologists) seeped into the soil below. Eric first led Guy into the woods, and after a short time we were called to bring our dogs into a small clearing where Guy was now pointing in a general direction. He had been told the specific location where the body had been; we were not.

This was going to be a real test for Keb, with our major crimes detectives watching our performance closely. I held my breath as Keb searched quickly before giving her trained indication by sitting in two places. Guy smiled and gave us a thumbs up. Good girl, Kebbie! While Guy and I debriefed, Keb was off to the side carefully inspecting a bush. "That bush is a K9 mailbox. I just saw two other search dogs pee on it," Guy volunteered. No doubt Keb was now trying to determine if one of her friends was the culprit, and if they perchance had left a message for her.

"Want a snack, Kebbie?" She immediately turned around looking quizzically at me. Did I hear a familiar word? "Snack." Did you say, "snack"? I fished out an old liver treat from my snack bag, which she grabbed out of my hand, ever the voracious dog. "Gentle, Keb, gentle."

We then stayed around to watch some of the younger dogs struggle to find the location of the ground "decomp" area. After the Fiasco of the Dead Fish, I was grateful we'd had opportunities to work "large source" and was feeling a little better now. The K9 search and rescue world is not for the faint of heart; the opportunities for humility are constant and unrelenting.

8
Search for the Hidden Grave
In Which Justice Is Served

"To accomplish the burial, the criminal will want to expend the least amount of physical effort balanced against the need to hide the body where he hopes it will not be found."

—EDWARD W. KILLAM, *THE DETECTION OF HUMAN REMAINS*

The evening news is on, but I'm listening with only one ear and half a brain as I try to fix Keb's dinner while she does tight laps around my feet. Then I hear the trigger words "Oso, Washington," and my attention is jerked to the TV screen. Two years ago, the violence of nature descended upon the quiet hamlet of Oso, Washington, in the form of a massive landslide. Forty-three lives were lost; the tiny community of Steelhead Haven was wiped from the face of the earth. Keb, Guy, and I deployed again and again over a monthlong period, searching for victims across bleak fields of mud and debris.

What I hear shocks me. In the outskirts of Oso, a young couple, Monique Patenaude and Patrick Shunn, are missing. Authorities now believe they've been murdered by their neighbor John Reed, an ex-felon who lived just down the road. I shake my head in disbelief. My God, hasn't that community been through enough?

The First Desperate Days

Early the next morning, I'm at home preparing for a client conference, when our SAR deputy, Charles Thayer, calls to ask if Keb and I are available for an evidence search. It's taken a long time to establish our credibility as an HRD team, and I take Charles's request as a hard-won affirmation. I feel the normal sense of anticipation. Will we find what we are looking for? Will we perform well under Charles's watchful eye? He provides an address on Whitman Road as a rendezvous point, but no other details. I know Guy is in Hawaii on vacation, so I call Dan from our K9 team to see if he can be my field support person for the mission. We agree to partner for the day.

When I enter the Whitman Road address into my car GPS, I'm struck by how close it is to the Oso Landslide where we searched just two years ago. As we drive north with Keb in the backseat, we can't help but speculate. "Dan, Charles didn't tell me over the phone, but I bet this is related to that double homicide we've heard about." Dan is a calm and steady type, but I see his blue eyes widen with interest. After a forty-five-minute drive north, we arrive to find Charles's white Jeep Wrangler parked on a shaded, quiet portion of Whitman Road. I notice that several members of our man-tracker team are also there.

Leaving Keb in my car, we walk over to get briefed by Charles. Our suspicions are confirmed: "You'll be looking for evidence related to a couple who have been murdered. That's their house, right across the street from us." My mind spins as Charles provides us with details. We hear that Monique and Patrick had planned to attend a concert on the evening of April 11, and when they did not arrive, their friends became concerned. The next morning, after finding Patrick and Monique's house empty, their cars missing, and their animals uncared for, the friends became alarmed and called Snohomish County 911. On Tuesday, April 12, sheriff's deputies began an initial missing persons investigation, interviewing friends and neighbors, and searching local logging roads for their vehicles.

On Thursday, observers in SnoHawk 1, our sheriff's two-seater Hughes 500-P helicopter, were conducting a visual search over the "Whitman Bench" area, miles of forested and logged terrain on the hillside above Whitman Road. They spotted two vehicles, part way down a ravine, concealed by brush. When deputies reached the vehicles, they confirmed that they were the Jeep and Land Rover owned by Patrick and Monique. The SUVs were unoccupied, but when the deputies looked inside, they saw blood. What started as a routine search for two missing persons exploded into a full-scale homicide investigation.

Major Crimes Unit detectives conducted forensic searching of the vehicles, while man-tracking experts from Snohomish County Search and Rescue combed the area. It became clear that the vehicles were not simply pushed over the edge. While the Jeep apparently rolled halfway down the ravine, the

Land Rover had hung up on small trees, and there was evidence that someone had made attempts to winch the SUV farther down. When this failed, cut branches were thrown on top of the vehicles. Not far from the ravine, the SAR man-tracking team located a camo tarp concealing boards, axes, and cables, and they quickly realized this was the gear used in attempts to move the SUV. Whoever did this invested a lot of time and energy attempting to conceal these vehicles. There is a growing concern that the criminals invested a similar effort to conceal the bodies of Patrick and Monique.

As Charles continues the briefing, Dan and I scan a large topographical map rolled across the hood of the jeep. We can see that Whitman Road runs from west to east, as it parallels two-lane Highway 530 for two miles and then ends 300 yards from where we're standing at the edge of the Oso Landslide. Immediately to our north, the densely wooded valley wall rises 900 feet to "Whitman Bench," a 1,400-acre forested plateau one mile wide by two miles across. Charles now points to the map. "You can see Reed's property here, it's right at the edge of the slide. The ravine where their cars were found is only a half mile up the hill from Reed's house."

Major crimes detectives Bernard Simms and Ambrose Barry now join our briefing huddle and provide us with additional background. We hear that our detectives learned of a long-standing property dispute between Reed and the missing couple, and that Patrick and Monique lived in fear of him. Simms stops and points down the road. "We also found bloody clothes and shell casings on John Reed's property, just down that dirt lane to the east of us. Based on accumulating evidence and interviews with Patrick and Monique's neighbors, John Reed quickly became our prime suspect. But there's more. Based on cell phone records, we believe Reed's brother Tony was also involved."

It's unusual for our law enforcement partners to share so much detail with us. Dan and I exchange a glance, feeling we're in the middle of a *CSI* episode. Simms continues with even more detail: "We also learned that shortly after Patrick and Monique disappeared, the Reed brothers drove ninety miles over the pass to Ellensburg, Washington, where they met with their parents and arranged to switch cars. They then drove to Phoenix, Arizona, where they switched cars again. A car license reader in Calexico, California, detected their plates and revealed they crossed over the border into Mexico. We've issued an international search warrant, and federal authorities in Mexico have joined the manhunt."

After the briefing ends, Charles leads a small convoy up and over ten miles of winding dirt logging road to reach the far eastern side of the Whitman Bench. The road twists and turns, then narrows down to a grassy two-track, barely wide enough for my Toyota 4Runner to squeeze through. We park near a large open field, surrounded by tall firs and cedars. Charles directs us to search the field and surrounding woods. Looking around, I see tall grass dotted with logged stumps and a drainage running close by. Temperatures are in the mid-eighties and I can already feel sweat running down my back.

I give Keb her "search for dead" command, and right away she's showing a distinct and recognizable change in behavior in the area closest to the ravine where the cars were found. I mention this to Charles, who is standing nearby, "It looks like Keb is detecting HRD odor in this general area."

Charles nods, "Yes, blood evidence was found in the vehicles. I want to see if Keb can locate anything more." This validates Keb's altered behavior, but holy smokes, this will be a first for Keb and me for sure. Will we be able to rise to the occasion? After an hour, we don't find anything of interest in the field and so expand our searching to the nearby woods. It's so hot that we have to intersperse searching with frequent breaks, but it's hard to find places to cool off. Keb's energy is dwindling quickly. Her head is slumping, her tongue is hanging out, and she is panting hard. OK, girlie, I bet you have run out of nosetime, eh? "Hey, Dan, I think we're burning Keb out. How about if we stop for now?" He nods in agreement. Soon we're back at my car, where we brief Charles on our negative results and take a belated lunch break.

It's early afternoon when we start the drive back toward our command van, parked in a wide spot on the dirt logging road. Along the way back uphill, we come upon two of our mountain bike team members, and we stop to chat. They've covered a lot of miles, but like us, have found no clues. I've let Keb out of the car for some just-be-a-dog time and notice out of the corner of my eye that she's bounding across the adjacent clear-cut with renewed energy. Good, she has cooled off. Or is she interested in something? Did I just see her nose rise into the air? I can see Dan waiting impatiently for us, so I call Keb back and offer her water from my bottle. She gulps down all that's left, and soon the three of us are continuing up the hillside in the comfort of my air-conditioned rig. Keb lounges contentedly in the backseat, lolling in the breeze of a small fan installed specially for her benefit. We are truly "done" for the day.

Our sheriff's department is far from done and continues a determined effort to find Patrick and Monique. That evening, Charles pages out a request for all available SAR ground teams, man trackers, and K9 teams for more searching on the next Saturday. Within our K9 team, emails start flying: "What handlers are available? Who can be field support?" I'm happy to see that Guy and June will be returning from Hawaii on Friday night. Guy tells me he's been commandeered by Charles to be OPS chief, so June will be my field support.

By 8 a.m. Saturday, a string of SAR vehicles and command trucks line Whitman Road, which will be our focus area for today's search. Man trackers and detectives will be canvassing Reed's properties and buildings. Ground teams will be searching fields and swamps in the area, while our Swiftwater team will be searching the banks of the nearby Stillaguamish River. Guy has assigned Keb, June, and I to search the hillside that runs behind Patrick and

Keb perches quizzically after popping out of the hidden bunker. "What's the fuss?"

Monique's house all the way east to the Reed property. It's steep and forested with thick underbrush. "Hey, June," I tease as we ready our backpacks, "did you bring any garden clippers; they could come in handy today!" We both hate traversing hillsides and suspect that the terrain we have to tackle will be thick with undergrowth and thorny devil's club. Even Keb disapproves of spiny devil's club, making little snorting sounds, sometimes looking back at me with a shriveled-up nose. You want me to go through this stuff? Really?

An hour into our search, June and I see a small grove of cedar trees running across the hillside. We know that the brush will be lighter under their shaded canopy, so we begin thrashing our way toward them. We cross a small drainage and my boot sinks into ankle-deep water. At last, we enter the open area. Keb has arrived ahead of us, and we see her sniffing at a strange-looking pile of black plastic bags. They're filled with something, but we're almost afraid to find out what. June gingerly pokes one of the bags with her hiking pole, and we're relieved to see that only dirt spills out. Keb shows no interest.

Around us, we now see more bags, braced here and there with timbers. Hairs rise on our necks, as we realize that we are standing on top of one of John Reed's bunkers. We've heard from our detectives that he has built several of them in the forested areas behind his house. We're curious about what they may have been used for. "Do you think it might have something to do with drugs?" We never really find out, but we've heard rumors that Reed bragged about being able to murder someone and hide victims somewhere in the mountains never to be found.

Abruptly, I notice that Keb has disappeared. We see a small ladder that leads down an opening to a tunnel. She's gone inside! I lean in to the hole and call her urgently, "Keb, come here, *now!*" I hear her moving below, now on my left, now behind me. I whistle to get her out of harm's way. "June, I don't like this at all; maybe she can't find her way back out and is stuck in some kind of maze?" The next sixty seconds stretch into an eternity. Fear rises in my throat as I contemplate descending into this evil hole to look for her. Then, like a rabbit out of a hat, Keb pops out at the tunnel opening, snorting a bit of dirt from her nose and looking up nonchalantly, as if to say, "What's the fuss?" June and I look at each other in a huge wave of relief. I roll my eyes and smile. Yeah, we narrowly avoided a catastrophe there. Let's go find something a bit less exciting to do.

We pause to collect ourselves and slow our heart rates. We expect that the detectives have already been up here, but Keb's opinion will provide useful information. "Team Keb to Command. We don't see a safe way for us to explore inside the underground bunker, but we want to report that Keb has not shown any behavior suggesting she smells human remains."

Keb has always been a confident dog, with a strong streak of independence. When looking for live subjects, Kebbie will follow up on human trails for long distances, which is exactly what I need her to do. When she was young, her propensity to range widely concerned me a great deal when she worked off-leash in urban areas, where traffic and other hazards can be a life and death issue for a dog. Now, at the age of six, she has matured, and with the help of a return-to-me-right-now whistle (a high piercing sound that can be heard far away), I feel she is under control. My handheld GPS is also connected to the transmitter Keb wears around her neck, so at any time, we can see her exact location on the map screen.

"Don't Move!" I quickly grab Keb's collar on the brink of the Oso Slide.

June and I leave the bunker behind us and keep moving uphill, with Keb ranging ahead of us. June is looking at her GPS map screen, and I see concern come over her face. "Suzanne, it looks like Keb is right next to a drop-off!" We round a corner and see Keb sitting on a rock ledge looking down. As I approach, I try to call her to me using a calm voice, but in my mind, I am shouting, *Don't move!* I reach her and grab her collar. As I lift my gaze, my jaw drops. Not only are we standing on top of a 200-foot cliff, but below us and as far as we can see, lies the Oso Slide. Memories of the weeks Kebbie and I searched through mud and debris flood over me. I see again the face of the dead woman that Keb found. We are silent and immersed in our own reflections as we start on the long trek back to base.

The Best Laid Plans

It's been two weeks now, and pressure is building on major crimes detectives, SAR deputies, and SAR volunteers to find the bodies of Patrick and Monique. John and Tony Reed are still missing and presumed to be hiding in Mexico. Our SAR deputies—Charles, Jack, and Stan—have been devoting most of their work hours and many of their days off searching logging areas up on the Whitman Bench. Guy has convinced Charles to try a different approach.

Gathered in the upstairs meeting room at our SAR headquarters are detectives from Snohomish County Major Crimes Unit, all five of our SAR deputies, and a few of our most senior SAR volunteers. There's a buzz of conversation in the room as I sit with the rest of the group on uncomfortable folding chairs and wait for Guy to connect his laptop to the sometimes-flaky overhead projector. He's hiding it pretty well, but I can tell how nervous he is.

Charles calls the group to order and then introduces Guy as one of our lead SAR planners, perhaps a hopeful stretch of reality at the time. "What I'm proposing," Guy begins as he scans the room, "is to apply lost person search planning techniques to find the clandestine gravesite. First, we're gonna list the 'What Happened' scenarios, and then we'll note the evidence for or against each scenario. After that, we'll use a formal consensus method to rank order our scenarios. This is a method used by SAR planners to combine every-body's perspective and opinion in a fair way." Looking around, I see several eyes are following with interest, more show skepticism.

Standing in front of the projector screen, Guy begins by showing a mapped representation of likely scenarios for what the suspects did with the bodies of Patrick and Monique:

> *Scenario A: Concealed near the victims' house.*
> *Scenario B: Concealed in woods surrounding the suspect's property.*
> *Scenario C: Concealed in forested areas up on the Whitman Bench.*
> *Scenario D: Thrown into the river.*
> *Scenario E: Concealed off forest roads on the south side of Highway 530.*
> *Scenario F: Driven out of the area entirely.*

With a bit of difficulty controlling side discussions, Guy leads the assem-bled group through the formal consensus process, which yields a probability score for each of the scenarios. We're all mindful of John Reed's boast that he could hide bodies where they never would be found. Our detectives remind us that residential security cameras showed Reed's pickup truck driving up the road that led to the ravine where the victim's vehicles were concealed. Not surprisingly, the Concealed in Forested Areas up on Whitman Bench Scenario has far and away the highest probability score. We have an organiz-ing consensus now, but still face a formidable challenge to turn this into an operational search plan: how do we prioritize searching over 1,400 acres of forested logging slopes?

Two days later, the same group meets back upstairs at our county SAR base. In preparation, planning wizards Arthur and Guy have used mapping programs and aerial images to locate six main dirt roads and over twenty spur roads up on Whitman Bench—we'll want to search every one of these. Using terrain analysis, they've also identified where each road passes above steep slopes or cross drainages—likely sites for a quick disposal of bodies. As the meeting closes, we have a list of thirty mapped search assignments, and I notice Charles sitting at the back of the room, looking pleased. We now have a ranked list of assignments for ground searchers, K9 teams, and the Swiftwater team. We have a plan, and we're going back.

Late in the afternoon of Saturday, April 30, we watch the sun descending through overcast skies in the west. The search for Patrick and Monique is now in its nineteenth day, and Charles, Guy, and Arthur have been implementing their new plan. The Swiftwater team has been systematically checking drainages on the downhill side of the main access road, while I and other HRD K9 teams are on standby should any clues be found. Guy, Deputy Jack Samuels, and I are standing on a small concrete bridge that crosses over what we've begun to call the "Big Drainage." Below us, our Swiftwater fanatics have downclimbed a steep watercourse and are poking and prodding in every slimy nook and moss-covered cranny. Arthur has noticed a faint trail and some fresh cuts in small brush at the top of this drainage. This is not natural, and Arthur considers this highly suspicious, so they're pulling out all stops.

As Keb wanders nearby, I watch Jack and Guy search the flat streambed ten feet downstream from the bridge. Jack stops short, then bends down. "I see some keys!" Guy hurries over to see Jack hunched over a tiny crevice between rocks in the stream. There, in two inches of water, lies a small key ring. Jack reaches down and, using his pen, carefully picks up the key ring to examine it. Pulling out his cell phone, he snaps a picture and sends it to our detectives. The "we found some keys" information is also radioed downstream to Arthur's Swiftwater team. Totally jazzed now, they redouble their efforts.

"We found some keys!" Guy above the streambed.

Jack and Guy continue a more determined microsearch of the flat streambed below the bridge. Amazingly, Jack makes another important find. Perched on top of a five-foot, moss-covered stump is a pair of glasses. They look relatively fresh and clean, but once again, we just can't imagine how they got perched there. Jack sends a picture via cell phone to our detectives; they continue their search but find nothing more.

Guy starts clambering back up to join me on the road and is spotted by Keb, who enthusiastically crashes down the slope to meet him halfway. Using a grip on Keb's collar for balance, he rejoins me looking a bit chagrined. "Damn. I walked right over those keys three times, it's a good thing Jack's got sharp eyes." Soon Jack joins us, kneeling briefly to rub Keb's ears, as his own dog, Justice, barks jealously from inside Jack's jeep.

We're excited, but at the same time a bit skeptical. We look back and forth between the bridge and the location of the keys. We look back and forth again. In a direct line between the keys and the bridge there is a ten-foot-high boulder. "Jack," Guy volunteers, "if the keys were tossed from a car window, they would've needed to fly in the air straight for about fifteen feet, then execute a 120-degree turn to drop into that location." Our eyes meet: it's hard to imagine that flight path. A darker suspicion comes to mind. If the victims' bodies were dragged downstream to a hiding place below in the drainage, keys could have dropped out unnoticed.

As the day winds down, the weary Swiftwater team climbs back up to us with nothing to report but a few tantalizing scrape marks. We're chatting with them as they peel off dirty dry suits, when Jack gets a call from the detectives who've shown the picture of the glasses to a friend of the victims. The friends say they definitely belong to Monique. The three of us look at each other, still skeptical. We know people will see what they want to see, and we've experienced such false alarms in the past.

The Big Drainage

After being on the Whitman Bench search all day, I arrive home with clothes full of dirt and a stomach full of hunger. Eat first, laundry second. It'll be nice to have tomorrow to rest. At 6 p.m. I'm finishing the crumbs of my gourmet dinner of Ritz crackers and cheese while relaxing in front of the TV. Keb is helping clean up stray crumbs when Guy calls, "Suzanne, I just got off the phone with Charles! The keys that Jack found fit locks on Monique and Patrick's property!" Guy continues enthusiastically, I can just see him waving his hands in the air. "With this hot lead, we're going to mobilize again for tomorrow with a search of the Big Drainage, using our Swiftwater rescue team, ground search teams, sheriff's office dive team, and HRD K9 teams."

The next day, Keb and I arrive before 7 a.m. to find our command van set up just west of the concrete bridge at the top of the Big Drainage. As

OPS chief, Guy has already posted plans and maps on the side of the command van and is working with Rob to start handing out team assignments. Arthur and his Swiftwater fanatics suit up and start descending the drainage, downclimbing in places, rappelling in others. Mid-morning the Snohomish County Sheriff's Office dive team arrives. They pull on their bright blue-and-yellow dry suits, grab shovels and digging gear, and head down to join Arthur's team.

Guy will be OPS chief today, so teammate Rolf will be my field support. Our assignment this morning is to search in the Big Drainage, starting down near the bottom and working our way upstream. We load up in my rig, consult the map, and locate an area about half a mile away from search base where we can descend into the lower regions of the drainage. We spend the next several hours in an epic struggle to search the lower parts of the ravine, first sliding down steep slopes on our butts, then scrambling across loose slippery rocks, then hauling ourselves back up grasping roots and shrubs. Keb easily traverses the slopes using her four-wheel drive, but several times I'm forced to swallow my pride and ask Rolf to haul me up.

Just before midday Rolf, Keb, and I return to base, and by now I look and feel like a wild woman. Twigs are sticking out of my hair, I have mud smudged all over my face, and the sweat is running down my back. And then—holy cow! There's the food truck! Our food truck and the volunteers staffing it under the able direction of Debra Draper are the envy of SAR teams from other counties. Today, Debra's team have outdone themselves, laying out fresh turkey and cheese sandwiches, breakfast muffins, a home-made berry cobbler, and trays of fruit and vegetables. I devour the treats served, glancing around me and hoping no one sees how many of one kind of delicacy I am stuffing my face with. I subversively tuck a turkey and cheese sandwich under my shirt, and head back to my furry four-legged partner with a little surprise for a job well done. Her ears perk up and nostrils flare as she smells these morsels and eagerly chomps sandwich, napkin, and all. "Good girlie, Keb." The sandwich disappears in two gulps.

I run into Deputy Charles, and he comments on my morning assignment. "It looks like the terrain you and Keb traveled this morning was quite something, eh?" He smiles and says, "Sometimes I forget that you're a member of mountain rescue and have special skills." Charles is himself a member of our mountain rescue unit. It warms my heart. In this world the compliments are few and far between.

Guy then approaches us from behind the command van. "Suzanne, I know you guys have been searching hard all morning, but do you think you, Keb, and Rolf could do another assignment? We need an HRD K9 team down where the Swiftwater team has been working all day. About 300 yards below the bridge, they've actually rerouted the stream to direct water off of a shallow pool. They now suspect something might be buried in the sandy bottom."

In a moment of insanity, I say, "Yes." In reality, Keb and I are beyond being burned out for the day. Saying no and knowing your limitations are probably the most important skills anybody can bring to search and rescue. Today, my ego and need to demonstrate stamina are getting the better of me. Guy walks me over to the large map on the side of the command van and convinces me the location is not far away. Hah! As it turns out, we end up having to clamber down yet another steep hillside. When we emerge from the undergrowth of the hillside to the area where the water hole is, I find about half a dozen Swiftwater and dive rescue folks looking up at us expectantly. The pressure is on.

After a brief consultation with Arthur (who clearly is enthusiastic about this hole in the stream), I give Keb her "search for dead" command and we start working the area. She's not very focused, repeatedly looking back at me for direction. She briefly checks out a bloated dead rat lying at the edge of the stream—yuck. "Kebbie, leave it!" Above us there are now half a dozen people standing on the rocks staring intensely at Keb and the water hole. So, the predictable happens: you have a burned-out dog, you have a horde of people cueing her by staring at the hole, and a handler that sends her down in the same place over and over again. To my horror she starts "throwing a sit": her trained indication for human remains.

Damn. Sorry, I don't really buy it, Keb. I try to explain to the Swiftwater peeps what I think is happening, but I can tell that some of them are still excited, now reinforced by seeing Keb alerting on the hole. What was I thinking? In hindsight, I should have declined the assignment. Having accepted, I should have sent Keb down the hole only once and trusted her negative response the first time. Lastly, I should have asked the people to not stand around in a ring on the boulders above staring and cueing. Lots of "should haves" there. Bottomline: handler error. It's OK, Kebbie; I'm the one who needs to be forgiven.

After another desperate uphill thrash, resulting in more dirty leaves in my hair and more dirt on my butt, Keb and I drag ourselves back into search base. Keb is soaked; her ears are drooping and speckled with mud. I brief Charles and share what just happened, carefully cautioning him that what I saw was a burned-out dog getting cued to give a false response. "I'm concerned that the Swiftwater peeps will read too much into what they saw. I would hate to see more resources thrown that way." Charles nods. He's a former K9 handler and understands. It happens. No dog is 100 percent. If anybody tells you differently, they are *full av skit*.

At day's end, despite the tantalizing find of the keys and glasses, nothing else is found in the drainage or the pool below. Arthur and his team are disappointed after having worked so hard, but critical search objectives have been accomplished, and we have substantially reduced the probability that the bodies are in the Big Drainage.

Big Dog Day

Guy and I are plotting in secret. After weeks of searching, Patrick and Monique have not been found. Our SAR deputies remain determined to find the concealed bodies. Yet even after the Big Drainage search, we still have much of the Whitman Bench area to be searched. "Suzanne, what if we could put a large number of HRD K9 teams into the area, covering miles of roads and spurs up on the Whitman Bench all in one effort?"

Guy has sparked my interest, and this is a recruiting task I can take on. Following the Oso Landslide, the K9 community in Washington State has come together in a very collaborative way. We all try to visit and train with each other intermittently, and many of us stay connected in private groups on Facebook. The Facebook group I started many years ago, K9 Search and Rescue Community, has over 4,000 SAR K9 handlers from throughout the world engaged in daily discussions.

Guy has been entrusted to lead more and more large searches in recent years, so we agree he will present our idea to Charles. Yes! He gets the green light, and we select Sunday, May 15, for what we are now privately calling "Big Dog Day." I start connecting with people using e-mail, phone, texting, and Facebook messaging, and in only a few days, we have over twenty of some of our finest HRD K9 handlers from throughout Washington State committed to help.

We do extensive preplanning of assignments. We want dog teams to traverse every road and spur in the area, in the hope that they will pick up some scent. We will also add as many ground teams as we can recruit to cover high-probability areas in the margins along the road system. And it's no surprise when we hear that Arthur wants to take his Swiftwater team back down into the Big Drainage.

Keb and I arrive early Sunday morning and immediately see a bunch of familiar faces. There is Sally Olsen from Kitsap with her chocolate Lab, Skye.

I recognize her at a distance by her bob and reddish-brown hair. I see Cathy Best, a handler with an easy and engaging smile, here from eastern Washington with her black shepherd, Izzy. Nearby is Ethan Denver from Kittitas County, with his distinctive gait and his black Lab, Jet, and the list goes on. Guy and I inventory our K9 responders and confer briefly. My first task today will be to help him match K9 team capabilities to specific assignments.

As the large crowd of searchers gathers, I see Guy by the command truck and for a moment our eyes and smiles meet. We have preplanned assignments ready for every K9 and ground team. Carter has set up a GPS map system that will show us the location of every team in real time. Guy has printed detailed search maps before leaving home. This is a first for Snohomish County, perhaps the largest preplanned K9 deployment of its kind in state history. As the point person for the K9 effort, I have a lot of handlers approaching me with questions and giving me an occasional hug. Soon we have all twenty HRD K9 teams and over 100 search personnel out on search assignments across the two square miles of Whitman Bench.

By 1 p.m. teams have finished their initial assignments and are back at base. As is usual on a large-scale search, K9 teams have occasionally reported "interest" by their dogs. Ground teams have found bits of trash and old clothing, but none of these clues have panned out. Not far from the command truck, our food truck volunteers have set out a spread of fresh sandwich wraps, fruit, cookies, chips, and drinks, and the teams gratefully stop for refueling and a short rest. As volunteers and dogs are rested and fed, I begin working with Guy to give the teams new assignments and send them out into the field again. We're standing close to the back of our command van, when suddenly we overhear radio traffic that shocks us:

"Team 6 to Command! (the team lead sounds breathless).

"Go ahead Team 6" (the radio operator sounds bored).

"Team 6 to Command, John has a long mustache!"

Guy leaps up into the command van as the stunned radio operator just looks at him. This is our secret radio code phrase for "*We found a body!*"

"Tell them to repeat their message!"

Leaning in at the command van door, Deputy Stan McKay is standing close by me now; our eyes meet in tense anticipation.

"Team 6 to Command, John has a long mustache!"

We can hardly believe it. After all these weeks of searching, we've found Patrick and Monique. Guy grabs the mic from the radio operator and asks Team 6 to radio location coordinates: Team 6 is about two miles down the twisty dirt road from us, very close to where the victims' vehicles were found. Detective Jack Samuels sprints over to his jeep, jumps in, and speeds off down the dirt road with K9 Justice barking loudly from the backseat. Stan uses his cell phone to call our major crimes detectives, tells them of the find, and arranges to meet them here at the command post and escort them down to the site. They in turn put in a call to the medical examiner's office to start their staff on the way, but it will take them at least forty-five minutes to get to us.

Guy, Stan, and I can barely contain our emotions. We're flooded with a sense of relief and accomplishment. The search personnel near our command van become aware that *something big* has happened, but we don't announce the news yet. I watch Stan and Guy anxiously pace back and forth for five more minutes, then I hear Stan turn to him. "Screw it, I'm not waiting; let's go down there!" Guy cautions me to keep the news quiet, then he eagerly hops into Stan's truck. I can see them high-fiving as they disappear down the rough logging road in a swirl of dust.

Ten minutes later Guy calls my cell phone, and I've never heard his voice sound so strange. "Suzanne, it's not it."

There's a long, long pause, and I can hear swearing in the background: "Who's on that team anyway? And what the hell were they thinking?"

Cell reception is bad, but I can hear Guy continuing, "Jack just arrived down at the scene and radioed us. It's a good clue, but it's not them. Damn, damn, damn. What they found was a bloody jacket, stuffed under brush and logs. From a distance it looked like a body, and the team decided not to approach any closer so as not to contaminate the scene. Suzanne, I need you to work with Rob to reallocate four additional HRD K9 teams, man trackers, and two ground teams, and start them down to our location. Then I want you and Keb down here as well. This clue is now our new ground zero!"

After relaying the message to Rob, I drive my rig to the newly assigned search area and realize with a shock this is near where Keb and I searched on our very first day! Later at home, I review my GPS tracks to see that Keb and I had passed about 150 feet away from where the jacket was located. This triggers waves of "what if" mind games: What if it had not been so hot? What if the wind had been drifting in the other direction? What if I had pushed Keb into that area? What if we had looked more carefully and discovered signs that someone had disturbed the vegetation?

For this assignment, I'm teamed with Sally and K9 Skye from Kitsap County Search Dogs. We decide to deploy from a road south of where the jacket was found and do a fairly tight grid search pattern, while keeping our K9s searching different terrain along the way. There's fresh adrenaline in the air now that everybody is aware an important clue has been found. But we return to our starting point hours later, tired and disheveled. It was another bushwhack from hell, and despite intensive searching, all teams have returned empty-handed. "Well, we gave it our best, and I'm beat now," Sally mumbles as she loads Skye into her truck for her long drive home. Totally fatigued, we give each other hugs and Sally gets on the road. "Drive safe. Don't fall asleep on the road."

As daylight fades, Guy calls teams back to search base to bring an end to Big Dog Day. We completed many of our priority assignments. We had over

100 searchers in the field with no injuries or mishaps. It was a well-organized effort. We didn't find Patrick and Monique (despite the heart-stopping false alarm), but the jacket found later turns out to be a critical piece of the evidence puzzle. Thank you, Team 6! You're forgiven.

Late that afternoon as we're heading home, I have mixed feelings: excitement that a major clue has been found, disappointment that we have not found our subjects, and satisfaction with how well our Big Dog Day search effort went. Over the years I've been instrumental in building our own K9 team and developing an informal regional K9 network, which today yielded a large turnout and served my county well.

The Grave Revealed

On Monday, May 16, John Reed's brother Tony turns himself in to authorities and is quickly transported back to Snohomish County to be interviewed by detectives. He explains that he was not present for the murders but confesses to helping his brother conceal the bodies of Patrick and Monique. It's something anyone would do for their family, right? On Tuesday, May 24, Tony Reed leads detectives to a clear-cut area up on the Whitman Bench. He leads them 160 feet from the road where the shallow grave is concealed under trees and branches. The gravesite is just 50 feet *outside* one of the search areas planned but not yet searched.

Would we have eventually found it? Guy thinks maybe, others disagree. On Thursday, May 26, Snohomish County Sheriff's public information officer, Angela Nichols, has arranged for Guy and me, along with our lead man tracker, to be interviewed by local TV news station KING. She wants to make sure our efforts are recognized by the community. By contrast, one national crime news commentator goes on the air to criticize our county's efforts during the search. She incorrectly claims that the grave was found close by the vehicles (it was actually well over a mile away) and bemoans the incompetence of the local hicks running the search.

When I hear that Patrick and Monique's bodies are found, it's hard not to think about what happened to them. For weeks Guy and I have been physically and mentally immersed in the search, but now that it's over, I feel at loose ends. Then, on Friday, May 27, the phone rings and it's Guy. "Charles just called! He and deputies Stan McKay and Jack Samuels are going out to the clandestine gravesite, and he's invited us to come along and bring Keb!" This may be exactly what I need to get some personal resolution. The next morning, we all meet at the rustic Oso Cafe for coffee and hot breakfast sandwiches. The atmosphere is easygoing, though somewhat subdued. We've all worked hard on this mission together. And while finding the grave has brought a level of closure, justice has yet to be served. Murderer John Reed is still on the loose.

Three sheriff's jeeps and our two cars slowly convoy up the logging road that we've all been up and down so many times in the last weeks. I'm curious about the grave location, and my looming fear is that the grave was in an area that Kebbie and I had searched. Guy has been maintaining the master search map, which now shows GPS tracks from every search team, like ant trails across the terrain. He assures me the grave is not in an area previously assigned to any K9 teams, which is a relief. I also want to see what the gravesite looks like. Hidden graves are typically shallow, with bodies less than eighteen inches below soil, and branches, leaves, debris, and whatever else is available tossed on top.

As our convoy comes to a halt, I look around, and realize this is the clear-cut where *on the very first day of searching* we had paused to chat with a couple of our bike team members. What if we'd searched into that clear-cut? What if we'd not been burned out and done for the day? We silently walk out to the gravesite and just stand quietly for a while. I know the bodies of Patrick and

Monique were recovered days ago by the medical examiner, but I can't shake the feeling: this is where evil took place.

After everybody has returned to the cars, with permission from Charles, I take Keb out of my rig and put her on her "search for dead" command. As she approaches the area where the soil is disturbed, her posture changes and she hunkers down near the hole, turns around, sits in her formal indication, and gives me her "look." I know had we sent Keb out here, she would have found the grave for us.

Aftermath

Time passes; other large-scale missions absorb us; we return to our routine of weekly K9 training. Gradually, our memories of the Oso Double Homicide Search begin to fade into the background. Then in July 2016, John Reed is captured by Mexican authorities and turned over to U.S. Marshals. In April 2017, his brother Tony Reed is sentenced to fourteen months in prison for helping to hide the bodies of Patrick and Monique. Reed's parents are convicted of withholding evidence and obstructing justice.

In early May 2018, John Reed's trial begins in Snohomish County Superior Court. Our deputy, Charles Thayer, recently retired after thirty-five years of service, has made it a personal commitment to attend all the proceedings. He feels it's part of his duty to the ever-present families of Patrick and Monique. Guy has worked with the prosecuting attorneys to provide evidence maps and is able to attend a few of the trial days. He provides a report back to me every evening. Each of the pieces of evidence our searchers found is introduced by our detectives and explained in context, along with photographs showing its setting, how it was handled, and its appearance in close-up. "Suzanne, I could see that even the smallest bits of evidence that our SAR teams and deputies uncovered were woven into the prosecution's strong case."

During the trial, we learn that Monique confronted Reed for trespassing across their property at the end of Whitman Road. Reed shot her, then waited until Patrick returned home later that afternoon. Reed then ambushed and shot Patrick in cold blood. After eighteen days of trial and just four hours of jury deliberation, on May 30, 2018, John Reed is found guilty of aggravated first-degree murder for the death of Patrick Shunn. He is found guilty of second-degree murder for the killing of Monique Patenaude.

Mission Debrief

Guy

Two weeks after the grave was found, Charles and I organized a formal debrief session for all our SAR volunteers. We felt it was important that they be recognized for their efforts, and we wanted to give them a unified picture of how their efforts contributed to finding a large number of important clues. The meeting room was packed, and the debriefing went well. Detectives Simms and Barry attended and thanked SAR volunteers profusely for their enormous effort during the extended mission.

The meeting ended, and I packed up my papers and laptop. As I walked by Charles's office near the exit door, he called me in with a serious voice. Minutes ago, the wife of one of our SAR volunteers had confided to Charles that her husband still felt badly about not finding the grave. Early in the search, his team had noted and verbally reported disturbed brush on the side of the road and suggested that it should be looked into. This disturbed brush was on a direct path into the clear-cut where the grave was later located.

As I entered Charles's office, he was struggling to contain a level of anger and frustration that I'd never seen in him before. Silently, I was thanking my stars that this happened early in the mission, while I was still in Hawaii. Rob, who was OPS chief for that day, walked by and Charles called him in. "Did you know about this report?" After some very uncomfortable conversation, we parsed out what happened. Yes, a search team had found this important potential clue. They reported it to a busy, distracted Rob during a verbal debrief, but did not clearly describe or request follow up in their written debrief. The written debrief was never formally reviewed after that operational period. That wasn't Rob's fault—it just wasn't our standard practice at the time. We lost a critical opportunity for finding the graves early in the mission. Damn. Damn. Damn.

Looking Back

Suzanne

In early 2017, Guy was formally recognized by the Snohomish County Sheriff's Office for his leadership in OPS and PLANS chief roles during the Oso Double Homicide Search. In recent years our SAR deputy, Charles Thayer, had grown to rely on him more and more to plan and organize search efforts, and I suspect that Charles had a hand in arranging this award. For my part, I was content with the personal satisfaction that my efforts had enabled one of the largest assemblies of K9 resources in regional history. Then one morning, at the annual Washington State SAR conference, I was shocked to hear my name called out for a SAR Leadership Award. Totally flustered, I walked back from the podium to see my team members applauding me, and in that moment, I felt immense pride that I had made a difference for my team and for my community.

9
Mystery of the Sol Duc River

In Which the Wizards Are Deceived

"When the boys back at the camp,
the sad news came to hear.
To search for our lost comrade,
downriver we did steer."

—TRADITIONAL BALLAD

You may not know it, but you've probably got one in your community: an informal grapevine of SAR volunteers, sharing news of developing search incidents, even before notifications come through official channels. "Have you heard about this search? Are they going to need search dogs? Do you think we'll be called out?" This morning, my grapevine is on fire with phone calls, Facebook posts, and text messages about a search in Olympic National Park, in the far northwest corner of Washington State. On a rainy April morning of 2017, park rangers were confronted with a mystery when they found a bicycle, along with camping gear, abandoned on a narrow park road that winds its way along the wild Sol Duc River.

The very next day, Clallam County sheriffs made a connection via a missing person report. The gear belonged to Jacob Gray, a twenty-two-year-old man originally from Santa Cruz, California. Because Jacob's bicycle had been found on the east side of the Sol Duc River inside the national park, initial hasty searching was conducted by park rangers. Following standard procedures, they searched roads, trails, and campgrounds on April 6 and 7, looking for any sign of Jacob. When nothing was found, they expanded their efforts by calling for assistance from Olympic Mountain Rescue (OMR). What began as a routine investigation soon blossomed into a search that would continue for many months and involve one of the largest searches in state history.

The Initial Search: April

OMR volunteers arrived the next day, and like the park rangers, they were puzzled by what they found at the Last Known Point, where Jacob's bicycle and gear were abandoned. Here, there was no campground, no obvious pullout, and no easy access to the river. Why would Jacob stop here? Why would he leave his gear here? It didn't make sense. OMR man trackers made their way carefully through brush down to the river's edge, and here they found something that caught their attention: scrape marks on a large moss-covered rock at the very edge of the river. To the trackers, it looked like someone sat on top of the rock and then slid down toward the river.

This was an ominous clue. The river was running high, fast, and cold, with currents that could easily sweep a person downstream. Close by, the trackers saw a huge moss-covered log that spanned the river. Jacob might have attempted to cross here, but the OMR trackers quickly decided they would not risk it. Unable to cross the river safely, they drove the six miles around to reach the opposite side, where they scrambled down steep slopes to find more suspicious scrape marks directly across from the same log. Did Jacob slip while attempting to cross that log? Was he swept down the river? Did he pull himself out of the water to make those marks on the opposite side? The searchers had no way of knowing.

Callout

As my grapevine continues to hum, I check out the search location with my mapping program. The Sol Duc Hot Springs Road winds for twelve serpentine miles along the dark river, from Highway 101 in the north to Sol Duc Hot Springs at its southern end. On the east side of the river is national park land, the home of old-growth forest, owls, bears, and ancient spirits. The west side is national forest land, the home of clear-cuts, forest roads, and gun-toting yahoos doing illegal target shooting. Because Jacob might be on either side of the river, Olympic National Park and the Clallam County Sheriff's Office are sharing jurisdiction for the incident.

By now, Jacob's family members have flown in from California. While the river is still unsafe to search, family and friends search the steep forest on the west side of the river, but no trace of Jacob is found. The family is now convinced that Jacob managed to cross the river and may be lost or injured in national forest lands on the west side. They put pressure on both the national park and the Clallam County sheriff to bring in search dogs, but none are available from that county.

The morning of April 13 is a typical Wednesday, starting with my 7 a.m. cardio weight training, an exercise routine I've religiously done three mornings a week for the last ten years. As I arrive, my trainer Jeff grins, and with a glint in his eye, announces, "Today we have a lot of lumber to chop." Later that morning, still aching from the lumberjack workout, and following a short hike with my two K9 partners (Bosse, the elder, and Keb, the younger), I'm physically tired as I sit at my desk in my home office. In addition to my executive coaching practice, where I work individually with senior leaders on emotional intelligence and leadership, I've run several executive roundtables for the last twenty years. Today's consulting challenge is to design a session on "Culture: More Than a Buzzword" for the thirty human resources leaders in my roundtable.

In the seventeen years I have helped build our K9 SAR team, one of my personal priorities has been defining and nurturing a strong and healthy culture. When asked what my role on our K9 team is, I often answer that I'm the "guardian of our culture." Suddenly my cell phone rings, interrupting my thoughts. I see this call is coming from an "unknown source," which means it's either an annoying robocall or our SAR sergeant, Charles Thayer, whose cell phone number is always masked. I decide to answer, and sure enough, it's Charles, who gets right to the point, confirming rumors I've already heard via my grapevine.

"Suzanne, a twenty-two-year-old male from Port Townsend has gone missing over on the peninsula. Olympic National Park rangers and Olympic Mountain Rescue folks have been searching since April 5, but they weren't able to thoroughly search areas along the river. The park just contacted me with a direct request for a single K9 team." My ears perk right up as Charles continues, "Would you and Keb be able to go?"

Pleased that Charlies has requested us specifically, I immediately answer, "Yes," while silently realizing this will postpone my work that generates needed income. Fortunately, my clients know about my commitment to search and rescue and will forgive my last-minute rescheduling.

I'll need to find a field support person, so I call Guy who, it turns out, needs a bit of convincing. "Suzanne, is this going to be worth the effort? It's already almost eleven, and we'll have to catch the ferry, and then we're gonna need to drive *at least* three hours to get to the search area. We're not even going to start searching until 4 p.m. at the earliest!" After a brief but intense charm offensive on my side, Guy agrees to be picked up in fifteen minutes, and we are soon on the ferry from Edmonds across Puget Sound to Kingston. All of us are now excited and committed to the task ahead.

Keb is so excited and committed that she spends the entire ferry ride snoozing unconscious in the backseat of the car. Guy and I ascend metal stairs from the car deck to the passenger deck to enjoy the view during the five-mile crossing of Puget Sound. Guy stops by the onboard cafe to pick up an Egg-Mc-Washington-State-Ferry breakfast sandwich and a bottle of orange juice. As the ferry churns across the sound, Guy munches on this late breakfast and scans the water for whales and wildlife. I remark that once we unload from the ferry, it will be a three-hour drive to the ranger station. Guy squints one eye: "Suzanne, I've looked at the map. I'm betting on closer to four hours."

Charles directed us to meet rangers at the Storm King Ranger Station on the west shore of Lake Crescent. After briefly getting lost (don't tell my SAR friends) and wandering around the wrong building, we find two rangers, one tall, one short. Short Ranger greets us like long lost friends and leads us to a messy office in the back of a rustic cabin, "Thanks so much for coming over on short notice. We know it's a long drive for you guys! We want you to check out the possibility that our subject somehow crossed the river near where his bicycle was found." His finger points to a spot on a large, well-creased topographical map spread across his desk. "We'd really like to get a dog team to search the riverbanks and forested hillside here on the west side of the river." He pauses to see if we're still with him and continues. "You'll be the only searchers in this area today."

This is a bit of good news, and I respond quickly, "It's actually ideal for us that no other searchers will be in the area. My dog is trained to find both live and dead persons, and we'd expect her to alert on anyone in the area." The rangers look at each other and seem pleased with this piece of news. The national park and the Clallam County Sheriff's Office are getting a lot of pressure from the family and would *really* like to get this case resolved.

Tall Ranger starts packing up maps and then fishes out a set of truck keys from a drawer in the beat-up desk we've been using for a map table. As we leave the ranger cabin and head toward my aging Toyota 4Runner, we see Jacob's family gathered in the gravel parking lot; we make brief introductions before loading up. Tall Ranger turns to me. "Do you want a scent article for your dog? We've emptied Jacob's backpack and hung the contents to dry right here outside the cabin. You can use any of those clothes if you want."

Dang it! This means those articles are worthless. I thank them, but respectfully turn down their offer. "My dog's nose is so sensitive, she's going to detect not only Jacob's scent, but also your scent or the scent of any family members who've touched his clothes. In fact, their scent may be the most recent and possibly the strongest. If they've been in the area that we're going to search, Keb may track *their* scent and not Jacob's." A few of the family members are nodding. I think they get this. Scent articles, I think to myself. I should be focused on the mission at hand, but my mind returns to a recent K9 deployment when scent articles erupted as an ugly issue.

Just a few months back, June and I had been the K9 first team to arrive on an urban search for an elderly woman missing from her mobile home park. As we waited to deploy, we noticed that the family of the missing woman kept moving in and out of the home, potentially contaminating any scent articles. The local law enforcement guy on scene also observed this and suggested we collect a scent article right away. We usually wait for our trailing teams to show up to collect their own scent article; it's something they are pretty fussy about. But this time I decided to go ahead and get one, so that we could start searching as soon as possible.

As a K9 operations leader with hundreds of missions under my belt and sixteen years of K9 handler SAR experience, I felt solidly qualified to take on this task. By this time in her career, Keb had undergone scent-discrimination training and had learned to search preferentially for one individual's scent. "June, I believe this is the right decision for our team. Let's make sure we secure a good scent article now while there is still a good chance to get one that's not contaminated by law enforcement and family. The trailing teams are still not due here for quite a while, and this search is urgent because our missing woman is at risk for hypothermia in this cold weather."

June nodded her head and agreed. "Yeah, they'd probably appreciate that, so you might as well. Do you have your scent kit?" Knowing the sensitivity of our trailing handlers, I made sure to follow proper protocol, gloving up, making sure I was not leaning over and shedding skin rafts (minute skin particles that all humans shed) over the article, carefully bagging a pillowcase from the woman's bed. When our K9 team coordinator Carter arrived minutes later, I explained exactly what I'd done. We agreed on a safe place to store the sealed bag containing the pillowcase. June and I got our assignment and headed out on our search of nearby yards.

We were out searching, blissfully unaware and totally focused on finding our lost woman, when *skit* hit the fan! Our first trailing handler arrived on the scene. In front of all SAR personnel, the public, and law enforcement, she angrily shouted, "Suzanne has no business collecting a scent article. She may have compromised this whole mission!" This was, in my

opinion, unprofessional. Our SAR expectation is to *never* engage in crit-
icisms or arguments on missions, especially not in public, and especially
not in front of law enforcement or a missing person's family. As if that were
not enough, the "pillowcase story" became one of the most repeated stories
around for months. I even heard about it from K9 SAR colleagues from
other counties. Damn! What should have been a quick internal discussion
was blown way out of proportion and damaged the credibility of our entire
team.

My mental focus returns as we follow the ranger's truck up Forest Service
Road 2918 on the west side of the river. I glance in my rearview mirror. "Guy,
see all those cars following us? I think that's the family!" Guy and I quickly
agree we need to ask that they be restricted to staying near their cars while we
conduct our search. Keb would be seriously distracted by a swarm of family
members wandering through the woods. When we arrive at our insertion
point, it's already late afternoon, and as we pull on boots and packs, we're
surprised to be told by rangers that we need to be out of the field before dark
at 8 p.m.

During our briefing, we were told that the river was only about 200
yards from the road, just a simple stroll through the forest. Hot dog! This is
going to be an easy one. But our euphoria is short-lived, as we soon realize to
our dismay that reaching the Sol Duc River from here actually involves first
following an old logging track and then descending 400 feet of an *extremely*
steep forested slope. After searching for twenty minutes with one of the rangers for a reasonable route down, we decide on a slope where we just might be
able to descend without falling and breaking our necks. Guy and I have by
now reassessed our Green-Amber-Red safety rating from green to amber due
to steep terrain. Helmet, gloves, eye protection, and hiking poles turn out
to be quite useful as we carefully and slowly descend the steep, rough slope.
Partway down, our ranger decides to turn around, saying cheerfully, "Well, I

Suzanne and Keb descending steeply toward the Sol Duc River. Minutes afterward, our ranger guide wisely decided to turn back.

think you guys should be able to make it OK from here." Guy and I silently exchange a glance. He's going to abandon us? Just before the ranger leaves, we confirm that our plan is to return to the insertion point and meet him at the vehicles before dark.

We're about halfway down the slope as I pick my way carefully between slippery moss and downed trees. I take the next step down and my boot keeps sinking and then sinking some more. *Jäklans skit!* My leg is now firmly wedged in a deep animal hole between two huge tree roots. I'm stretched in a painfully awkward position, and as I struggle, my leg sinks deeper and deeper. Keb senses my discomfort and has come back up the slope to offer comfort and encouragement. Guy, on the other hand, has not noticed, and is well below me down the slope toward the river. I sheepishly holler out to him, "I'm stuck!" and am relieved when my knight in shining armor (actually dirty hiking clothes) is able to return up the slope and perform a rescue by pulling me up by my arms.

As he pulls, Guy grins and mutters something about "getting this on video." I do not find the remark humorous. My foot is actually hurting, you dolt, I think, letting my frustration get the better of me. Soon I'm out of the hole, and the rational part of me has returned. Lucky thing I was not doing this mission alone. This is a good reminder of why we always deploy as a team of at least two humans. Guy knows how to rig a rope-rescue pulley system. Keb does not.

After my quick but humbling rescue, we reach the riverbank and determine by looking at our GPS map screen that we're about 300 yards downstream of the scratch marks found by the trackers. These are our goal, so we start our search moving upstream. The river level is now a bit lower. We'll be able to search cautiously along it where the banks allow access. This involves walking over slippery river rocks and clambering over forested hillsides where steep slopes edge right down to the water. Visibility for objects in the river varies between pretty good and zero as the lighting shifts from open sunlight to dark shade. A light wind flows down the river, carrying the scent of cool water and decaying leaves. Keb is having a great time splashing through the shallows. Guy and I are worried that she might get over enthusiastic and end up floating down the river, so we keep a close eye on her.

It's a near impossibility to avoid water on wilderness missions in the Pacific Northwest. Water comes at us in a variety of forms: rain, streams, rivers, lakes, snow, and glaciers. It follows that our training must include K9 water safety and water search strategy, so Keb and I have trained for water searching since she was six months old. Whether working on a boat or from the shoreline of a river or a lake, handlers must understand how terrain, wind, and currents impact where our dogs will detect scent. These environmental variables create different challenges and require nuanced approaches to K9 problem solving and training. It ultimately gets down to reading the minute behavior changes of our dogs to understand what they are trying to communicate, while intuitively leveraging our experiences and training. I often say that K9 search and rescue is as much an art as it is science. As handlers, we engage in an intricate dance with our dogs, and when there is synergy, it's a beautiful thing.

Today we're searching along a mountain river that winds back and forth for miles before emptying out in the Pacific Ocean. As Keb and I work our way upstream, I'm using all I've learned about water searching to help guide and interpret her searching. In rivers, bodies are often caught in underwater roots, log "strainers," or other debris, and may be found relatively close to where the subject was last seen. Where will scent be eddying? Where might a body be entrapped? This is the puzzle Keb and I need to solve.

Did Jacob try to cross the river on this log? Would we ever know?

After an hour of searching, we arrive at the general location of the scrape marks found by the man trackers. "Guy, look, we're in the right place! That's the large downed tree that spans most of the river. That's the log that Jacob might have crossed over!" We stare at the tree with the river flowing fast beneath it, and quickly agree it's something neither of us would attempt to cross. In my imagination, I see someone slipping off that log, and I wonder if Guy can see me shudder.

Daylight is waning. Guy and I have seen nothing for the past two hours, but Keb is now suddenly showing increased energy and a change in behavior suggesting she detects "live scent." Is it possible Jacob is somewhere nearby? In this world of steep, overgrown forest, we humans could walk right by an unresponsive person without noticing. We're completely dependent upon Keb's talents to find anyone out here. I stop to make sure Guy understands my search strategy. "I want to give her a lot of room to do a 'ranging' search, followed by more detailed gridding in areas where I want her to explore more."

"I'll be a second pair of eyes," Guy volunteers. I nod in appreciation. It's so great to have a field support partner experienced in working with K9s. No need for elaborate explanations. Keb's energy level persists but she keeps wanting to move up the slope, which will take us back toward our beginning point. Guy checks his watch. "Suzanne, if we want to get back to the vehicles before dark, we need to start the climb back up now. It's going to be slow going."

As mountaineers, we've learned to ascend steep snow by "kicking steps"— punching your boot toe into the snow to create your own foothold. As we climb back up the steep mossy hillside, we are literally kicking steps in the soft forest dirt, and in places, hauling ourselves up by pulling on any available roots or branches. Keb, on the other hand, effortlessly scrambles up and across the slope. There are times I catch her perched impatiently on a rock looking down at me quizzically, as I'm grunting and heaving myself up the hillside. Come on, slowpoke, what's the problem down there?

Our ascent winds its way up faint ramps and grooves in the hillside, and we keep seeing evidence of moss scraped off rocks and occasional heel-sized depressions in the loose dirt. As we continue to follow Keb uphill, Guy pauses. "Suzanne, I think that she's actually following the scent trail of a human. It's conceivable she's following a path that Jacob traveled, but I'd bet my last donut she's following the trail of a searcher or family member. We know they were in this area just yesterday."

Good job, Kebbie. Not only has she followed human scent from yesterday, she's led us up what probably is the easiest path, and I am silently grateful for her. Once up the steep slope, we follow compass and GPS, navigating our way west through dense green forest. We make it back to the vehicles just before twilight and debrief with the NPS Rangers. I then see that family members are still waiting near their cars, so I walk over to engage in some small talk. But it's hard to know what to say. It is obvious our search has not been productive. How do you share that message and still leave hope? Shortly before we leave, one family member approaches me. Her face shows sadness and strain; she is radiating frustration. "Why didn't you use the clothes we offered so your dog could follow Jacob's scent?"

Did she not hear me earlier? I repeat my explanation as patiently as I can. "My dog will smell the odors of *anyone* who handled the clothing recently. If family members handled the clothing, and you've been searching in the same area, Keb might follow your scent, and not lead us to Jacob." I hope she understands me, but I realize that sometimes people will cling to simple beliefs when they are more comforting than the truth. Engaging with family in situations like this is a delicate proposition. Fears of the worst can get the better of family members and channel their thinking. I do my best to empathize and inwardly cringe at the thought of being in their situation. What if it was my daughter we were searching for? What would I feel? What would I want to hear?

By now, Jacob's family is profoundly concerned and is growing deeply disappointed with the park's efforts. They're unhappy that it took three days to get search dogs involved in the search. They're unhappy that even then, it's only one dog. They're unhappy we didn't show up until 4 p.m. They're unhappy we only searched for four hours. Well, I'd be unhappy too. They've been told incorrectly that Keb only detects dead persons, which is an unfortunate misunderstanding, but they are unhappy about that as well. What they don't realize is that Keb, with her ability to respond to the scent of *either* live or dead persons, with her ability to search across steep wilderness terrain, with her ability to detect scent in water, is the *perfect* dog for today's search.

The family's dissatisfaction no doubt stems from another widely held misconception—that our National Park Service has a large cadre of SAR staff, ready at any moment to respond when needed. This is simply not the case. When this large cadre does not appear, people demand to know where all their tax dollars are going. Well, they're not going to the national parks, which are poor as church mice. Olympic National Park, like most national parks, very often must rely on local volunteer SAR resources to staff their searches. Some of the time, these volunteer SAR resources need to take a one-hour ferry ride, then drive another four hours to reach the search site. So, when they search for four hours, and then have to drive all the way home again without dinner, they too grumble about the National Park Service.

When Guy and I arrive at the Kingston ferry dock it's almost 11 p.m., and we have over an hour wait for the next ferry across the sound. It's quiet and peaceful in the small harbor town. The dark streets are empty. After searching all afternoon and driving most of the evening, we are *starved*! "It looks like everything is closed. *Skit*," I grumble.

Just then, Guy spies a pub across the street that looks open. Our hopes soar as we walk over in the light rain, abandoning Keb who is sleeping in her backseat dog bed. Guy starts to mutter something that sounds like "veggie burger with cheese," while I dream of a healthier salad. Inside, the place is almost empty. We ask the waitress for menus, only to be crushed.

"Hon, our kitchen closed at 10 p.m. All's we've got are chips and peanuts."

Guy's voice blends pain and resignation. "Four bags of each, please."

The Search Continues: July

From mid-April through June, we hear via my K9 grapevine that additional searching is being conducted by Clallam County SAR and is supplemented by private search efforts driven by the family. Jacob's father performs heroic searching of the river itself, returning again and again to use his diving skills to search in ponds and under waterfalls. No sign of Jacob is found. No clues are found. The mystery deepens. This is the worst possible scenario for any family—not knowing, not knowing, not knowing.

In late July, Keb and I are again in my home country of Sweden, visiting family and new friends in the Swedish SAR community, when I get an uncharacteristically long email from Guy. In response to a statewide request from Clallam County, our deputy, Charles, asked Guy if he would be available as PLANS chief for a return search of the Sol Duc River. Water levels are much lower now, and the Clallam SAR deputy wants to put ground searchers and K9 teams in the river basin, wherever safe. Guy contacted Arthur, the leader of our Swiftwater team, and explained the objective was to search eight miles of riverbed downstream from where Jacob's bicycle was found.

Arthur then did something amazing. He used Google Earth satellite map imagery to virtually fly down the eight-mile river section, zooming in to identify and locate river bends, pools, and logjams that might trap a "negatively buoyant object." He then emailed Guy a table of over twenty "trapping locations," each with a description of the river feature, its likelihood (high, medium, low) of trapping a person floating downstream, along with latitude/longitude coordinates.

Guy was able take Arthur's data points and plot them on his master search map. Once all of the trapping locations were plotted, he divided the eight-mile downriver stretch into eight zones, and we could see clearly which zones had a higher density of trapping locations. He then planned a series of river search assignments, along with detailed maps identifying target locations to be searched within each river zone. Our planning wizards were on a roll.

Guy's planning formed the basis for the largest river search in Clallam County history. K9 teams, ground searchers, mountain rescue teams, and Swiftwater teams from throughout the Puget Sound Region all assembled on Saturday, July 29, on a search run jointly by Olympic National Park and Clallam County Sheriff's Office. Searchers found bones in the riverbed—lots of 'em. But they were all animal bones. A pair of hiking shorts was found in the riverbed, abraded as if washed down the river for miles. Two K9s showed strong interest in a log pile not far downstream from the Last Known Point. Arthur's Swiftwater fanatics probed the depths of the log pile as deep as they were able and reported to Guy that it was a highly likely place for a floating body to get trapped forever in unreachable nooks and crannies.

Jacob's family was on site that day, and they were impressed and grati-fied with the sizable turnout of volunteers and with the large, well-organized search effort. In the email from Guy, he includes a clipping from the local newspaper, the *Daily Peninsula News*. They've published a thank-you letter from Jacob's family.

> We want to thank search teams from Clallam, Snohomish, Kitsap, Pierce, Mason, and Jefferson counties, volunteers from the Clallam Bay and

Olympic corrections center's Inmate Recovery Team, Olympic Mountain Rescue, Northwest Disaster Search Dogs, Olympic Project / Ridge Walkers Unlimited, the ATV Club, the American Red Cross Northwest Region, Olympic National Park, and all volunteers who came out to support the search effort for Jacob, and extend a special thanks to Clallam County Sheriff's Office's SAR Coordinator, Lyman Moores, for superbly orchestrating the undertaking. It was evident by how flawlessly this very large operation was executed—even with counties and volunteers joining late in the process— that Sergeant Moores' team spent days of preparation and planning.

Mission Debrief

Guy

As the river search ended, the effort provided Jacob's family with no findings, no comfort, no closure. The pain and mystery remained. It would be easy to conclude that our endeavors were fruitless and meaningless, but in a way that's difficult to explain to the family, Jacob's disappearance provided a far-reaching value. During the large and complex search, the command staff learned, the operations staff learned, the K9 handlers learned, our search dogs learned, our planners learned, the park rangers learned, and the sheriff's deputies learned. All gained important experience that will be carried forward the next time there is a missing hiker or missing child. All of this value is being paid forward as we plan and execute future searches.

And one absolutely vital thing to understand about search planning is that you can't search everywhere—there are never enough resources. So, you need to use information, experience, and intellect to focus your limited resources where the probability of finding your subject is the highest. Arthur's virtual flyover of the eight miles downstream from Jacob's Last Known Point provided us with the key to doing this on the river search for Jacob Gray.

This eight-mile distance was derived from the work of SAR genius Dr. Robert "Bob" Koester. Over many years, Bob has analyzed international SAR incident data and has quantified and characterized typical behaviors for over thirty different categories of lost persons (e.g., children, dementia subjects, lost hikers). For each category, he has also analyzed the historical data, which provides planning wizards with probability-based distances. So, for "lost persons in a river," I could see in Koester's classic book *Lost Person Behavior* that in 95 percent of historical cases the subjects were found within eight miles of the Last Known Point.

I was able to accurately plot all of Arthur's "trapping locations" using SARTopo, an online mapping program created by Matt Jacobs, another SAR genius from California. By now, the astute reader will be realizing that we planning wizards are mostly faking it. We simply use the work of other SAR geniuses to make ourselves look like we know what we're doing.

Looking Back

Suzanne

I'm back from Sweden in early August, when I get an excited call from Guy: "I just got an email from the Clallam SAR deputy! Family members identified the hiking shorts we found as being *identical* to a pair given to Jacob!" The gear found near the river, the "slip marks" on the rocks, the K9 interest near the suspicious log pile, the shorts that match—sadly, all of these are pointing to the same conclusion: Jacob was swept down the river, never to be found.

During the river search for Jacob Gray, search dogs showed clear and intense interest in the same log pile that Arthur reported was in the perfect position to trap a person floating down the river under high-water conditions. The Swiftwater team ferried one of the K9s across the river on a float board so that the dog could get direct access to the log pile. The K9 handler reported that her dog showed extreme interest and actually wanted to leap into the water immediately downstream of the log pile. The wind was coming downstream through the log pile and the dog was straining to get inside. When they moved upstream of the log pile, the dog's interest disappeared. It was no surprise to hear that in late August, Olympic Mountain Rescue and Clallam County SAR volunteers returned to deeply probe the suspicious log pile. They searched all day in hazardous conditions, using pry bars and chainsaws. But no trace of Jacob was found.

It was not until April 2018 that we learned our planning wizards were deceived. The K9 handlers were deceived. The demons of time, weather, and mystery prevailed. Over a year after our search of the Sol Duc River, a team of field biologists are studying marmots in Olympic National Park. On a high ridge above Hoh Lake, among the hardy pink heather and late season wildflowers, they find clothing and gear. Park rangers are alerted and return the next day, when more careful searching reveals scattered human remains. The remains are transported to the King County medical examiner, and within a few days, dental records are matched to Jacob Gray. Initial conclusions are that Jacob died of hypothermia—high in the mountains, and over eleven miles from where his bicycle was left, and far away from the Sol Duc River.

10
The Case of the Swedish Skull

In Which Keb Goes International

"It is important to have an HRD dog exposed to all different classes of decomposition, and realize that some phases are more difficult to detect."

—C. Judah and T. Sargent,

How to Train a Human Remains Detection Dog

Keb doesn't know that the Earth is round. In fact, I'm pretty sure her concept of geography is limited to home, neighborhood walks, car rides, and new forests to be explored when searching for human smells. And because she snoozes most of the time while in the backseat, for her, the twenty-minute ride to a nearby urban search is the same as a three-hour drive to a Mount Rainier mission: home, car ride, new forests, and new smells to be explored.

As a native of Sweden, my worldview is a bit broader. I'm constantly mindful of the family and friends I left behind 4,700 miles away on the other side of the planet. As old age crept up on my parents, Scott and I became more determined than ever to visit them every summer and to bring Keb along. For us, it's a commitment of money and a long plane ride. For Keb, it's just another long car ride followed by new forests to explore.

The Swedish Possibility

In early 2012, I was on the phone making plane reservations for my annual summer visit to see my parents in Sweden. An idea started forming in my mind. Is there such a thing as a Swedish K9 search and rescue organization? What if I became involved and—even better—what if I could bring Keb to train with fellow K9 SAR colleagues on my summer visits! Could I carry my life passion for the K9 SAR community across the globe all the way to Sweden? As I pondered the possibility of going international with my K9 SAR experience, I realized how everything in my life had led to what I was contemplating. What if I could actually build the K9 SAR community across countries, closing the circle on the path of building international community I started in graduate school at the University of California?

Possibilities began to swirl in my brain, and a nervous excitement buzzed in my core. This was the opportunity I had been looking for! Keb, who had been lying by my feet, perked up as she sensed my "Aha!" experience. "Would you like to go to Sweden, Kebbie?" *Thump, thump, thump.* I took her tail wagging as an enthusiastic "yes." This moment of insight was the origin of our annual K9 training pilgrimages to Sweden. Over the next six years we would train and deploy with SAR K9 handlers from Sweden and Denmark, develop lasting friendships, and help solve a deep mystery.

I started internet research on SAR in Sweden and discovered that even though Sweden was a small country, more than 7,000 people went missing every year. And yes indeed, they had a volunteer search and rescue organization! Missing People Sweden (MPS) had recently gained attention by helping solve several well-publicized cases. In a four-day period in 2012, MPS volunteers located three people in three separate searches, including the high-profile case of Anna, a nine-year-old girl who was abducted from school near Gothenburg. This initial burst of success sparked recognition and credibility and led to the steady growth of MPS.

Using my social media sleuthing skills, I persisted in exploring Swedish SAR and, after multiple dead ends, befriended Lena Olsson on Facebook. She turned out to be the perfect contact for me. Lena lived in southern Sweden, not far from Nyhamnsläge, the little fishing village my family is from. After we exchanged texts over several months, an invitation popped up on my Facebook Messaging screen: "*Vill du träna med oss i sommar är du hjärtligt välkommen?*"

Keb scrambled from under my feet as I leapt up and ran into the kitchen. "Scott, Scott! Lena has invited us to train in Sweden this summer! She says their team would love to have Keb and me train with them! In Sweden! Keb and I could go to Sweden!" Scott just grinned quietly; he knows I repeat myself when I'm excited. But it was easy to see that he too was intrigued with the idea. I pulled Keb's head close and looked into her dark eyes. "Kebbie! Do you want to be an international traveler?" *Thump, thump, thump.* Her tail and my heart beat with excitement. Totally energized, I promptly started researching the ins and outs of flying internationally with a dog. If all the logistical challenges I later ran into had been known to me at that time, I might have reconsidered this international adventure. But I'm an eternal optimist. Over the next several years, "If there is a will, there is a way" became an oft-repeated thought as I tapped into my personal affirmations to make my plan come together.

The Search for Vikings

Keb and I first traveled to Sweden in the summer of 2013. Upon arrival, Lena introduced us to the rest of her Swedish K9 team: Bitti, Henrik, and Kattis. They were a small but committed team made up of salt-of-the-earth people, and we eventually became fast friends. I was thrilled to my toes when almost immediately Keb and I were thrown into our first SAR deployment in Scandinavia. Smiling enigmatically, Lena turned to me: "Want to go on a mission? We have a missing person case, and I will be heading out with my dog, Buster, tomorrow. It would be just the two of us, unless you and Keb would want to join."

While Lena looked at me hopefully, I sat for a moment in stunned silence. "You mean it? That would be so cool! Can I bring my husband as field support?"

We set out on our search early the following morning. Scott and I were amused by the Swedish cows mooing and chewing their cud in green meadows lining rough gravel roads. Spending the whole day with Lena introduced me to some of the peculiarities of searching in Sweden. "No, no, Suzanne, you cannot let Keb off leash! We have strict leash laws." Keb, who had already taken off on the narrow dirt road ahead of us, was not too happy about being put back on leash. But after facing off with a protective bull in one of the fields, she decided her leash could be tolerated and stayed close to us on the road.

Initially, I pushed back gently. "But, Lena, Keb is an air scent dog. She almost always searches off-leash and has a rock-solid recall. Are you sure I can't let her range free? She'll be able to cover much more ground that way." I started to explain how Keb often roams far from me on wilderness searches and how I can track her on my handheld GPS. Then I stopped myself, noticing that Lena was opening her mouth to say something while at the same time crossing her arms. I realized this was not the time to be ethnocentric or argumentative. Cool it, Suzanne. We are guests here, and you need to stay in a learning frame of mind.

As we walked the rural dirt lane, Lena shared more information about the constraints of deploying search dogs in Sweden. Later in the day, we found ourselves inside a fenced meadow, and Lena judged it safe to "let slip" the dogs for an off-leash run. Buster and Keb took joyful advantage of the opportunity, and after getting the zoomies out of their systems, they both sprinted into a shallow stream and rolled in pools to cool off from the summer heat. "Check them out, Lena: they are frolicking with pure joy!"

I learned an important lesson on that first day. In hindsight, one of the reasons I had been getting along famously with the Scandinavian dog handlers was because I've stayed true to my commitment to not push our United States way of doing things on them. Our cultures, contexts, and histories are very different, so it makes sense we were at different stages of evolution. In the United States, for example, K9 search and rescue dates back to the 1950s, while in Scandinavia, use of volunteer search dogs has emerged only very recently. Over the years, the Swedes, Danes, and I have shared perspectives from our home countries and reflected on similarities and differences in how we train, and while doing so, our respective K9 toolsets have been expanded and enriched.

When Keb and I next returned to Sweden in 2014, I learned my MPS K9 friends and I had been invited to spend a weekend in Denmark. I was flattered when our Danish counterparts asked me to do a presentation about K9 human remains detection in the United States. The Danes and Swedes sat in rapt attention while I shared my experiences at the tragic Oso Landslide in my home county just months earlier. With memories still fresh, I was able to intersperse my presentation with vivid stories and personal learnings from participating in such a huge disaster with Keb and my Snohomish County K9 team.

Even though I grew up speaking Swedish, I remember being worried about my communication skills. "Lena, it's embarrassing to me that the Danes all understand what I say, but I have a heck of a time understanding when they ask questions." Danish has an unusual number of vowels, and to make matters worse, modern Danes freely leave out lots of the remaining consonants that make for better distinction between words. "They just go too fast," I complained.

Lena listened patiently. "Just relax, they all know English." This may have been true, but some of them were less than excited about using this opportunity to practice. We often ended up speaking all three languages, with Lena acting as my interpreter. I'm sure an outside observer would have scratched their head at the verbal mélange, but it worked for us, and it seemed our dogs were able to follow along pretty well. That weekend in an old Danish farmhouse, we thoroughly enjoyed training together, and new friendships began to form.

Over the years we typically congregated at Lena's house in the county of Skåne, amid waving green fields of wheat, barley, and rye as far as the eye could see. The Danes would bring packages of *röda pölser* (long, skinny, red hot dogs). They had been quick to take note of my (and Keb's) infatuation with this local delicacy. Our summer gatherings often involved beer, wine, and an occasional schnapps as we relaxed together after long days of training. I remember one evening sitting in the yard with Lena, Agneta, Bergitte,

Anneke, Bente, and Vicki reveling in the sunset, when I heard Niel and Balder calling from inside. *"Hallå Suzanne, vill du ha en schnapps?"*

Truth be told, I *hate* schnapps. It tastes like kerosene. But being a real Swede, I've learned to endure, and so I reluctantly accepted the brimming shot glass handed to me. "OK, but I need one of the *röda pölser* and a beer to wash this down with!" I secretly dreaded having to drink the stuff with its horrible aftertaste but could tell they really wanted to toast with me. We lifted our glasses, our eyes met in good Scandinavian style, and we drank to new friendships. Wooooooh! My throat burned; my skin was tingling. I just loved this group, though, and I was willing to make this sacrifice! They had no hidden agendas; it was so refreshing! It was a welcome relief to have drama-free time away from the continuing personnel hassles on our K9 team at home. As the schnapps burn faded slowly in my throat, I reflected on the month prior to this trip, in which we all suffered through "The Battle of the Leg," a bizarre episode illustrating the lengths to which a small group appeared to resist efforts to evolve our K9 team.

Over the years, we had recognized a serious deficiency in the way we trained our dogs. In our typical Pacific Northwest wilderness and rural environments, mere days or even hours of exposure could cause the death of a lost person. We could never be certain if we were searching for the living or the dead. On several painful (and for us, embarrassing) incidents, some of our K9s who were trained only to find the scent of *living* humans actually walked right by *deceased* subjects. You can just imagine how this impressed our sheriff deputies.

We needed the ability to train our dogs to find a missing person, whether alive or dead. To address this problem, our team had recently acquired a human leg, the result of a kind and generous donation from a man who lost his limb after years of battling diabetes. This was a unique opportunity for us to expose our dogs to "large source" (whole, or large parts of human bodies) during trainings. Unfortunately, in the months before I left for Sweden, one of our members, who had been entrusted with its secure storage in a large freezer, appeared to hold the leg hostage. Week after week, she dismissed requests to get the leg to our trainings, providing one excuse after another. Our carefully planned training schedule was delayed and disrupted. What left a bitter taste in my mouth was the fact that "battling for a human leg" was so disrespectful.

As we handle body parts, tissue, blood, or human bones in our trainings, we need to be constantly mindful of the fact that we are dealing with substances that belonged to a living human being, someone's son, daughter, wife, or husband. Training with donated source is an honor and privilege bestowed upon us that we should never take for granted and *never* exploit for personal interests.

During our 2015 summer visit, I was excited to find that our opportunities to search in Sweden continued to expand. Shortly after our arrival, Scott, Keb, and I deployed with Lena and K9 Buster, along with other K9 handlers, to Sösdala, a bucolic farming community on the far southern tip of Sweden. Sösdala, with only 1,800 inhabitants, is an example of small railroad towns prevalent during the history of my home country. We searched that day for a possibly suicidal man, and our K9 assignment was to walk nearby railroad tracks. Some time into the mission, several dogs showed marked changes in behavior, but we quickly discovered this was due to a dead deer in the brush alongside the tracks. We did not locate the missing man that day. I heard from Lena that months later he was found where he had hung himself, in a location nowhere close to where our dogs were deployed.

During this search I gained more insight into how large missions are conducted in Sweden. I was surprised to learn that anybody over eighteen can volunteer for grid searching when the call for searchers goes out. They just show up and are assigned to search teams! This is a dramatically different approach than in my home county, and in most of the United States, where SAR volunteers have to meet strict requirements, which often includes hundreds of hours of training. On that Sösdala mission, I was amazed at how efficiently the mission was organized and that civilians with little to no training were unhesitatingly deployed in the field.

Two days after the Sösdala mission, Keb and I traveled to Uppsala, the fourth largest city in Sweden, where we had a fascinating opportunity to work with 1,000-year-old bones from the Viking era, as well as burnt bones dating back to the Iron Age (the fourth to first centuries BC). That summer, my five "besties" from high school and I had our annual three-day weekend together at a hotel just a block from Uppsala Cathedral. Eva, Battan, Mia, Lena, and Marre all still live in Sweden but are spread out all over the country. Eva is an archeologist. She had been able to borrow a collection of ancient bones. She was excited about articles she had recently read about K9s specializing in finding historical graves and turned to me with a grin: "Let's give Kebbie a test!"

On the second day of our reunion, following an evening of wine, talk, and loud songs (we all used to be in the choir together), Eva set up a three-bone search problem for Keb and me in the small park below our old hotel. I instructed her on how to handle the bones. "Please don't touch any of the bones with your bare hands. Always use gloves. We want no contact with your skin. In fact, I'd prefer you don't even lean over the bones, because you might shed skin rafts. To keep myself honest, I also don't want you to share *any* clues with me as to where you place them. OK?" I was feeling a bit nervous about this test and prepared them for the possibility that Keb simply would not recognize the scent of bones this old. I explained, "Human remains are made up of chemical composites, many of which have been scientifically proven to be recognized by dogs. I just don't know if the composites are still there after 1,000 years."

Will Keb be able to find centuries-old Viking bones?

To my surprise and delight, Keb nailed all three bones in short order, sitting at those locations, with perfect trained final responses. As I rewarded Keb with her ball, inwardly I was jubilant and could hardly contain myself.

"Vilken superhund!" Eva exclaimed in her typically exuberant way. Keb indeed got super dog treatment and happily munched on *röda pölser* treats for the rest of the weekend.

The Search for Bengt

Late that same summer, Keb and I were chatting with our Swedish colleagues when Lena mentioned the mysterious disappearance of fifty-two-year-old Bengt Jönsson. In January 2015, Bengt was seen getting on Bus 222 from Helsingborg north to Mölle, a small harbor town on the remote tip of the rugged Kullaberg Peninsula in southern Sweden. Why Bengt got on this wrong bus remains a mystery, but witnesses reported seeing him at a bus stop in Mölle in the darkness of a late wintery afternoon. From this Point Last Seen on that fateful day, he disappeared without a trace.

Official searching started a few days later, and searchers were excited when Bengt's glasses case was found on a path behind the Mölle Chapel. Swedish law enforcement searched nearby forests and coastlines for weeks until they ran out of resources. Subsequently, volunteers from Missing People Sweden continued the search in collaboration with law enforcement. The search went on intermittently for another eighteen months, utilizing hundreds of MPS volunteers, coast guard boats, divers, helicopters . . . and search dogs. But nothing more of Bengt was found.

When Lena explains that he was last seen at the Mölle bus station and that his glasses case was found on a trail near the community chapel, my interest soars. "This is just ten minutes away from my parents' house! That bus station is but a stone's throw from the house of my best childhood friend Tjatte, and she was married in that very same chapel!" Lena listens intently, unlike Buster and Keb, who sprawl nearby on the floor, tired after a day's training and paying no attention whatsoever. Soon Keb is snoring quietly by my feet. I stroke her head softly while continuing, "I remember as a teenager hiking and bicycling the trails outside Mölle, even the ones that ran north and south along the shores of the Kullaberg peninsula. Lena, I know that area!"

As we continue to scheme, the beginnings of a plan take shape, and the next day, Lena, Kattis, Henrik, and I decide to search the area. We spend an afternoon behind the quaint little church, searching along well-trodden trails adjacent to recently harvested barley fields. I leap aside when a horse cart comes racing toward me on one of the narrow dirt roads, but other than that our stroll is peaceful. Our three dogs are well behaved, and shortly past mid-day (after carefully looking around for any game wardens) we decide to let the dogs off leash to search nearby hillsides. Imagine that! I've been influencing my Swedish friends with my tales of "loose dog searching!" I think I can hear Keb sighing with relief that she can now move around freely to do her job. At the end of a pleasant afternoon of searching, we return with hands empty, but with hearts full of camaraderie. I had no way of knowing that Keb would later play a role in solving the mystery of Bengt Jönsson.

Bengt's mysterious disappearance remains a major topic for discussion within my circle of Swedish comrades. I listen with growing intrigue as my friend Tjatte shares the tales and stories of the locals and their varying opinions of what happened to him. As we're sitting at her kitchen table, she is painting beautiful patterns on coffee cups she has recently thrown in her adjacent ceramics studio. Oh, how I adore this woman. She is crazy fun, direct, and we simply click together. Her black Labrador retriever, Hedvig, is lying on the floor watching us as we talk, laugh, and share old childhood memories. In the meantime, Keb is romping around in the yard chasing butterflies.

While continuing to paint with incredible precision, Tjatte shares questions raised by the locals. Did Bengt fall off coastal cliffs nearby? Did he get back on a bus? Was he eaten by a wild boar, or worse, by evil forest spirits? We have a grand time discussing these theories, as Tjatte speaks in the broad

Between the serious business of searching in Sweden, Keb and I find time for some love and relaxation.

dialect typical for the area that at one time was a part of Denmark. Her language is flavorful, perhaps even crude, with many unique cuss words and sayings harkening back to farming days.

The summer draws to an end, and we return home to the Pacific Northwest. Six months later, I am once again making plane reservations for Keb and me for our 2016 planned trip. Before we started flying internationally, we had become seasoned pros, traveling several times a year throughout the United States for specialty training in places such as Colorado and Texas. Kebbie is convinced she is human, but airline employees are not easily fooled, so traveling to Sweden with a four-legged companion requires careful logistical planning.

Arranging our international air travel to Sweden is much, much more complicated, but over time, Keb and I have been able to fashion a workable approach by flying Iceland Air from Seattle to Copenhagen, Denmark (via Iceland), then driving over the bridge to Malmo, Sweden. When we travel overseas, I have Keb travel as "excess luggage," rather than in cabin. It actually seems like the kindest alternative for such a long flight. I cannot imagine how Keb would feel being stuffed under my seat for twelve hours. She is no doubt much more comfortable snoozing in a roomy crate in a heat-controlled luggage area. In fact, I might be more comfortable back there with her, rather than in my cramped economy class seat.

Flying Iceland Air, with a layover in Reykjavik's relatively small Keflavik airport, also allows me to see when Keb is transferred between planes. I always, *always* ask to see the captain's manifest when I board to make sure Keb is on the airplane with me. I'll forever remember the one flight when I pestered the flight attendant to check the manifest, and to my horror and in the nick of time, we discovered that Keb had been forgotten in the quarantine area!

Over the years I've developed a relationship with Iceland Air staff, and cannot praise Jessica, the dog-friendly Seattle-based area station manager, and Jean Pierre, my Iceland Air travel agent, enough. One year, Keb and I got stranded overnight in Reykjavik due to bad weather. Iceland requires all dogs entering the country to go through quarantine, so Keb was confined to an underground quarantine area for a long, worrisome day. Thankfully, Jessica sprang into action with long-distance phone calls. I was given special permission to make frequent visits to Keb's basement "jail cell," while at the same time Jean Pierre worked his Iceland Air magic to get us on a continuing flight, hours earlier than what I had been originally told.

Usually though, our overseas travel goes smoothly. Once I've gone through customs in Copenhagen, I make a beeline for the oversized luggage area to wait for Keb who comes traveling toward me on a conveyor belt. After a long and arduous trip, I can hear her tail banging against the walls of the crate when she catches sight of me. As she gets closer, I hold up a *röd pölse*, which we both love so much. It's become a ritual to greet her with this Danish hot-dog morsel when arriving in Scandinavia. She gobbles it down and I let her out of the crate. She immediately goes all-out with big slobbery kisses all over my face. Truthfully, I really don't like getting the full-face-lick treatment and have tried, to no avail, to train her to lick only my chin. Sigh, impulse control has flown out the window after the long trip, and I am too exhausted

Keb's *röd pölse* treat at the end of her long intercontinental flight.

to protest. All the while her otter tail is swishing back and forth with the power of a weed whacker. A fellow passenger waiting for her oversized luggage quickly jumps out of the way to avoid getting whipped.

By now Keb has knocked me over, and I'm sitting on the floor, fruitlessly trying to take her enthusiastic greeting down a notch. "You know, Kebbie girl, you're now a seasoned international traveler and need to start behaving like one." More licks and now she is nibbling on my left earlobe. "I'll tell you what, you haven't peed for twelve hours, want to go potty?" I have covertly inspected the crate and confirmed that no accidents have taken place. The licking stops abruptly as Keb hears a familiar word: "potty." With me hanging behind on the leash, we sprint out of the Terminal 2 entrance, where we are both relieved to spy one lone bush in the middle of a large planter. Keb squats and continues to squat for a long time. "Feel better now, girlie?"

By this time, I'm exhausted. Even when everything goes smoothly, these long trips wear us both down. I have Keb on leash in one hand, while pushing a huge cart with the dog crate and suitcase in the other hand. Curious passengers stop to stare as we slowly make our way to the rental car counter. We end up with a small station wagon, barely big enough for the crate and luggage, and then drive carefully toward the bridge to Malmo, which will take us from Denmark to Sweden. My parents' house is on the coast a couple of hours north. I am already dreaming of a deep, long sleep in a bed with sheets and a pillow. Oh, the luxury of being able to stretch out in a horizontal position! Once at my parents' house, both Keb and I sleep fourteen hours straight.

While my air travel to Sweden with Keb usually goes off without a hitch, the week preceding each flight is always exceedingly stressful. It sounds easy enough: just make sure your pup is up to speed on vaccinations and has a health certificate approved by the United States Department of Agriculture/ Animal and Plant Health Inspection Service (APHIS). Two days prior to our 2016 trip, I'm with our longtime veterinarian, who is licensed to complete required documents for international travel. "Dr Sodhi," I ask, "have you made sure everything is accurate and complete? You know how finicky and unhelpful the APHIS clerks have been in past years. I only have forty-eight hours until my flight leaves."

While feeding Keb a treat for good behavior, he responds in his strong Indian accent, "I know this is an annual nightmare for both of us. The bad news this year is that APHIS will no longer accept advance phone calls or faxes to verify we have completed everything according to their ever-changing guidelines before you go down there. You'll just have to drive down to their office, submit Keb's paperwork, and hope for the best." Keb seems unconcerned about this bad news and rolls over on her back for a tummy rub from this nice man who always delivers heavenly treats.

Early the next morning, Keb and I are on our way to the APHIS office in Tumwater. We have all our documents in hand, but now face a three-hour drive through Seattle rush-hour traffic, then another three-hour drive home. Once at the office, an unfriendly face glowers at me from behind a glassed-in booth. "We don't accept drop-ins. The next appointment you can get is three months from now," she says rather nonchalantly while distractedly thumbing through today's mail. My cheeks burn as I hear this totally new requirement. I stand my ground and refuse to leave. The clerk disappears behind doors for a half hour, presumably checking with a supervisor, or perhaps just filing her nails. She returns with a sour look and reluctantly agrees to process our application. We leave with the approved document in hand and start the long drive home with frayed nerves and seething anger. "Kebbie, what a damned sour puss!"

Just prior to my next summer's flight, I encounter the *very same* clerk, who refuses to accept my application because I've filled it out in both English and Danish. She points at her tattered manual: "See, it says, the application has to be in English." She is looking smug. Her eyes tell me she is enjoying her power over me.

I am now shriveling like an ill-watered plant. Logic has little chance of winning in this situation. Nevertheless, I try. "The form my veterinarian filled out *is in English*, and it is the current, revised form. It is also in Danish. So, it has what the guidelines require and then some." My attempts to influence her are met with stony resistance. Desperate now, I resort to submissive pleading: "If we don't get this signed, I'll have to cancel my trip! It's impossible to get a dog sitter for three weeks on just a day's notice!"

My pleas have no effect. "Nope, it is not in accordance with the guidelines," she retorts and then disappears into the back office.

I return home totally panicked, feeling frustrated and powerless. Fighting back tears, I manage to reach my vet on the phone and explain what happened. Dr. Sodhi is a true hero. He listens sympathetically and agrees to meet me in his office that very evening to create an "English only" version of the paperwork. The next morning, with my heart in my throat and blood pressure sky high, I make the same three-hour drive to Tumwater once again. It takes every ounce of self-restraint not to throw the form in the APHIS clerk's face, but this time we leave with a notarized copy. Kebbie and I are out of purgatory and once again on our way to Sweden!

In July 2016, I happily reunite with Lena, hugging her while Keb runs happy circles around us. "Suzanne!" she breathlessly shares, "Last week they found some articles in the woods near the Mölle Chapel, and the police now think they might belong to Bengt Jönsson!" Keb is totally distracted by getting pets from her, but my ears stand straight up at this news. "Another major Missing People Sweden search is planned for next Sunday. Would you like to go out for a K9 search on Saturday? The police have approved a K9-only search prior to a larger official search."

"Would I! *Röda pölser!*" I quickly use all my charms with my husband and daughter, Linnea, and convince them that this is a much better way to spend Saturday than whatever our original plans were. They somewhat hesitantly agree, and when Saturday arrives, they are assigned as field support for Keb and me. On the way to our rendezvous at a trailhead just outside of Mölle, we drive by Krapperup's Castle, a few minutes' drive from my parents' house. This castle was built in medieval times and is steeped in old ghost stories. Growing up, I remember the hair standing up on my neck when hearing stories about the ghost Vita Damen, the White Lady, who appears once a year immediately before midnight on New Year's Eve. "Stop the car!" shouts Linnea, as she sees not a ghost but a sign offering *fika* (coffee and pastries Swedish style), which we savor while taking in the ancient castle, moat, and suspension bridge.

With our appetite for coffee, pastry, and ghosts temporarily satisfied, we link up with the rest of the K9 teams at the trailhead. Lena has a rough idea of where the articles were recently found and explains, "The police have taped off the area, so it shouldn't be too hard for us to find." Lena leads us down a trail that begins as an easy stroll along a wooded path. It's been a year and a half since Bengt went missing, so I fully expect we are looking for bones. Keb has been trained on a lot of human bones. Swedish K9s Buster and Fido have not.

The laws governing human remains in Scandinavia are strict. One thing I learned from training in Sweden and Denmark is that my friends have very limited access to real human remains: typically only hair and teeth. Even with the limitations faced by my Swedish comrades, I'm amazed at how effective and committed their dog teams are. They train hard and make optimal use of the sparse human remains they have access to. They turn green with envy when I tell them we have access to placentas through a birthing center and have more lenient laws about using human remains for search and rescue dog training. Their eyes grow wide and their jaws drop when I tell them about our body farm facilities that allow HRD K9s to become exposed to full bodies in various stages of decomposition. "By training with other teams in our region, and by going to high-quality workshops with nationally recognized trainers," I explain, "I've been able to expose Keb to pretty much every part of a human body, from bones, brain tissue, internal organs, and blood to whole body parts such as feet or a leg."

Lena stops and points into a forest of widely spaced birch and alder, dotted with knee-high shrubs. "I think the roped off area is in there somewhere." Our dogs are still on leash as we start bushwhacking in the general direction she has suggested. Keb is eagerly pulling me along. Within minutes, we come upon the marked off area. One by one, we have our dogs search in the area. We haven't been told exactly what has been found here, and while our dogs show slight changes in behavior, none of them give a trained final response. As our searching continues, I ask Lena about wildlife and animal trails. "When you hike through this area," she explains, "you may well spot foxes, badgers, roe deer, and red deer. In recent years there have also been incidents with people and dogs running into aggressive boars." I recall my friend Tjatte telling me of such an encounter. I don't know how Keb would react to a wild boar, but I'm sure I don't want to find out.

Lena points out what she thinks is a fox trail heading west, and I suggest we head that way. Animals will move bones along trails, and I know from my training this is an important factor to consider on our searches. As we continue to search slowly, our group of three handlers, three K9s, and support searchers Scott and Linnea spread out for wider coverage. It's only thirty minutes later when, out of the corner of my eye, I notice Keb suddenly slowing down and systematically starting to investigate an area. Hmm, this looks suspiciously like a change in behavior. "Lena, Bitti! Can you bring your dogs over to double-check this area?" They quickly agree and direct their dogs, but neither shows any behavior change of significance.

"We passed by a dead animal just a little while ago," Lena says. "Maybe that's what Keb was reacting to." I know my Kebbie, and strongly doubt this, but don't say anything. We split up again, and then suddenly I see Keb hunch over something, turn around, give me the Where's My Ball? look and then sit: her trained final response! We are now about seventy-five feet away from where I first observed a change in behavior. I quickly approach and sneak a peek at what is hiding behind her back: a skull! Kebbie's found a human skull!

Linnea is close by, and I call her over excitedly and ask her to confirm— after all she's the only orthopedic surgeon on our search team today. "Yes, yes, it's definitely a human skull," she assures me. We look at each other with thrill lighting up our eyes and chills running down our spines. At our feet, Keb is totally unconcerned, but she is getting impatient for her ball to appear.

By now, Lena, Bitti, and Scott have rushed over to join us. Each in turn bends low to stare at the skull. Lena quickly pulls out her cell phone to call the nearest police station in Hoganas, six miles south of us. She's almost shouting into the phone: "We've found a skull! We've found a skull!" She listens to the response, takes several deep breaths, and begins to carefully describe how to get to our location. It takes an hour or two before an officer shows up. After only a moment examining the skull, he quickly concludes that we may have solved the mystery of Bengt Jönsson's disappearance. He thanks us profusely.

All of us are flushed with a sense of achievement. Like with my K9 team back in Washington, the culture with my Swedish colleagues emphasizes the effort and achievements of the entire team. "This was a team find!" We all agree, but I'm so proud of Kebbie I can barely contain myself. We sit for a while in the now quiet forest, reflecting on how all of our training and hard work is so rarely rewarded with finds like this. After another hour, we see that one of Bengt's relatives has arrived at the site. A police officer gently escorts her to the location of the skull, where she lowers her head and appears over- come with emotion. Later, she approaches us one by one, thanking us for our efforts, and pausing to gently stroke Keb's head.

Mission Debrief

Guy

Search planning wizards always focus on answering one fundamental question: "Where should we look?" And while complicated, answers from modern probability-based search planning can be summed up in the phrase: "Let's search in the most likely places."

"That's all well and good," you say, "but how do we know which are the most likely places?" One effective method is to use data from previous searches for individuals similar to our current lost person, an approach formalized by Robert Koester in his book *Lost Person Behavior.*

Early in my SAR career on a snowy March morning, we were searching for an elderly woman who had wandered from her house in the middle of the night. The weather was cold; the family believed their missing grandmother was barefoot and clad only in a nightgown; all of us felt an atmosphere of desperate urgency. Two hours into the search, Carter was 100 yards west of the house at the base of a steep blackberry-covered slope when K9 Mav started pulling him uphill. Carter tried to move in that direction but was blocked by thick brush and sharp thorns.

Shortly thereafter, man trackers arrived on scene. After carefully circling the house, they concluded that the missing woman walked out the west-facing front door. As other searchers combed the neighborhood streets and woods, the man trackers followed faint footprints across the street, continuing to lead directly west, where they disappeared into the blackberry thicket. Searchers forced their way another ten yards through the mass of vines and thorns. The missing grandmother was found alive, huddled and cold—and in a direct line between her front door and Mav's nose.

What I didn't know then is that the location of our lost grandmother could have been predicted by application of Lost Person Behavior Analysis.

Turn to page 161 in Koester's book: "Dementia wanderers' trademark behavior [is] essentially moving straight ahead. Direction of travel predicts a dementia subject's location better than in most other subject categories."

When Suzanne emailed me details of her Search for Bengt, I was intrigued enough to apply Lost Person Behavior Analysis. Bengt Jönsson had some degree of mental deficiency, and he was last seen at the bus station in Mölle. On my search map, I plotted two circles: the inner one showed the distance from the Point Last Seen within which 25 percent of lost persons similar to Bengt were found in past searches. The outer radius showed the distance in which 50 percent of lost persons were found in the past. These circles formed the basis for defining the "most likely areas" for the search.

During the 2015 searches for Bengt, his glasses case was found on a trail in the woods behind the Mölle Chapel. Could this help us improve our search planning? You bet. When I mapped the location of this important clue, it allowed me to draw a hypothetical "direction of travel"—a bearing line from the bus station through the found clue. For Bengt, this direction of travel was consistent with the hypothesis that he was attempting to walk back in the direction of his home, many miles to the southeast. Is this a sure thing? Of course not, but it's a valid use of an important available clue.

Once the direction of travel was mapped, I could return to the historical Lost Person Behavior dataset and add the "Dispersion Angles," showing how far off of the direction-of-travel line similar subjects have been found in previous searches. Using the distance-of-travel range rings in combination with the dispersion angles, my search map now provided a richer view of "the most likely areas."

Was it fair to do arm-chair second-guessing from 4,000 miles away and more than a year after initial searching? Some will be quick to say, "Of course not." We arm-chair planners are not on scene; we don't have first-hand knowledge of many unknown variables and factors that might make a search unique. And yet when I added the location of Bengt's remains to my planning map, the picture screamed for attention. Keb found the skull just outside the 25 percent Lost Person Behavior radius and dead-center of the highest probability zone based on direction of travel. Might the course of the initial search have been altered by this planning? Suzanne is right. It's not fair to speculate.

Looking Back

Suzanne

Two days later, Keb, Linnea, Scott, and I are on the long flight home. Kebbie is no doubt snoozing below in her roomy travel kennel, dreaming of all the *röda pölser* we gave her the night we returned in wild celebration from our successful search. Lights are dim in the quiet aircraft cabin, but I can't sleep. For me, it's still sinking in: Keb and I had a major find in Sweden. The skull was positively identified as belonging to Bengt Jönsson, the search officially ended, and the mystery was solved. Official credit for the find is given to Missing People Sweden, and we are fine with that. In reality, the vast majority of our K9 search assignments don't result in a find, and we replay our successes over and over during the quiet times. It's part of what keeps us going. It's what we live for.

11
Disappearance on
Vesper Peak

In Which a Mountain Hides Its Secrets

"The wee birdies sing and the wild flowers spring,
and in sunshine the waters are sleeping.
But the broken-hearted ken nae second spring again,
Though the world may not know of their weeping."

—Traditional Scottish Ballad

Imagine you're alone in the deep woods. You have no map, no compass, no radio, no cell phone. There are no trails to follow, no landmarks to guide you. Oh, and one other thing: you're a dog with eyes only two feet above the ground. In every direction, all you can see are trees and shrubs. Everywhere you look, the view is the same. How are you going to find your way back to your search team? Who could overcome such a navigation challenge?

Using only her nose, eyes, and ears, Keb does this on every training and every mission. After finding a human (usually a volunteer hider), she may pause for a quick face-lick and then will dash off to find me. As I continue to move through the woods on my own course, I'll hear a rustle of brush and faint tingling of her collar bell as she approaches. Keb will stop me with her ever-enthusiastic jump alert "I found someone!" then we dash off together as she leads me back to the lost person. After years of working together, I know Keb will find her way back to me every time. I know her nose is the key to this marvel, but exactly how she does it is unknown to us mere humans.

First Operational Period

With Keb happily hanging her nose and pink tongue out the back window to inhale the sweet mountain air, we drive east from the small town of Granite Falls and follow the Mountain Loop Highway for thirty miles as it winds along the Stillaguamish River, first through small farms and green pasture lands, then into densely forested foothills. Shortly before Barlow Pass, I turn right at the hard-to-see entrance to Forest Road 4065 and wind my way slowly for two miles on a primitive dirt road, squeezed in by brush on both sides and strewn with potholes and small washouts. At the road's end at an elevation of 2,300 feet, I see a weathered picnic table, a forlorn wood-plank outhouse that has seen much better days, and a battered wooden sign reading "Vesper Peak Trail."

We arrive on scene at 8 a.m. to find our command van already set up in the cramped road-end. SAR volunteers are beginning to trickle in, finding barely enough room to park their vehicles along the narrow dirt road. Today will be the first "operational period" (full search day) in the search for Samantha Sayers. Leaving Kebbie in the car, I walk over to greet Deputy Jack Samuels, who has taken over as incident commander, relieving our new SAR Deputy Alan, who's been up all night. After thirty years, Charles Thayer has retired; Alan is now stepping up to fill some pretty big shoes. I see that Guy has pulled on his bright orange down jacket against the cold and we take notes while Jack relates what he's been told about the incident.

Yesterday morning, twenty-eight-year-old Samantha Sayers left for a solo hike up the Vesper Peak Trail. When she did not return at the end of the day, her fiancée Kevin dropped everything and drove two hours to the trailhead. He found Sam's parked car but no sign of her. His concern rising, Kevin immediately started hiking up the trail, calling out her name. The forest was dark and quiet. Without a light, without any gear, he made it about a mile up the rocky trail when he slipped and fell. Realizing that help was needed, he hiked back to his car and drove as quickly as he could to the nearest pay phone—twenty miles back at the Verlot Forest Service Center. The 911 dispatchers contacted our SAR deputy, Alan Miller, who then met Kevin back at the trailhead around 3 a.m. Alan recommended waiting until SAR teams arrived, but Kevin insisted on going right back up the trail by himself. Alan gave him a helmet and headlamp, plus a spare SAR radio, and Kevin headed up the trail again to search for Sam, while Alan radioed into dispatch to page out a request for all SAR resources in the county.

Guy and I have hiked the Vesper Peak Trail before. Peggy Goldman's climbing guide, *75 Scrambles in Washington* (Seattle, WA: Mountaineers Books, 2001), describes it as a ten-hour round trip, with a rating of 5 out of 5 on the "How Strenuous" scale and a rating of 4 out of 5 on the "Technical

Skills Required" scale. Nevertheless, it's attempted by many hikers each year. It's easy for us to imagine what Sam experienced on her ascent. Leaving the parking lot, the forest floor is mostly open, covered by thick fallen needles and downed branches. Soon, you come to the rocky crossing of upper Still-aguamish Creek, where you carefully tread slippery rocks and grasp thick tree roots to climb up the dirt bank on the west side. The trail then winds its way up through the low brush of mountain ash and twisted vine maples, leaving the tall evergreens behind.

As you gradually climb up the high mountain valley, snow-tipped Sperry Peak appears ahead on your right and Morning Star Peak high up on your left. Vesper Peak remains hidden by the ridge looming above you. The trail now becomes a fainter path that turns here and there through rock fields as it steadily leads southwest up the valley. Then, at a turn you might miss if you aren't paying attention, the trail angles sharply to the right and climbs toward what looks like an impassable wall of granite. But there is a trail of sorts—a steep zigzag through loose rock and dirt. The edges of this almost-a-goat-path are soft scree that slips away underneath your boots. The path is strewn with rocks that have fallen from the steep cliffs above. You have to place each step with care, as a slip here could mean a nasty fall. Using your hiking poles for balance, and breathing hard, you finally edge over the top at 4,700 feet and onto the narrow, treed ridge that is Headlee Pass.

The path now traverses a rough boulder slope, then crosses the origins of Vesper Creek, close below the outlet of snow-covered Lake Elan. And it's here that the hike becomes a climb, as the route ascends snow slopes and winds up rock slabs steep enough that handholds must be used for balance. Some-times you can see where worn rocks mark the path to the summit of Vesper Peak, or you can follow boot prints of others who have passed this way in the days before. Steep cliffs and ravines lurk on all sides. Sometimes the route up the final ascent to the 6,200-foot summit is unmarked and confusing. And

Headlee Pass rises ominously above any approaching hiker.

sometimes, if the clouds descend, or if you are weary or distracted, the safe route home can be hard to find. This is the terrain where Samantha got lost; this is the terrain that we now have to search.

At search base, Dan and Guy will be PLANS and OPS this morning. We've responded many times in the past for lost and injured hikers here, and our initial SAR deployment will be guided by "reflex tasking"—sending our search teams to the most likely places. As I listen in, Guy reviews initial search scenarios. "The highest probability is that Sam is lost or overdue, perhaps hunkered down near the trail when caught by darkness. Another possible scenario is that she's tripped or fallen. It would be damn easy for someone to slip while descending the loose, steep switchbacks just below Headlee Pass. They're just terrible."

Our first priorities will be to get "hasty" teams up the trail all the way to Headlee Pass and then, if we can, to the Vesper Peak summit beyond. When a hiker is missing, it's standard practice to send hasty teams for a quick search of nearby trails and roads—locations where subjects are typically found. We know we can't send just anyone up into that mountainous terrain, so as

SAR volunteers trickle in, Guy looks for strong, experienced members of our mountain rescue team who can handle this assignment. As OPS chief, one of his responsibilities is to make sure that teams have the fitness, experience, and gear needed to complete their assignments while staying safe. By 9 a.m. we're relieved to see two members of our mountain rescue team, Mark and Andre. Guy quickly pairs them with two fit but less experienced SAR volunteers, makes sure they have VHF radios and GPS units, and then sends them up the trail as Hasty Team 1.

An hour later, we have three air scent K9 teams and several additional ground teams available. Guy sends one mountain-capable air scent K9 team up the trail to the basin below Headlee Pass, with the hope that if Sam is anywhere in the basin, the dog will pick up her scent. He assigns the other two air scent K9 teams to investigate the "Sam took a wrong turn" scenarios: up the less-traveled route toward the old Sunrise Mine and north along the upper tributary of the Stillaguamish River. Both of these assignments put teams into extended thrashes through downed trees and thick, streamside brush, but after hours of searching, they find no signs of Sam.

After I've helped Guy organize the initial K9 assignments, he gives me the heads up that he wants Keb and me to deploy soon, so I return to my 4Runner to find her eagerly thumping her tail against the backseat. "Are you ready, girlie?" As I'm getting Keb's harness and GPS collar set up, I reflect on memories that Vesper Peak holds for me. Years ago, Scott and my son-in-law attempted a climb of the peak, and when they had not returned after dark, I called Charles to ask if he could send someone out, just to check the trailhead. To my chagrin (and Scott's embarrassment), Charles ordered a full SAR callout "One of our own is missing!" only to learn they had merely been delayed by route-finding problems.

On this first day of searching for Samantha, Keb and I will be joined by Gail Holmes and her golden retriever, Davy, who are now on scene and ready to go. Guy explains that for safety he wants us to deploy in the field as a single team with two K9 handlers and two dogs. This we can manage easily, but we're concerned to also hear we'll be accompanied by one of Sam's family members. This adds an unwanted element of complexity. Who is it? Can this person keep up in the rugged terrain we will be traveling through? We have to be cautious about what we say and take some time to feel this person out. What is his or her mental state? Will the family member take our focus away from the task at hand, our need to observe closely what our dogs are trying to tell us?

While Gail and I study the map and devise tactics for our assignment, we're relieved to hear the family member has been reassigned. Keb, in the meantime, has managed to escape her leash, and I have to use my shrill whistle to get her to return from whatever it is she is exploring. After a couple of whistles, she jauntily strolls into the staging area chewing on some unknown delicacy. I silently hope she has not snatched an energy bar from someone's pack, all the while reprimanding her in hushed tones. "You're making us look bad, girl!" Unfazed by this criticism, Keb happily hangs her tongue out and wags her tail.

Terrain often funnels lost persons into drainages or along streams, and the assignment Guy has handed us is to search along the drainage formed by the South Fork of Stillaguamish River. Peeking over the side of the trail, I groan silently. Even before entering the drainage, I can tell it's going to be steep scramble terrain with lots of large blown-down trees all the way along the banks of the stream. I see twelve-foot-high stands of thorny devil's club and quickly head back to my rig to make sure I am geared up appropriately for what is ahead. Devil's club (scientific name *Oplopanax horridus*) is a mean, nasty shrub endemic to rainforest gullies and swamps of the Pacific Northwest. Its thick stems are just the right size to grab for support as you cross a rocky gully, but the undersides of its huge prehistoric-looking leaves are covered with tiny sharp spines that pierce and stick in human flesh. Many SAR volunteers new to the northwest learn a painful lesson when they first encounter devil's club. Thick leather gloves and chaps are a must for this one. I wince—when I realize that my chaps are tucked away in a drawer in my garage. But I must go on, regardless.

As we expected, our assignment turns out to have treacherous steep areas, and there are times we have to slide down cold wet stream banks on our rear ends. Other times we end up having to backtrack when the devil's club is so thick there is no way to move forward. Without my chaps, my legs are being stung by the sharp spines. Hmm, a machete would not have been a bad idea on this one. K9s Davy and Keb are blissfully ignorant of our struggles. They work beautifully side by side, ranging independently through brush tangles in all directions. We are tracking both of them on our GPS units, which are receiving signals from their dog transmitter collars. Toward the end of our assigned area, we're stopped dead in our tracks by a steep ravine and truly impenetrable vegetation. Sweaty, tired, and frustrated, we take a bearing on the forest road that leads back to the staging area and return to download our GPS tracks, write a brief report on our assignment, and move on to what's next.

After making sure Kebbie has water and her favorite snacks, I walk stiffly to the command van where I find Guy, Jack, and Dan deeply involved in planning additional search assignments. Guy shows me the master planning map on which he's sketched a search area boundary and divided it up into multiple search regions. Each region roughly represents an experience-based guess at how Sam may have interacted with the mountain terrain. "If Sam lost the trail here when she started down the mountain," he points to just below the summit, "she might have been funneled down this drainage, mistakenly thinking it would lead her to Headlee Pass."

Dan and Guy are both experienced planners, but as the morning wears on I can see hints of concern on their faces. The demons of time and weather are arrayed against us. Guy's bent over the mapping laptop in front of him, studying the mountainous areas that still need to be searched. "All of this planning is well and good," he mutters, while sitting across from us in the cold, cramped command van, "but this damned overcast weather is just killing us. We may not be getting *any* helo searching done today; we'll be lucky if our pilots can just do flybys at lower altitudes. And it's so foggy and cloudy near the summit we're not going to be able to use helos to transport any searchers up there."

Guy lifts his cap and rubs the top of his head. "Dan, I've been up to Headlee Pass before, and even for fit mountain rescue teams, it's at least two hours to hike up and over the pass and get to the summit area. For our normal search volunteers, it's gonna take them *three or four hours* just to get up to their assigned search segments. They're going to be tired before they even start searching, and they're not going to have much time and energy to search. We're just not able to get much searching done."

Dan nods in agreement and adds, "Well, doing nothing is not an option. We'll just have to send teams out today and give it our best shot. Maybe the cloud cover will lift tomorrow or the next day." As I leave the command van, Guy and Dan are staring unhappily at the map, hoping it might magically provide some answers, or at least some improved weather.

Late in the day, searchers encounter and interview a group of hikers camping below the summit, close to the trail just south of Lake Elan. The hikers are convinced they saw Sam heading past them westbound toward the summit. They did not see her returning eastbound, and are convinced that if she had returned, they would have seen her descending the trail. This report is important and useful, and for purposes of planning, Guy moves the mapped PLS (Point Last Seen) to this location and plots lost person behavior probability distances from this point.

Operational Periods 2 through 4

It's Friday morning, the second day of searching. Our operations are now geographically split into two coordinated efforts: searching up on the mountain itself and searching down in the two major river valleys below. To support these geographically separated search efforts, we need to do something we've never done in our county before: set up and staff two separate incident command posts. At the Vesper Peak trailhead, Alan Miller will be incident commander, with Dan as OPS chief. Eight miles to the southwest at Spada Lake, Jack Samuels will be deputy incident commander, with Guy as OPS chief. To coordinate efforts between the two command posts, we have radio communications, which work—well, most of the time.

Keb and I are assigned to Spada Lake, and in order to be at the command post before 7 a.m., we need to leave home before 4 a.m. Thick fog envelops us as I gingerly drive the final miles over twisty dirt roads to the command post. The narrow dirt road seems to go on forever. Am I driving off the end of the earth? Finally, I arrive at Spada Lake just as dawn is breaking. Our command post is in an ideal setting for our SAR operation. The forest has been cut back to make a huge gravel parking lot. In the northwest corner, a long boat ramp leads past two modern pit toilets down to the shore of Spada Lake. Water district authorities have closed the gate two miles back to all but SAR personnel. We've taken over the east side of the lot with our command vehicles and have marked out the west side for volunteers to park. The center of the gravel lot is being kept clear for helo operations.

By mid-morning, most teams have deployed into the field, and we're entering a quiet time. I've been helping get K9 teams assigned, am itching to get out searching with Keb, but encounter an unexpected detour. Sam's mother and father have flown out from the east coast, and they are at our staging area today, along with fiancé Kevin. We've set them up at a picnic table, away from the command trucks and on the far side of a grassy field.

Jack and Guy agree it's time to brief the family. "Suzanne, can you come with us?" They recruit me on the way in case the family has questions about search dogs. Families always ask about search dogs. I join them, and we walk over together.

I admire Guy's calm clarity as he begins the conversation with a general explanation of how searches are planned. He describes how planners combine local knowledge and analysis of terrain to form a "best guess" at what happened and where Sam might be. He tells Sam's parents that the main scenarios are that she is lost or injured up on the mountain, and that we've got search teams assigned to high-probability areas near the summit, as well as possible routes off of the mountain. As he continues while pointing out locations on the map, I see nothing but worry and fatigue on the faces of Sam's mother and father. "We've also got teams starting to search along Williamson Creek on the west *here* and the Sultan River Basin on the south *here*. These are major drainages that should funnel Sam, if she wanders off the wrong side of the mountain."

Guy pauses in his explanation and looks into the eyes of Sam's parents as Jack takes over. As a deputy, part of his role is eventually to prepare families for what might be a worst-case outcome, that Sam may have met with a fatal accident. Guy and I exchange a glance when Jack broaches the topic on just the second day of the search. Does he have a bad feeling about this one? "We've got lots of search resources today, and we're doing all we can. I know it's hard to hear this, but you need to understand that there are cliffs and ravines all over the mountain. All of these are places where a fall could lead to injury or worse." Sam's father and Kevin sit silently through this. Sam's mother, Lisa, is overcome with emotion and walks away from the table. Minutes later she returns and with wet eyes apologizes to us, but there is no need. We try hard not to personalize our SAR missions, but I can't help but think of my own daughter and how overwhelmed with concern and fear I'd be. Our meeting ends, and I too need a few minutes of solitude to collect myself.

In the late afternoon as search teams begin to return to search base, I can see Guy and Jack pouring over the map posted on the side of our command van. They're beginning to plan for another day of searching. No new clues have been reported, there has been no sign of Sam, and I can see they are getting concerned. It's not unusual for a lost hiker to spend a night out and get found the next day. But Sam's been missing for two nights now on high mountain slopes, and the tone of the mission is turning more somber.

The next day, Saturday, is our third day of searching. To better manage search efforts high on the mountain, the Vesper Peak Trailhead command has been moved three miles north of Vesper Peak, to Big Four Ice Caves, where there is more room for multiple command trucks and a field for helicopter landings. With two separate search bases (Big Four and Spada Lake), the members of our command staff are stretched thin. Our Snohomish County deputies take turns as incident commander for the two operations, while Guy, Dan, and Carter alternate as PLANS and OPS chiefs at the two sites. We keep on searching. All of us are starting to get worn down.

And yet there is still optimism and hope in the air; you can feel the energy in the search teams that show up each morning. You can sense they are all thinking the same thing: Today, my team is going to find Sam. Theoretically, by now Sam has had more time to travel down the mountain, so for this third operational period, our focus on the river basins below Vesper Peak has increased. I've helped Guy develop a plan for deploying a large number of K9s: east along the Sultan River Basin (below the southern slopes of Vesper) and north along the Williamson Creek Basin (below the western slopes of Vesper). We still believe that if Sam managed to descend into these basins, she would try to work her way downstream, rather than to cross and move uphill on the opposite side. In SAR terms, this is called "containment by terrain."

Decorated with SAR gear, and wincing from the cold water, Guy scouts across the Sultan River.

In the past two days, I've reached out personally to recruit high-quality, mountain-capable K9 teams from other counties. Our SAR deputies in Sno-homish County have been very pleased with the new approach to getting large numbers of dog teams for missions like this. This morning we have about a dozen dog teams show up. I'm the overall K9 operations leader and have asked Candice, a relatively new and very capable handler-in-training, to assist me in organizing the teams. We work well together and in short order have charted what teams are here and what their capabilities and limitations are. We need to know how experienced the teams are, which teams are certified in both air scent and HRD, and which teams are capable of searching in rough mountain terrain. As OPS chief, Guy defines what K9 assignments need to be filled, and we help match teams to these tasks. Less-seasoned handlers and dogs are paired up with strong field support volunteers, and I designate a couple of teams with strong mountaineering skills for insertion by helo at higher altitudes on the mountain.

The weather has finally improved, and, *thank the stars*, we have both our helos flying today: searching across large swaths of the mountain and also transporting SAR teams up to near the summit. Our K9 team trains for deployment by helos because it makes all the sense in the world in our mountain terrain. I'm committed to having K9 team interactions with the helo team be professional and smooth. And I would just love to get helo-inserted with Keb. But an old foot injury has been acting up all summer, and there have been times lately when, totally unexpectedly, I'm overcome with a sharp shooting pain, hobbling me for short periods of time. The last thing a search and rescue member wants is to become a liability on a mission. So, no helo ride for Kebbie and me today.

Once Candice and I get all K9 teams assigned and out in the field, we get ready to deploy ourselves. Keb has been waiting in my Toyota 4Runner, and I've been hearing occasional impatient barks from the backseat as the morning has worn on. We've been assigned to search a 1.5-mile-long segment in the Williamson Creek Basin. Our ears perk up when we learn we'll need a boat ride across Spada Lake before hiking into our assigned area. Not as good as a helo ride, but Kebbie loves boat rides, and this might be a scenic crossing.

After a long wait in the warm morning sun by the Spada Lake shore, our boat driver, Bud, motors up in a fourteen-foot Public Utility District skiff and waves for us to climb aboard. During the ten-minute boat ride to the northern shore, we enjoy the mountain scenery while Keb happily hangs her nose over the side, inhaling the scent of the water. We get dropped off on a grassy marsh beach, do some brief scouting, and shortly find the faint trail that we attempt to follow as we work ourselves north along Williamson Creek.

The trail is easy in some places and totally overgrown in others. A ground search team has already been through here, marking their route with orange flagging tape hanging from ferns, bushes, and tree limbs. When we have opportunities to easily branch from the trail to search game trails, we do so as Keb happily dashes ahead of us. She's been well trained to ignore even the recent scent of animals and to let me know if she finds *any* human in this wilderness terrain. If she finds Sam today, we'll be thrilled. If she finds another SAR team, I'll reward her just the same and stop to compare notes with them.

Candice does a superb job as field support, competently handling radio communications and navigation, allowing me to devote myself totally to observing Keb. As we arrive at the turnaround point of our assignment, we decide to have lunch on a rock overlooking the stream before heading back. It's been a sunny, pleasant day, but we're both thinking about Sam and wondering where she is. Late in the afternoon, we're returning down the Williamson Creek Basin to catch our boat ride back across Spada Lake when Candice stops me. "Suzanne, I think Keb is on to something. She's slowed down, and look at her tail! The way it's wagging, I can tell her energy has perked up."

I've noticed this too and am pleased that Candice is being so observant. "Yes. See how she's sort of weaving back and forth, and how her posture is more erect now? I think she's trying to figure out a complex scent picture." As we're discussing how we can best partner with Keb to solve this problem, we see her dart over some rocks and disappear out of sight behind a wall of green rain forest.

We attempt to follow, not being able to keep pace, but observe on Candice's GPS how Keb is traveling in one direction at a fast speed. "Candice, look!" I say, as the GPS shows Keb has stopped and is now rapidly moving back toward us through the forest. Once she sees us, she does her *I-found-a-live-person!* jump alert. "Show Me!" I shout, and Kebbie immediately dashes off in the direction from which she came. I think I discern human voices in the distance—several voices. Is it possible? Could it be? I start having a faint feeling of hope, only to have it crushed. The voices turn out to be another SAR team heading back from an assignment farther up the creek. We're disappointed, but after rewarding Kebbie for her find, we stop to compare notes with the other group, then we all head off down the drainage toward Spada Lake.

Bud, our friendly boat driver, shows up about half an hour later. We're tired and immediately stretch out on the floor of the boat, watching the sky and listening to the din of the tiny outboard motor. Keb has probably run three to four times the distance that Candice and I have hiked, and she is quickly asleep beside me. Her damp fur is tickling my nose as she snuggles close. I love my girl. I can see her eyes moving under her lids. What is she dreaming about? Is she sensing the seriousness of our mission, or has she just been out for another day of engaging in her favorite search game?

The very next day, Sunday, will be Operational Period 4, and Guy, Dan and I are assigned to the Big Four incident command post, with Alan as incident commander. From here, we'll be deploying teams to search the summit areas. The sheriff's office has closed off the Big Four Ice Caves parking lot, which is now filled with command vans and the cars of SAR volunteers. A nearby lawn area has been designated as a helo LZ (landing zone). For most of us, it's the fourth continuous day of waking before dawn, driving two hours to search base, searching all day, then driving two hours back home to get a few hours of sleep.

At the snack table outside our command van, I'm contemplating a third cup of lukewarm coffee, while I see Guy looking wistfully at a half-empty box of day-old donuts. Alan rushes over. "Hey Guy, we may have something hot here. A hiker has seen media reports with pictures of Sam; he called 911, who managed to transfer him to my satellite phone. He's telling me he was up on the Vesper summit on Wednesday and saw Sam up there! He says he saw her just below the summit, heading downhill toward the west." Guy and Dan exchange a glance. West? This is the opposite direction of the safe route back to the trailhead!

Alan pauses for just a second, and Guy interrupts. "OK, this may be the best information we've had for days! If he actually saw Sam, this might give us a new PLS and a direction of travel! Give me ten minutes to update my master planning map and plot high-priority search areas on the western slopes of Vesper."

Alan has asked the hiker to drive out to our Big Four staging area, so we can have him show us on the map where he last saw Sam. After the hiker arrives, we can tell he's having difficulty finding where he was on the map. Guy pulls Dan and Alan aside for a private conversation. "We need to put this guy *on the ground* on Vesper summit. We need to have him verify *exactly* where he was standing and have him point to *exactly* where he saw Samantha."

We glance over at the LZ and see that SnoHawk 10 has just returned from deploying a search team. Alan quickly walks back over to the hiker and points to our big helo. "Are you willing to be flown up to the summit?"

The hiker's eyes grow big, and after a brief hesitation he nods. We scramble to arrange for Dan and two mountain rescue volunteers to accompany him, while Alan radios the pilots with this new request. Within minutes, Dan, the mountain rescue team, and our wide-eyed good Samaritan are strapped tight inside the helo and whirring up toward the Vesper summit.

At the summit, the helo sets down and unloads, and our hiker is carefully escorted over to the spot he had pointed to on the map. Initially, he's disoriented. He looks around west, then south, and then suddenly his face changes in recognition. "I was standing *here* and," he points, "she was walking downhill in *that* direction." Dan is stunned. Our hiker is pointing *south*, not west as we originally had been told. Dan quickly scribbles marks on his map, and all scramble back to the helo for the quick flight back to Big Four ICP.

Dan unloads from SnoHawk 10 and sprints over to us waving his map. "South! She was heading south!" he says, pointing to the marked PLS. We hastily climb into the back of the command van and review the master planning map. We've previously identified potential assignments down the hazardous slopes and gullies leading south from the summit. Guy now elevates these to high-priority assignments and will send more teams into those areas.

As Sunday afternoon wears on, our fourth full day of searching is winding down. Searchers are returning from their assignments. They debrief at the command van, leaving us a record of where they have searched, what obstacles they encountered, what clues were found. All SAR volunteers begin every search day with high hopes. This will be the day we spy Sam from the air. This will be the day we locate Sam on the mountainside. This will be the day my K9 leads me to Sam. This will be the day. But so far, each day has ended in quiet resignation.

Tired and hungry, volunteers stop by the food station, gratefully grabbing cups of coffee, snack bars, sandwiches, fruit, and small bags of potato chips. Search dogs are brushed off, rested, belly-rubbed, and watered. They climb up into backseats or kennels for a well-deserved sleep on the long ride home. In the command van, Guy and Dan review what searching has been accomplished (a lot), and review what has been found (almost nothing). Their thoughts begin to turn to *what now?*

Stand Down; Blow Up

It's the decision that every incident commander fears having to make: When do you terminate a search if the subject has not been found? It's a decision that has no right answer, provides no comfort, and always leaves lingering doubt. It's a decision that pits SAR safety and resources squarely against the survival chances of the lost person and the hopes of a worried family. This is Alan's first time as incident commander on such a large-scale search. He's seen exhausted searchers returning day after day. He's seen volunteers and command staff falling asleep during brief quiet periods at search base. Hundreds of SAR volunteers from all neighboring counties have joined the effort. He realizes we've burned through most of the region's SAR resources during these intense four days of searching. Alan makes a decision that none of us want to ever have to make. There were no doubt multiple factors involved: volunteer fatigue, sheriff personnel costs, helo fuel expenses, and the need to conserve SAR resources for other missions. We don't know what consultations with or pressure from sheriff's department superiors were involved.

Alan suspends the search. He informs the family that SAR efforts have been terminated. The world explodes.

While the Snohomish County sheriff's office must juggle multiple conflicting demands and priorities, Samantha's family has only one: find Sam. They call county officials. They call Washington State officials. They call national politicians. A "Find Sam Sayers" page is created, and Facebook erupts with comments and condemnation. Someone posts Alan's cell phone number on Facebook. Calls from all over the country flood in: relatives and friends pleading to continue the search, complete strangers angrily denouncing the sheriff's office. Alan ends up needing to turn off his phone to get some sleep on Sunday night.

The social media firestorm is like nothing we've ever experienced in our SAR history, and it's taken the sheriff's department completely by surprise. Posted comments are high in emotion, but low in information.

"I see Sam in my mind—she's near a rock and a tree." (We'll get right on that.)

"Have they searched nearby trails?" (No, that never occurred to us.)

"Have we searched using infrared sensors?" (Head slap.)

"Are they using search dogs?" (Dang, we missed that one too.)

"I've got a good hunting dog in Alabama, should I drive out to help?" (Thank you, no.)

According to statistics from the International Search and Rescue Incident Database, after four days the probability of survival for lost hikers drops to 50 percent. So our glass might be half empty—or half full. But this figure is an average across all types of environments, from benign woods to extreme mountain terrain. Vesper Peak is well toward the ugly end of this continuum. Sam carried only a typical day-hiker pack. She had little gear for an emergency bivouac, not much extra food, and only a few extra clothing layers. Make no mistake, we don't single out Sam here for being unprepared—this is how most day hikers in the Pacific Northwest would be equipped. Unfortunately, this means they are barely ready for what might go wrong on a day hike, much less to survive an extended period.

Sam's family has a lot of grit and passion, as well as the ability to use social media to make their case. Their Facebook presence goes viral, as Samantha's mom begins early in the mission to post daily videos. She is a uniquely charismatic woman, and I can't help but watch the videos, often with earphones in bed after Scott is asleep. He thinks I'm too obsessed with this mission, and maybe there is a grain of truth to that. Though I'm not privy to the interactions between our law enforcement and the family, what I read in Facebook posts suggests it's not a friendly relationship. It usually isn't in these situations. Law enforcement, while compassionate, also is dealing with finite resources and their own bureaucracy. Family has infinite love and unending commitment to find their loved one.

On Monday, the sheriff's office has called for a 10 a.m. planning meeting at our SAR operations base. Guy is attending as lead planner and will be presenting a set of slides detailing our search efforts on Operational Periods 1 through 4, Thursday through Sunday. As I cross the bridge east over the Snohomish River, I can see that the weather is clear. I know that some of us—myself included—are wondering why we aren't out searching.

Alan and Guy sit near the front of the upstairs classroom, and as the meeting starts, I survey the packed audience from my chair in the back row. All four of our SAR deputies are here, along with three of our helo pilots. Also sitting near the front are Chief Nanten and Bureau Chief Branson, "the brass" from the Snohomish County Sheriff's Office. Leaders of the man-tracking team are here, along with a half-dozen of our mountain rescue experts who bring firsthand knowledge of the Vesper Peak terrain. Alan starts the meeting by thanking all of the volunteers, providing an overview of the incident, and discussing the media firestorm and resulting pressure from politicians. Then Chief Branson assures us that both the county sheriff and the state governor are totally supportive of our efforts. Although the internet is wild with speculation, Alan adds that investigative work, careful interviews of friends and family, along with a review of phone and credit card records have all but ruled out foul play in Sam's disappearance.

Guy then takes over from Alan and reviews the search operations and findings for each of the previous four operational periods. Each slide lists assignments for each day and includes a map showing where search teams have traveled on the mountain. He outlines areas that might warrant more searching. Even before the meeting winds down, I sense the atmosphere has shifted. What started as a postmortem on a suspended search has kindled the beginnings of new hope and effort. Our SAR deputies leave to start arranging for statewide resources. In the back of the room, Guy assembles his planning team to begin prioritizing and mapping specific assignments. We've been asked to recruit as many K9 teams as we can get. We're going back, and we are going back tomorrow.

Operational Periods 5 through 14

For Operational Period 5, we will continue to run dual search operations: high up on the mountainsides and lower down in the two river basins. Even though this is a workday, we get a good volunteer turnout for the search: ground searchers and K9 teams from multiple counties, as far away as Chelan and Yakima, east of the Cascades. Everett Mountain Rescue has been joined by volunteers from sister organizations Seattle Mountain Rescue, Olympic Mountain Rescue, and Tacoma Mountain Rescue.

Sam has been missing for six days and six nights. This will be the longest search in recent county history, and for all of us—deputies, dogs, and volunteers—initial optimism has given way to bleak worry. I can tell that Guy and Dan are concerned that their planning efforts aren't yielding any results. On my visits to the command van, I overhear them asking each other if they are missing anything.

Our plan today for mountain rescue teams is to send them into harm's way. From the summit of Vesper, steep rocky ravines and granite slopes lead down all sides of the mountain. We know each one of these is hazardous, yet we want to search every one of these ravines on the southern slopes. One-by-one, Guy and Dan identify these on the topographic map and assign them to teams. I can hear the stress in their voices and see it on their faces. Along with Alan, they fear they're putting search teams at risk for a subject now beyond rescue. In addition to search urgency, command staff always need to assess the risk/reward balance. Are we looking for a recently missing child in the woods at risk from a rapidly approaching storm? We send searchers without hesitation. Are we searching in extremely hazardous terrain for an adult who may already have perished? This is a much harder *Go / No Go* decision.

Today our mountain rescue teams are getting some unexpected help. There are, in this world, men who are trained to jump out of airplanes and rescue people from active combat environments. These are the Air Force

Pararescuemen of the USAF Special Operations Command. These are the "PJs," the para-jumpers. We don't know what political forces were involved, but today our search is joined by twelve PJs from the 304th Rescue Squadron, out of Portland, Oregon. Young, strong, and unassuming, they receive assignments from us and gear up for their helo deployments. Guy assigns them to rappel down steep dangerous ravines; they agree to do so without question. They spend all day on the mountain, camp at search base overnight, and come back the next day ready for more.

As the day wears on, Guy and Dan repeat the cycle of debriefing returning teams and capturing their GPS tracks on our master planning map. The cumulative picture of what has been searched continues to build. The main and terrible problem, though, is that the mountain terrain is so rough that our confidence of finding someone in areas covered by search teams is disappointingly low. We could search the same steep ravine again and again, and still miss finding Sam.

By Wednesday, August 8, Sam has been missing for seven days. We continue full search operations from Big Four and Spada Lake. On this Vesper Peak search, something happens for the first time in our county history: we launch a large-scale deployment of drones from multiple counties. Each drone must be deployed by a two-person (pilot plus observer) team. These teams must be inserted near the Vesper summit by helo and escorted from launch point to launch point by mountain rescue personnel for safety. Each drone has a flight time limited by battery life, and hence by the number of batteries teams can carry into the field. Strict FAA regulations stipulate that the drone cannot be flown beyond the visual range of the pilot or observer.

Despite these limitations, the drone flights provide detailed images of places on the mountain that otherwise would remain unsearched. But no signs of Sam are seen. At the end of each day, volunteers spend hours reviewing high-resolution images. They occasionally spot searchers on the high, rough terrain, but no Sam. They learn that spotting searchers wearing red or orange parkas is barely possible. They learn that searchers in dull colors are effectively invisible.

On Wednesday afternoon, I look over to see Sam's family arriving at the Big Four command post. Guy spies me and hurries over. "Suzanne, Alan wants me to help update the family. Can you come over and sit close by? You know they always ask questions about the search dogs." I nod and join Guy and Alan to walk over to the covered picnic tables near the lawn that we're using as the helo LZ. Guy looks uncomfortable. Meeting with families is not his favorite thing to do, and he's acutely aware of how upset they've been. As we approach, Sam's mom, Lisa, recognizes Guy and, to his surprise, greets him with a hug. He later confessed to me that this is something he would remember for a long time.

The atmosphere at the picnic tables is uneasy, reflecting tension between the family and the sheriff's department. Snohomish County Sheriff Chief Davis has now been assigned as family liaison, and I see that Lieutenant Nanton and Bureau Chief Branson are also here. Guy starts by providing an overview of where we have searched to date, and where we are currently focusing our efforts.

After the briefing ends, I see Lisa approach Guy. She's holding a small notebook and speaks so softly I need to lean in to hear, "Guy, I have a list of tips from a psychic that has contacted me. Would you be willing to look at them?"

Wow, where's this going to go? Guy is a hardheaded scientist type. In the past he's freely shared his opinion that psychics are worthless charlatans who at best provide false comfort and at worst prey upon people in their darkest days. To my surprise, I see him sitting patiently with Lisa, nodding, and carefully recording each suggestion, one-by-one, in his planning binder. When the list is finished, he pauses, then looks up at Lisa and promises he will compare the psychic suggestions to the search scenarios and findings.

Back in the command van, Guy describes the list as a classic case of psychic bingo: a long, scattershot of "I see a rock," "I see water," "She's near a stream," "She can hear searchers," "I see a tree," "I think she's in shade," "She can see the sun," "I'm feeling something green," and on and on. Guy sputters, "If Sam's found under *any* of these conditions, the psychic gets to claim her visions were correct. Never mind the 99 percent that were totally off base!" Then, after this brief raving, Guy sits down at the planning table and carefully reviews each suggestion to make sure that no thought has been ignored—and to keep his promise to Lisa.

Wednesday's efforts start to wind down. Again, our volunteers have accomplished a lot of searching under difficult conditions. But again, we've found no trace of Sam. Samantha's fate is touching me deeply, and as hard as I try, it's difficult to turn my thoughts off. Where is this radiant, young woman I keep seeing all over social media? How can she just disappear on a mountain? Has she fallen into a crevasse, never to be found again? Did she wander off the mountain and is lost and alone far away from where the search is taking place? Will she be found? Is she alive? Will she be found in an area already searched by K9s?

Late in the day, we meet again with sheriff deputies and chiefs to address the "What next?" question. We've searched large swathes of the mountain, we've worn down most of the regional SAR resources again, and we've burned through this year's helo fuel budget and are well into next year's. The deputies are tired, the planners are tired, the searchers are tired, and the dogs are tired.

Earlier, Guy had pulled me aside. "Suzanne, the vibes I'm getting are that after this extensive two-day push, the Sheriff's Department is again leaning toward closing the search down." He's devised a sneaky plan to steer thinking away from shutting down the search. Back in the command van, he's prepared a table showing a ramping down of efforts that extends for several more days. This starts with low-level trail and boat patrols for Thursday and Friday, a tactic to intercept Sam if she is alive and wandering down near Spada Lake. This is a commitment that is fairly easy for the Sheriff's Department to accept. Guy includes the possibility of searching the snowfields below the steep north wall of Vesper, something that can be done with a small team from Everett Mountain Rescue. At our meeting, his plan works, and shifts the sheriff's thinking from "shut down" to "ramp down."

As the day closes, we learn that the Air Force PJs will be leaving for home tonight. Guy and I walk across the Big Four parking lot to find their young captain. We thank him profusely for his team's efforts and tell him how much they are appreciated. He nods and smiles, but I think we've embarrassed him a bit. We start to walk back toward the command vans, when he turns and calls out to Guy. "Sir!" (No one ever calls Guy "sir.") "I just wanted to tell you that this is one of the best run civilian SAR incidents that we've ever participated in." I see the set of Guy's shoulders change and can tell how much this unexpected praise meant to him.

Early the next week, Guy and I continue discussing how our search dogs could help find Sam, even after hope has faded. The seeds for another search effort take root. We work with Alan and other SAR deputies to envision and organize a return to Vesper, this time with an emphasis on K9s searching for human remains. The unpleasant scenario now is that we're searching for a deceased person. In general, wind and scent will rise as the air warms during the morning, then fall as the afternoon cools. We plan to take advantage of this by placing K9 teams to expose our dogs to these natural scent currents, both high on the mountain early and low in the river basins later in the day.

The regional call goes out for HRD teams to respond for searching on the upcoming Friday and Saturday. To support this effort, we will set up just one command post at the Spada Lake site. We plan on thirteen K9 teams: eight to be deployed in the river basins, four to be deployed across the tops of ravines and slopes near the Vesper summit. We arrange for mountain rescue volunteers to escort the summit K9 teams. We arrange for both our helos, SnoHawk 1 and SnoHawk 10, to be available. We arrange for boat transport to ferry teams across Spada Lake. We're going back yet again.

We devise an intricate schedule of helo deployments that will insert teams at the right time of day. As the day proceeds, I'm relieved to see that loading and unloading of K9s is going well. I'm totally thrilled when I hear that our lead SAR pilots, Gary and Martin, complimented June, who is coordinating K9 helo deployments, on how well K9 teams were prepared to follow their instructions. June relates some important learnings. She learns that a full fuel load at the beginning of the day limits the helo's capacity to lift people and dogs. She learns that when the helo doors slide open (sometimes high above the ground in preparation for landing), some dogs will bolt for the door! So hold down those dogs!

Some of the mountaineering-capable K9 teams are assigned to search technical terrain high on Vesper Peak. They will attempt to lead their dogs across the tops of steep gullies to detect any scent that might be wafting up from ravines below. Our large helo, SnoHawk 10, transports these teams to a high saddle at 6,000 feet. With humans roped-up, and dogs on long leashes, they travel across steep snowfields, above knife-edge ridges and steep gullies.

By now, Sam has been missing for over two weeks. Her mother and father have reluctantly returned home to the East Coast. On Saturday, Sam's fiancé, Kevin, arrives at the Spada Lake ICP and is overwhelmed to see the number of volunteers and dog teams assembled. Guy walks him over to our command truck with all of our assignments and maps taped to the side and reviews our plans. Kevin thanks us sincerely for our efforts. And we appreciate this, but the fact remains that we have not found any trace of Sam. The Friday/Saturday HRD K9 effort ends. Once again, we have accomplished a lot of difficult searching. Once again, nothing has been found.

Endings

The Snohomish County Sheriff's Office finally terminates the search for Samantha Sayers. After official efforts end, Sam's family continues their own. Sam's fiancé, Kevin, organizes non-SAR volunteers who are willing to search high on the mountain. Kevin organizes his own drone sources, which capture hundreds of images from the mountain slopes. Analysis of these images is crowd sourced out to volunteers on the internet—an approach that, while it yields a large number of false positives ("I think I can see someone in this picture"), turns out to be an innovative and productive way to get many images searched by many eyes. For months, I see that Sam's family keeps interest alive via Facebook posts, and Kevin continues ground search efforts in steadily deteriorating fall weather. Finally, winter snow arrives in the Cascades and, like a shroud, closes the door on any more search efforts.

On the Vesper Peak mission, as on so many others, controversy over the way dogs are used arose, fueled by both misguided opinions and well-founded concerns. How many search dogs should be deployed? Is one breed better than another? When should the switch be made from air scent (search for the living) to HRD (search for the dead)? The reality is it's complicated, very complicated. Our dogs are merely one tool among a wide array of resources.

In spite of extensive deployment of K9 teams, Sam was never found. Was it the dogs' fault? Did a handler miss a subtle cue from their K9? Did thick vegetation block scent from reaching the dogs? Were our dog teams simply not deployed close to where Sam was? We may never find out. Our dogs are not superheroes, but they gave all they had, as did their handlers. I so wish we could have brought closure to Sam's family. Their suffering was raw and palpable. Our hearts ached for them and still do.

Mission Debrief

Guy

Some searches never end, really. The effort gradually fades away. The hope gradually fades away. What remains is the mystery and pain for the family. Eight thousand hours from hundreds of volunteers over three weeks wasn't enough to find Sam. The largest helo deployment of searchers in state history wasn't enough to find Sam. The largest SAR drone deployment in state history wasn't enough. Ferrying search dogs by boat and helicopter wasn't enough. Crowd-sourced review of aerial images wasn't enough. Using some of the best search planners available in the state wasn't enough. Searchers wading cold rivers, rappelling mountain slopes, and thrashing through thick brush— none of it was enough to find Samantha. The demons of time, weather, and mystery won again.

Historically, over 85 percent of searches are successful within twenty-four hours via straightforward tactics (just looking in the usual places). The vast majority of remaining subjects are found within two to three days. While internal and external reviews of our search efforts on Vesper Peak find no fault, in my mind, I inventory where we weren't perfect and wonder what might have made a difference. Should we have continued to search past our initial four days, and through the first Monday that we paused for rest and planning? Should we have sent search teams and search dogs into more dangerous terrain? Should we have been better at setting up a formal search command structure? Could we have better integrated county efforts with family-driven search efforts? Could my plans have been better?

Looking Back

Suzanne

In my dream, it's now late in the day. Keb and I have been on our assignment for hours, and we are far up the Williamson Creek drainage below the west slopes of Vesper Peak. The brush in the drainage is thick and disorienting here, and in places I have to force myself through. I'm having trouble seeing Keb, and for some reason my GPS tracker is not showing her position. My legs feel like lead, and I'm struggling to keep my footing on the slick, rounded rocks of the creek bed. I hear a soft bark and look up to glimpse Keb in the distance. She looks at me, then disappears. Moments later, another bark, another look, another disappearance. I don't understand why she's behaving like this, but I feel an overwhelming sense of fatigue, which prevents me from puzzling this out.

I sense Keb is ahead of me upstream, so I continue to follow as best I can. Unbelievably, the brush gets even thicker, and I have to push through to gain each step. I hear Keb's bark in the distance and wonder if she's found something. I look up just in time to see her disappear yet again. It's almost as if she is leading me to something, but I'm confused that she's not coming back to me to give her trained indication. I'm so weary now that things just don't make sense. I think maybe Keb is close on a scent, but as I try to follow her, she keeps moving farther and farther away from me.

Unexpectedly, the brush opens into a small clearing in the streambed. Ahead of me the creek flows peacefully over low granite ledges, adorned with pink penstemon wildflowers and deep purple bog gentians in a beautiful natural garden. The sun shines down from a blue sky, revealing Keb sitting near a low waterfall at the far side of the clearing and looking back at me. I splash through the shallow stream to join her. I'm so sleepy now—this looks like a wonderful spot to just close my eyes and rest peacefully.

Keb is still staring at me as I draw near. Suddenly my vision clears, and I see Samantha.

And then I wake sobbing, with Keb licking tears from my cheeks.

Afterword

"If I cease searching, then, woe is me, I am lost. That is how I look at it—keep going, keep going come what may."

—Vincent van Gogh

My journey with Keb and Guy as an HRD team had begun when natural disaster fell from above in the form of the deadly Oso Landslide. Our journey as an HRD team almost ended when changes in the Sheriff's Department and Snohomish County SAR leadership resulted in a sudden cascade of events that decimated our K9 team.

August was a month in which our years of slowly building K9 team resources and engagement had paid off. Day after day, during the weeks-long Vesper Peak mission, our law enforcement partners complimented us on our efforts. Throughout the region, our K9 leadership team had developed good personal relationships and a strong presence in the K9 community as a thirty-member, high-quality, professionally run team. In the search for Samantha Sayers, we called for search dog resources from across the state, and they responded. On scene each day, we orchestrated deployment (by land, by water, and by air) of air scent and HRD dogs in terrain ranging from densely forested river valleys to hazardous slopes and treacherous ravines high on the mountain.

While we were pleased with the turnout and organization we provided, in the wake of the protracted and ultimately barren Vesper Peak mission, we continued to analyze and speculate about the mission for weeks. We reviewed our search plans; we second-guessed our second guesses. Guy and I lost sleep wondering what we could have done better.

Across the state, weary SAR volunteers recovered in the way they always did after missions: they cleaned their gear and rested sore muscles. As I chatted with K9 team contacts in other counties, I could sense that they mentally let go of the mission and gradually returned to their normal lives. For our K9 team, however, recovery never came. As we started to recover physically and mentally, behind the scenes, we suspect that our small group of K9 team malcontents convinced the Snohomish County SAR leadership to move against us.

With the steady hand of Charles Thayer no longer present, the styles of the new lead SAR deputy and newly elected SAR president clashed unchecked with the values of engagement, open communications, and mutual respect, on which we had built our K9 team. We were shocked when, with no consultation, no recognition of our years of dedication and service, Carter, Guy, myself, and the rest of the ten-member leadership structure of our team were replaced without notice or explanation.

Our repeated attempts to discuss alternatives and to work toward compromise solutions were rebuffed. We were commanded to accept the new dictates without question. One team member spoke up in mild opposition and was immediately and publicly expelled. Within a week of the dismissal of our leadership team, Guy and I, along with half of the K9 team representing our most senior handlers and field support with over 100 years of SAR experience, resigned as a matter of principle. We found ourselves unable to serve in our home county, not allowed to tell our side of the story, and shunned by some neighboring K9 teams after being falsely smeared as rebellious troublemakers.

We were hurt, sad, and disappointed. Yet we never hesitated in our resolve to stand up for what we believed so deeply in. No longer members of an authorized K9 team, we were unable to deploy our dogs on searches. In our home county, the elderly continued to wander and children continued to get lost in the woods, and we—including the most committed K9 members, as evidenced by mission and training participation, with some of the most seasoned dogs—ended up sitting at home.

After leaving the Snohomish County K9 team, those of us who resigned formed a new nonprofit search organization, Cascadia Search Dogs, with the mission of contributing to positive, high-quality training for K9 search and rescue in our region and beyond. As a group, and individually, we reached out to become authorized as K9 handlers in other counties in Washington State, and within a year, we were able to start deploying again with our four-legged partners. It felt like being reborn. In addition to supporting Cascadia Search Dogs, Guy focused his energies and talents on building a new statewide SAR planning team, which is now supporting complex SAR missions and criminal evidence searches throughout Washington State.

In the meantime, the dissolution of our Snohomish K9 team allowed me to take stock of my own SAR career and decide on a path forward for me and Keb. While remaining involved with Everett Mountain Rescue, I have increasingly come to recognize that the work Keb and I have done as a human remains detection team is what resonates the most with me now. On our search and rescue journey, we've encountered victims that died doing what they love, victims consumed by animals in the mountains, and still others who have been viciously murdered by criminals or psychopaths. I have decided that going forward, Keb, I, and my newest addition—K9 Kili—will be dedicated to finding those who have perished, and in some way bring them home.

Ever the introvert, Guy seldom talks about his resignation, but I can tell his spark for search and rescue is still strong. Despite occasional mutual frustration and arm-wrestling over fashioning our book ("Damn it, Suzanne, there are still too many words in that chapter!"), we've remained teammates and friends. I remember sitting with Guy in my dining room, planning the content of our last chapters, with papers strewn across the table and Keb wandering from chair to chair, surfing for pets. He paused for a moment while absently stroking Keb's forehead, then looked up with a sly grin: "You know, Suzanne, we've got enough stories here for a second book!"

Looking Forward

While these years with my sweet girl have been an unbelievable rollercoaster ride, our partnership has deepened. Keb has turned eleven and is slowing down some. Most SAR dogs retire sometime between nine and twelve, and this is the time when K9 SAR handlers start looking for their next partner. In late November 2018, Scott and I found ourselves driving ten hours north to British Columbia to pick up my next search dog, "Kili," the newest member of our family. Keb has become a big sister to this young, wiggling newcomer. We have big plans and adventures ahead of us and are currently specializing in forensic human remains detection. In addition to searches involving missing people in general, we are now much more focused on supporting crime scene missions and also searching for historical burials. I am so honored to be the spiritual guardian for both my pups.

Writing these chapters with Guy has been a journey of remembrance and reflection. It's allowed me to relish some of the unique experiences, ranging from tragic to exhilarating, I've had in search and rescue over the last twenty years. Do we have regrets? Of course, we do. Would we do it all again? Of course, we would. Would we do something differently? Perhaps. What's important, though, is all that we learned from our experiences—about death and dying, about the courage and incredible noses of our dogs, about pursuing our passions and being a part of a committed team of volunteers, about having the grit and resilience necessary to explore new paths.

The work Keb and I have done together with Guy and others has helped me live with greater urgency, explore my purpose, and find a meaningful way to make a difference in the world. Rather than engaging in the shallow and the mundane, I prefer to greet the day with questions: *What is my WHY in the world? How do I want to be remembered when I am no longer here? How can I continue to positively influence the world and people after I am gone?* I strive to live with enthusiasm in alignment with my values, to live ethically and with integrity, and to go to sleep every evening knowing I did my best.

As I am writing this, faithful Kebbie snoozes innocently at my feet. Her eyelids and legs twitch gently as she dreams about chasing her favorite ball and munching on delicious *röde pölser* hot dogs.

I love you Keb. Thank you for coming into my life and helping me become the best possible version of myself.

A Dog's Devotion

Photo Credits

Cover and Back Cover

Cover image (Keb standing on rock): James Guy Mansfield

Back cover image (Suzanne with Keb and Bosse): Scott Welton

Inside Jacket Cover (Suzanne and Keb): Dan DeVries, DeVries Photography

Inside Jacket Cover (Guy on summit): W. Gary Mansfield

Dedication

Bob Fuller and K9 Peer: Suzanne Elshult

Table of Contents

Background image of Keb: June Mansfield

Preface

Map of Chapter Locations: James Guy Mansfield

Glossary of Search and Rescue Terms

Assembled SAR Volunteers: James Guy Mansfield

Chapter 1

Chapter title image (Keb digging in snow): Jon Mercer

1.1 Assembled avalanche training group: James Guy Mansfield

1.2 Keb impacts with her jump alert: Dan DeVries, DeVries Photography

1.3 Suzanne and Keb in snow cave: Suzanne Elshult

Chapter 2

Chapter title image (Suzanne and Keb on debris field): James Guy Mansfield

2.1 Keb agility training: Suzanne Elshult

2.2 Oso log pile: James Guy Mansfield

2.3 Cookies for dog heroes: James Guy Mansfield

Chapter 3

Chapter title image (View of Oso landslide): James Guy Mansfield

3.1 Suzanne and Keb amidst a sea of devastation: James Guy Mansfield

3.2 Our assigned search area: James Guy Mansfield

3.3 Marsh master landing: James Guy Mansfield

Chapter 4

Chapter title image (Suzanne and Keb searching): James Guy Mansfield

4.1 Keb disappears into the forest: Suzanne Elshult

4.2 Keb searches inside a huge stump: Suzanne Elshult

Chapter 5

Chapter title image (Guy and Keb on snowfield): Suzanne Elshult

5.1 Guy at Mount Rainier: Kevin J. Quinn

5.2 Keb loading into helicopter: James Guy
Mansfield
5.3 Descending to Indian Bar: James Guy
Mansfield

Chapter 6

Chapter title image (Suzanne and Keb search
at night): Suzanne Elshult
6.1 Our command van: James Guy
Mansfield
6.2 Keb wearing her SAR harness: Walter
Snelling

Chapter 7

Chapter title image (Keb in the back seat):
Suzanne Elshult
7.1 Suzanne searching with Keb: Dan
DeVries, DeVries Photography
7.2 Guy, Keb, and Suzanne under tree: Scott
Welton

Chapter 8

Chapter title image (Keb standing on rock):
James Guy Mansfield
8.1 Keb perches outside bunker: June
Mansfield
8.2 On the brink of the Oso Slide: James
Guy Mansfield
8.3 Guy searching above the streambed:
Chris Terpstra

Chapter 9

Chapter title image (Suzanne and Keb on
steep slope): James Guy Mansfield
9.1 Suzanne and Keb descend steeply: James
Guy Mansfield
9.2 Tree across Sol Duc River: James Guy
Mansfield

Chapter 10

Chapter title image (Skull on the ground):
Suzanne Elshult
10.1 Keb searching for Viking bones:
Suzanne Elshult
10.2 Suzanne and Keb relaxing in Sweden:
Suzanne Elshult
10.3 Keb enjoys Danish hotdog: Suzanne
Elshult

Chapter 11

Chapter title image (Helicopters landing):
James Guy Mansfield
11.1 Headlee Pass Trail: James Guy
Mansfield
11.2 Crossing the Sutan River: Dan
Merrifield

Afterword

Chapter title image (Suzanne and Keb on
the grass): Suzanne Elshult
A.1 Suzanne and Keb: Dan DeVries,
DeVries Photography

Index

Page references for photos are italicized.